Breakthrough Inc

To Shiraz,

There are rewards for sticking your neck out.

Excellent best word!!

Herb Rubenstein
Growth Strategies, Inc

September, 2002

**I see there must be a social revolution.
A new kind of order must come into the world
and I must figure out how to bring about that order.**

J Krishnamurti, *Author*
The Awakening of Intelligence

Every person in your company, your non-profit organization, your educational institution should be encouraged to be a strategic planner, a strategic thinker focusing on developing high-growth strategies for the future.

Strategic planning is a continuous process, a learning process, an adaptive process, a revolutionary process that promotes intelligent action.

Strategic planning does not accept history or the status quo as anything but starting points for improvement, growth and fulfillment.

The point of law is not to create laws, but to guide and govern behavior to lead to a better society. The point of strategic planning is not to create a nice plan, but to create the context and ability and energy to work at a higher level than ever before toward making the world a better place.

Strategic planning promotes more successful spontaneous behavior by preparing us and opening our eyes to look for the future we want to create. The basic concepts and flow of strategic planning are as useful for guiding individual behavior as they are for guiding behavior in groups, teams, companies and organizations in the business/non-profit/education world.

Breakthrough Inc

High-Growth Strategies for Entrepreneurial Organizations

HERBERT R. RUBENSTEIN

and

TONY GRUNDY

FINANCIAL TIMES

PRENTICE HALL

PEARSON EDUCATION LIMITED

Head Office:
Edinburgh Gate
Harlow CM20 2JE
Tel: +44 (0) 1279 623623
Fax: +44 (0) 1279 431059

London Office:
128 Long Acre, London WC2E 9AN
Tel: +44 (0) 171 447 2000
Fax: +44 (0) 171 240 5771
www.business-minds.com

First published in Great Britain in 1999

© Pearson Education Limited 1999

The right of Herbert R. Rubenstein and Tony Grundy to be identified as
authors of this work has been asserted by them in accordance
with the Copyright, Designs and Patents Act 1988.

"Council of Masters" is a registered trademark
of Growth Strategies, Inc. under US law.

ISBN 0 273 63885 8

British Library Cataloguing in Publication Data
A CIP catalogue record for this book can be obtained from the British Library.

10 9 8 7 6 5 4 3 2 1

Typeset by M Rules
Printed and bound in Great Britain by Biddles Ltd, Guildford & King's Lynn

The Publishers' policy is to use paper manufactured from sustainable forests.

About the Authors

Herbert Rubenstein is a Phi Beta Kappa graduate of Washington and Lee University. He received a Rotary Foundation Fellowship and a graduate degree in Sociology at the University of Bristol, in Bristol, England. He was then awarded the Lyndon B. Johnson Scholarship to attend the Lyndon B. Johnson School of Public Affairs of the University of Texas at Austin where he received a Master of Public Affairs degree. He received his law degree from Georgetown University in 1982.

He has conducted research and policy analysis for the National Academy of Sciences, the American Institutes for Research and the US Department of Health and Human Services where he helped design a new welfare system for the United States that had, as its center point, "Workfare" and job creation programs. During his 15 years of practicing law, he served as General Counsel and Litigation Counsel to numerous businesses and non-profit organizations.

In 1997 he created Growth Strategies, Inc. a consulting firm that advises businesses and non-profits on how to grow and achieve breakthroughs in their productivity, their bottom line and their top line. Growth Strategies, Inc. has offices in Washington, D.C. and Austin, Texas and is comprised of a core staff and 50 consultants using a virtual enterprise model to deliver consulting services.

Tony Grundy graduated from Cambridge in Philosophy and Social Sciences. He became a Chartered Accountant and worked in general management and in finance with BP and ICI. He has consulted with KPMG and PA and continues to work with major clients independently with his company, Cambridge Corporate Development.

He has an MBA, MPhil and PhD from three Business Schools and an MSc in Organizational Behaviour from London. He is now also a Reiki Master and Seichem Master of the subtle human energies. He is Senior Lecturer in Strategic Management at Cranfield School of Management.

Contents

Preface   ix
Introduction   xi

1   High-growth strategies – *where do we begin?*   1
Introduction   3
Phase one: the context for growth – the role of defining your
    market and mission and vision statements   4
Phase two: a closer look at the objectives of growth for your
    organization   15
Entering phase three: beginning to develop "the plan"   18
Completing phase three: completing the strategic plan and
    crafting strategies   19
Promoting the success of phase three: implementation of your
    strategic plan   27
Conclusion   31

2   High-growth strategies – *what are the tools?*   33
Introduction   35
Physics and high-growth strategies for entrepreneurial organizations   36
The implications of physics for strategic planning   39
Strategic tools made simple – 12 strategic tools   42
Conclusion   76

3   Achieving organizational breakthrough   79
Introduction   81
Stakeholder analysis   83
The Internet   87
Human capital, intellectual capital, and attitude capital   89
Knowledge management – the management of knowledges   91
The role of teams and virtual teams   92
Values-driven growth model   93
New selection process and paradigm for boards of directors   96
Councils of Masters/advisory boards   98
Spinoffs/spinouts   99
Outsourcing and new labor force practices – contract employees   100

Consolidation and roll ups 101
Profit zone analysis 104
Globalization 106
Conclusion 107

4 Money and resources 109
Introduction 111
Increasing dollars and resources available to an organization 111
Recognizing value 112
Raising money for companies 116
Raising money and increasing revenues for educational
   institutions 118
Raising money in the non-profit world 121
Compensation of employees and equity participation 124
Strategic partnering and the coming avalanche of mergers in
   the non-profit and educational worlds 125
Mergers and acquisitions, strategic alliances, joint ventures
   (MASA-JVs) 126
Strategic cost management 129
Economic value added (EVA) 131
Conclusion 136

5 Toward the high-growth future of your organization 139
Introduction 141
Recruit 143
Organize 152
Manage 158
Deploy 167
Conclusion 187

Appendix: mission and vision statements 189
Annotated bibliography 191
Index 235

Preface

Life is made for growth.
The Sages' Guide to Living

The days when there were three separate economic sets of rules for businesses, non-profits and educational institutions are over. Today they share common concerns about revenues, quality, employee and customer satisfaction, innovation and success. Their managers, employees and board members are all looking for ways to survive and even thrive in our rapidly changing economy.

This book makes the radical assumption that businesses (regardless of their size), non-profit organizations (regardless of their mission or policy orientation), and educational institutions (regardless of their location or strengths) all must be run in accordance with the same basic, fundamental laws of commerce and use similar "business" strategy tools. In fact, over the next ten years the distinctions among for-profit, non-profit organizations and educational institutions will be of little relevance to anyone but lawyers and tax agents. Therefore, throughout this book we use the term "organizations" to mean for-profit companies, sole proprietorships, non-profit organizations and educational institutions alike.

Competition between non-profit and for-profits is heating up. One of the fastest-growing businesses in the US at the turn of the century is the for-profit educational sector. Non-profits are now being judged on their "results" to such a great extent that evaluation of their success and productivity is often tied directly to funding decisions by foundations deciding to support the non-profit organization. Non-profit organizations, educational institutions and for-profit companies are all forming strategic alliances, affinity relationships, joint ventures, collaborative agreements and ties at such a fast pace that the lines between these types of economic entity are blurring rapidly.

Around the world, successful managers and employees at businesses and non-profits are working with a new set of tools. Terms like SWOT analysis (strengths, weaknesses, opportunities and threats), gap analysis,

ROI/ROE (return on investment/return on equity), human capital (the skills, knowledge and abilities of our workforce), knowledge management and "virtual" organizations are becoming more commonplace in most forward-thinking organizations. There is no reason, however, for these "business strategy" tools and concepts to be limited to graduates of MBA programs. The business-oriented tools we describe in this book are not difficult to use. They are practical. They can be used by front-line employees as well as senior management to assist you and your organization in planning and successfully implementing high-growth strategies.

We take for granted that you and members of your organization work hard, have integrity, value quality, want excellent service for your customers, insist on efficiency and that you have (or will soon create) a compelling vision for the future of your organization. These are the givens for growth. They are necessary, but not sufficient for high growth. The chapters that follow will give you important tools to use in developing the high-growth strategies that your organization needs to achieve its vision.

Acknowledgements

The authors gratefully acknowledge the large number of businesses, nonprofit organizations and educational institutions in which we have served as officers, chairmen and regular members of the board, legal counsel, consultants, advisers and employees. In addition we thank those companies and non-profit organizations that collect and disseminate information on the future of business including the World Future Society, the Strategic Leadership Forum and the universities where we have studied. This book could not have been written without the wisdom provided to us by the management of MicroStrategy, Inc. and the American Society for Training and Development who opened up their strategic planning processes to us and shared their working knowledge of how to create, develop and manage successful entrepreneurial organizations. The authors are fortunate to have had the experience of working with many people dedicated to improving how organizations operate, develop and most important, grow.

This book is written for everyone who is involved in creating or managing businesses or non-profit organizations, everyone who wants to make their business or non-profit organization work better and students of business and organizational development. For those of you who have been in the trenches doing this work and leading this work, it is to you that we dedicate this book.

Introduction

Entrepreneur – a person who organizes and manages any enterprise...one who undertakes.

Webster's

If you, as an individual, or in association with an organization, undertake to accomplish some goal on a regular basis, you are an *entrepreneur* and the organization is *entrepreneurial*. Using Webster's definition, all businesses, non-profit organizations and educational institutions are entrepreneurial in their nature. Welcome to the age of the entrepreneur. Everyone is included.

This book focuses on how you and your organization can develop strategic plans and successfully implement high-growth strategies. Throughout this book the fields of business, sociology, psychology, economics, accounting, organizational development, law, technology, finance, and others will be combined with "street sense" gained from the authors' study and experience with hundreds of companies, non-profit organizations and educational institutions. This book is designed to introduce you and your organization to a strategic toolkit that will improve your operations and assist you in developing and implementing better high-growth strategies. This book will also assist you in creating a more empowering, creative place of work for you and everyone associated with your organization.

It is our goal for this book to be as applicable to the person wanting to start his or her own first business or non-profit organization as it is to teams of executives at GE, IBM or CARE. This book presents examples of successful strategic planning activities and high-growth strategies from many organizations. One company, MicroStrategy, Inc. and one non-profit organization, The American Society for Training and Development (ASTD) have been selected for particular attention throughout this book due to their extraordinary success over the past several years. MicroStrategy, Inc. is a leader in the field of "decision support systems," a new business format where organizations are beginning to collect, warehouse and analyze large volumes of data to assist them in making business decisions. Success in this field over the next 20 years could make some aspects of businesses and non-profit organizations run on "auto pilot." In addition to having the potential for radically shifting the way business decisions are made in the future, MicroStrategy has grown from 150 employees in 1995 to 950 employees in 1999 and successfully raised $48 million in an initial public offering that gave up only three percent of the voting rights in the corporation. The American Society for Training and Development, the leading trade association in the field of training with 70,000 members, has also grown rapidly and is developing measures of the impact and effectiveness of training programs in an area where no reliable measures have previously existed. The ability of an organization to pinpoint, with precision, the impact and effectiveness of training efforts in improving employee productivity and improving an organization's bottom line, could radically improve not only the $55 billion training industry in the US, it could spread quickly around the world and lead to dramatic improvements in our ability to provide effective training to address world social and business needs. ASTD is an entrepreneurial non-profit organization that doubled its membership from 35,000 to 70,000 members between 1994–1998 and has recently begun an extensive international program to expand its scope of operations worldwide.

This book includes the "tools" you can use in guiding your business or non-profit organization to make the best strategic decisions possible. These are tools that can be used by managers, employees, consultants, volunteers or anyone affiliated with your organization. These tools can be used by groups or can be first used by individuals to bring organized, strategic thinking to the group or full organization. Throughout the book we share insights directly from companies and non-profit organizations where we have had direct experience in witnessing growth over the past three decades. These examples were selected because they come from a cross section of organizations in the economy, because they are have produced significant growth and, most importantly, because these examples carry with them insights that can assist you and your organization in creating and executing high-growth strategies.

Defining "high-growth strategies"

A high-growth strategy requires five distinct elements. First, it requires "change." Growth is change. It requires organizational change, a change in perception, a change in standards, a change in what workers and managers do and in how they do it. There cannot be high growth without significant change.

Second, it requires significant, measurable economic growth for the organization. For example, we have established a benchmark of 25 percent growth per year in revenues (membership) as a somewhat arbitrary line for earmarking "high-growth strategies." For start ups, the benchmark could be 100 percent growth for a few years since the base of operations is so small. However, as companies and organizations grow, the conventional wisdom is that high growth is harder and harder to achieve. Through strategic partnering and the new economics of the information age this conventional wisdom is giving way to a new reality that growth based on knowledge and improvement actually fuels further growth.

Third, high growth requires that "strategy," "strategic thinking" and "strategic planning" all play a significant role in the growth process and in producing strong economic results. We would be the first to admit that serendipity, synchronicity, chance, experimentation and those "things" that cannot be managed or planned for such as "luck," all play a significant role in determining just how much growth a company or non-profit will achieve in any particular year. However, we agree with the great golfer, Gary Player, who said, "The more I practice, the luckier I get." There are great similarities between what Gary Player called "practice" and what we call "strategic planning."

Fourth, the term "high-growth strategies" requires that an individual, company, non-profit organization, or educational institution has some picture of where it wants to go, how it wants to get there and by when. In this book we discuss "vision statements," "mission statements," "strategic plans," and other documents that put in writing not only the *goals* of the organization, but also the *values* of the organization. We are clear that growth must be done in a manner consistent with an organization's known and agreed upon values and culture or it will not be sustainable.

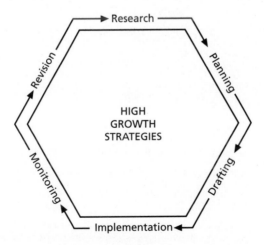

Fig. 1 Six sides of the coin

Fifth, "high-growth strategies" are dynamic. They both change the business environment and are changed themselves by what we learn daily about the economic, social, technological and political environment relevant to our organization. "Strategies" as we use the term in this book includes both the research, planning and drafting of the strategy and the implementation, monitoring and revision. These are six sides of the same coin.

Therefore, the goal of this book is to assist you and everyone in your organization in creating and sustaining the most productive decision making and implementation environment possible. In an age where more information is available to more people than ever before, it will be your ability to develop and implement high-growth strategies that will determine whether your organization achieves and can sustain high growth. Welcome to the journey.

High-growth strategies – where do we begin?

- Introduction

- Phase one: the context for growth – the role of defining your market and mission and vision statements

- Phase two: a closer look at the objectives of growth for your organization

- Entering phase three: beginning to develop "the plan"

- Completing phase three: creating the strategic plan and crafting strategies

- Promoting the success of phase three: implementation of your strategic plan

- Conclusion

I believe the business community has a unique role to play in bringing about the transformation in consciousness that must occur if we are to survive. Business is the most flexible and change-oriented segment of our society. Constant interaction with marketplace realities makes it necessary for executives, managers and entrepreneurs to reassess policies at regular intervals, evaluating them in terms of the costs, benefits, and risks involved. Successful business leaders must be ready to abandon unworkable policies and adopt new strategies to meet new challenges.

Harold Willens, *The Trimtab Factor*, 1984

Introduction

There are three basic phases of strategic planning. The key to developing a good, flexible strategic plan is the understanding that while phase one should be undertaken before phase two and phase two before phase three, in essence the ideas your organization develops in phase two and phase three will require changes in what you produced in phase one and two. Each phase is related and totally interdependent.

In *phase one*, organizations should prepare mission and vision statements and develop clarity and commitment in defining:

- why it is that your organization wants to grow
- your market
- your business
- what kind of organization you are now and
- what kind of organization you want to become.

In *phase two*, your organization must define and reach alignment on what constitutes "high growth." Is it a strong increase in profits, revenues, members, units sold, services delivered or some other "metric"? The answer to this simple question may be surprising when it is rigorously pursued and the implications of how your organization answers this question, and the priorities that it sets, will be profound.

The *third phase*, which is unfortunately where most organizations start, is the process of drafting the strategic plan and related, background documents and crafting the strategies necessary to implement the strategic plan.

In this chapter we define "strategy" in a practical, useful way that is just as applicable to the person who is thinking about starting a business, non-profit organization or educational institution as it is to the CEO of a major multinational organization with hundreds of thousands of employees and millions of customers.

Phase one: the context for growth – the role of defining your market and mission and vision statements

Why does the American Society for Training and Development (ASTD) need to be *the leader* in generating, discovering, gathering and disseminating the best knowledge regarding training, as stated in its "red book," its strategic planning document?

Why does MicroStrategy need to be *the leader* in the field of data warehousing and data mining? Why does it need to stay ahead of the field in the "decision support system" movement engulfing American businesses and why does it need to become a ten billion dollar company as its President and Chairman Michael Saylor promises?

Why does your business or organization *need* to achieve a particular result? Why does it need to achieve "high growth?"

These questions lead us to the primal importance of "context" when it comes to creating and sustaining high-growth strategies. Without the proper context, sustainable high-growth strategies are not only impossible to achieve in the long run, they are impossible to even start in the short run.

Our research and work over the past three decades has shown that organizations must grow or they will become insignificant, because *growth fuels vitality and leadership*. Progress toward and success in reaching goals gives confidence, creates meaning in the workplace and gives an organization the opportunity to achieve a strong financial footing. Growth can also create "growing pains" including cash flow problems, disorganization and chaos and take an organization to a level that is not sustainable. Strategy often is the link that differentiates successful growth from destructive growth. Strategy and the successful use of the tools that we provide in this book can make the difference between high, sustainable growth and no growth at all.

Jim Moore's book *Death of Competition* gives a great insight into the life of a business or organization when he says there are four stages in a business or organization's life.

1 Create the vision for the organization and start operations.
2 Market expansion with the goal of attaining critical mass, sustainability, leadership and significance in the marketplace.
3 Resist the inevitable market challenges to your market position, or to your authority.
4 Death or renewal.

Most growth-oriented people, companies and organizations agree, at least conceptually, on stage one – every organization needs a vision and needs to undertake the steps necessary to start its operation. It is in the second stage of an organization's life where our research shows that most organizations fail to pursue the proper strategy. Most companies and organizations believe that the goal of stage two is simply "market expansion" and that *any* growth means success in stage two. Moore's treatise that an organization in stage two must seek to achieve strong growth and achievement of a critical mass in the marketplace is confirmed by our research. Most of the organizations we have seen falter or struggle just to survive, fail in stage two to emphasize that the purpose of market expansion is not just to grow a little or even to grow steadily, but to grow to the level where your organization can achieve *significance* in the marketplace, can achieve a *critical mass* in the marketplace, can achieve *sustainability* and can achieve a level of *"authority"* where your organization's actions are important to your employees, to your customers and to the entire market that your organization serves.

Defining stage two in this way is as critical for small businesses, small non-profits and even sole proprietorships as it is for the larger organizations in this world. The goal of simple market expansion fails to lead to successful and sustainable high-growth strategies for several important reasons. First, a company or non-profit can attempt simple expansion in a given market without ever clearly understanding the full scope of the market. Selling a few more bicycles or computers, recruiting a few additional church, mosque or synogogue members, and providing a few more meals on wheels can easily be attained through the simple market expansion approach.

However, to begin thinking clearly about attaining market significance, becoming an authority in the market, achieving critical mass and sustainability, it is necessary to develop an excellent understanding of the market in which you or your organization participates. ASTD's plan to be the leading knowledge brokering organization in the training field requires it to figure out in advance what knowledge is needed 5, 10 or even 20 years down the road in the training industry. ASTD has done that, focusing on the need for reliable measurement systems to measure the effectiveness and impact of training programs worldwide. MicroStrategy's plan to be the leader in the field of "decision support systems" requires it to understand how we can use information in the future to aid businesses, government and individuals in making and implementing better decisions. MicroStrategy has done that by focusing on developing new technologies and new approaches to link the decision maker with the information he or she needs when the decision maker needs the information and in a manner that the decision maker can use on the road, in the car, in meetings and in the office. By seeking market significance and a position of authority within a market, an organization is called upon to undertake significant research, keep abreast of trends, customer wants and technological advances that can reshape the industry. Most importantly, the goal of market significance or authority in a market creates a brilliant context for growth that even the smallest organizations can develop and sustain. Small organizations, such as a school PTA or a small grocery store should define their "market" in terms where success is achieved by being a leader, by becoming the authority in their well-defined market and by making sure that their efforts make a real contribution to their members, employees, owners and customers.

This approach of seeking to attain and maintain a strong position in your market has the added advantage of helping you and your organization identify the "gap" between where your organization is today and where it intends to be in the future. The "gap analysis", explained in Chapter 2, creates what some call "creative tension" between what you and your organization have achieved in the past and where it must go in order to achieve high-growth strategies. The "gap" is one of the central elements in creating the necessary context for high growth in an entrepreneurial organization.

The "context for growth" thus starts a new way for you and your organization to think about your vision, your mission and your goals. Achieving a position of market importance, not merely expansion or some additional revenues, will become a central tenet of your high-growth strategy. When your organization begins to address the questions "What market do we want to lead?" and "How can we make a more significant contribution to our customers, members, employees and owners?" then your organization is well on the way to creating a meaningful, supportive context that can lead toward the successful development and implementation of "high-growth strategies." As you will see throughout this book, ASTD and MicroStrategy are well on their way toward answering these fundamental questions for their organizations.

The second basis for a high-growth strategy is the compelling reason behind your company or organization's commitment to growth. Usually, this reason is found in an organization's mission or vision statement. ASTD believes that improvement in training programs and in the way we measure the impact of training programs are essential in order to make organizations more efficient, equitable and productive. Through improving training, ASTD seeks to improve the quality of our worklife, the products and services we buy and the world's standard of living. MicroStrategy believes that it can make businesses, non-profit organizations and individuals more efficient and productive by creating systems that improve the ability of human beings to make better, more informed decisions and to carry them out routinely, quickly and efficiently. Everybody agrees that airplanes are safer because of autopilot systems. MicroStrategy's goal is to assist businesses and decision makers worldwide to make many of their inventory, purchasing, selling, resource allocation and even customer selection and customer relationship decisions using data analysis and decision-making systems that look and operate, in principle, like the autopilot systems used to fly airplanes.

An organization must develop a compelling reason for attempting to embark on a high-growth strategy. Why seek to lead a market or become significant in a given market? The answer will be different for each organization and each market. However, the quality of your organization's answer and the alignment it can create among employees, customers, members, owners and other stakeholders in support of that answer will be an essential contributor to your success in developing, implementing and sustaining high-growth strategies.

How does any organization go about the process of creating the context for growth? How does it create the compelling reason to grow? How does it define the market that it wants to lead? The process begins by going back to fundamental questions such as the following.

- What is the business we are in?
- What is our purpose? Our vision?
- How do we intend to achieve our mission?
- What growth objectives are the organization attempting to achieve?
- What growth objectives are complementary?
- What growth objectives are conflicting?
- What are the highest priority objectives to be achieved?
- What are our organization's most widely held beliefs or values?
- What distinguishes our organization's culture from other organizations?
- How do we want to be different, better than other organizations?
- What is our schedule for achieving specific targets for growth?

The vision statement will describe in qualitative terms the overarching goals of your organization and how the market in which you participate or the world at large will be changed as your organization begins to accomplish and then later expand its vision. The mission statement will discuss the values that your proposed activity will adhere to and describe some of the major steps toward achieving your goals. Via the Internet, it is possible to access other organizations' mission and vision statements easily. Appendix A contains the vision and mission statements of Growth Strategies, Inc., a consulting firm for businesses, non-profit organizations and educational institutions. In order for your organization to develop and implement high-growth strategies, it is essential that it creates and solidly agrees, on its own unique vision and mission statements.

Mission and vision statements do not cost much money to produce and may not take a long time to write. These statements form an important part of an organization's creation of a compelling context for growth. How does an organization know that it has created a strong context for growth, and how does it know when it needs to revisit and renew that context for growth? The answer lies in getting input from the people involved at all levels of your organization, including volunteers if your organization uses them. Are your employees, members, customers, volunteers and suppliers aware of the vision and mission of the organization? Do they support it? Does it motivate them to work together toward achieving the mission? Do they stay with your organization as employees and customers in part because of the vision of the organization? Does the vision provide meaning to the employees and help serve as the social glue in your organization? Is the vision simple, concise and consistent with the operations of your organization? The answers to all of these questions will shed light on whether the organization has created a strong enough context for growth.

The next question is how to achieve high growth once the context is properly established. To do that requires a strategic planning process that produces a great, readily implementable strategy that is flexible and changeable based on early feedback regarding its implementation successes and difficulties.

What is strategy?

A recent book *Strategy Safari* outlines the many schools of thought on strategic planning that have evolved in the business world. *Strategy Safari* identifies over 11 different types of roles that strategic planning serves in organizations. Seven key roles of strategic planning include:

- as a tool for creating vision for the organization
- as a device for collective input into creating and promoting the direction of an organization
- as a reactive tool to respond to environmental factors
- as an analytical device
- as a power assessment or negotiation support tool
- as a transformational device designed to reinvent the organization
- as an emergent device to guide the flexible organization by plotting policies and direction while empowering a broad range of decision making as new information and opportunities arise.

Since we promote the view that strategic planning *should not be any more complex than absolutely necessary*, we have created three groupings of strategies based in part on the work of Murtzberg and our own adaptation. The three groups are as follows.

- *Intuitive strategies*. These strategies are often not written, and are based on little systematic analysis of the environment, the current situation or organizational capacity. These strategies are based on an idea of the ultimate goal and a feel for how to achieve that goal.
- *Umbrella strategies*. These strategies are usually written and global in nature. They take into account some key aspects of the enviroment, the current situation and organizational capacity and set the direction and major policies an organization is to follow in seeking to achieve a particular result.
- *Planned strategies*. These strategies are always written, They take into account in detail the relevant internal and external environments an organization faces, the organization's resource needs and current organizational capacity to achieve growth, the allocation of responsibilities, the steps and the timetable regarding how to achieve a particular result. In addition, these strategies include a strategy to monitor the results of the implementation and to use the information received about the implementation of the strategy in a systematic way to improve both the strategy itself and the implementation of the strategy on an ongoing basis.

High-growth strategies often combine the strengths of each type of strategy, often placing a greater reliance on planned or umbrella strategies. The strength of a high-growth strategy for an entrepreneurial organization will be the result of using the proper mix of intuitive strategies (making the right decision on the fly when data are not available), umbrella strategies (good policies and directions) and planned strategies (careful analysis and detailed plans as necessary to coordinate activities).

While the commonly held belief is that the larger the organization the greater the need for reliance on a planned strategy, in fact, the opposite may be true. Small organizations, if they intend to achieve a high-growth strategy, have such a large gap to overcome in order to achieve their high-growth goals that planned strategies are often essential to chart the course for high growth. Large organizations may be able to grow quickly with the successful implementation and coordination of the organization around one key strategic decision, such as changing the compensation system of employees (bonuses or employee stock options), improving the quality and efficiency of manufacturing through increasing the use of quality monitoring systems, outsourcing, team assembly systems or other manufacturing innovations. While the effective implementation of one key decision can make a huge difference, planned strategies may be somewhat less important for high growth in big organizations. However a series of decisions coordinated among many participants of many organizations may be necessary for a small organization to achieve high growth.

All strategic planning processes must achieve a balance between continuity and change. The worlds of business, non-profit organizations and educational institutions are changing faster than ever. In fact, they are becoming one world of "commerce." Continuity of values that an organization stands for has never been more important. Strategic planning must take into account an organization's "adaptive capacity," i.e. its ability to absorb and implement change. The strategic planning process must promote flexibility and strive to increase an organization's ability to change. The strategic planning process must support the individuals in the organization in being able to develop the new attitudes and the skills necessary to accomplish the new behaviors that are require to achieve high growth. Strategic plans must be sensitive to an organization's core values and core competencies. In addition, they must, where required, seek to change the core values and operational culture, when these values and culture impede high-growth strategies. The most ambitious strategic plans are those designed to lead change in an entire industry or non-profit sector and that have extraordinary, innovative ideas built into the vision that drives the strategic planning process.

> **The most ambitious strategic plans are those designed to lead change in an entire industry or non-profit sector and have extraordinary, innovative ideas built into the vision that drives the strategic planning process.**

Strategic plans can be non-starters or even be destructive unless they:

- have sufficient support of stakeholders
- have a well-articulated, compelling reason behind them
- are supported by the view that the future for the organization and its market or the world at large will not be acceptable or desirable unless the plan is successfully implemented and the goals achieved
- successfully take into account the human factors involved in implementing strategic plans.

The human factors – including personal dynamics, psychology, communication, enrollment, empowerment, learning and the willingness and ability that humans have to adapt to new circumstances – are critical and should be assessed and taken into account in the strategic planning process. All high-growth strategic plans create a process of change that requires that human beings gain new skills, change their behavior, confront the unknown, experience loss of security and comfort and do all of this while not reducing their productivity, satisfaction or commitment to the organization. *This is no small order*. This book not only makes you aware of how tall an order strategic planning and its implementation is, but also gives you guidance, through both the external landscape and the internal organizational environment so that you can develop better strategic plans and reap the rewards, in terms of high growth, that the successful implementation of high-growth strategies can bring to you and your organization.

With the Internet and the explosion of world-wide communication, the entire arena of strategic planning and high-growth strategies is changing for many organizations, although not all. Today, one can put up a website and theoretically have fifty million customers tomorrow. Even if this growth seems magical, it is not. Companies such as Amazon.com and America Online have developed corporate strategies that combine strong elements of intuitive, umbrella and planned strategies. In Darryl Conner's books, *Leading At the Edge of Chaos*, and *Managing At The Speed of Change*, he states that organizations today must be "nimble" in order to take advantage of market opportunities and avoid market pitfalls. The flexibility of an *intuitive strategy* is critical and the experimentation that this type of strategy promotes rapidly increases our learning and experience base to create new products and services on a regular basis to meet changing customer requirements. *Umbrella strategies* keep organizations without large strategic planning departments focused, and allow employees to be empowered to make good business decisions consistent with the company's overall strategic plan. *Planned strategies* provide excellent guidance and in essence are "decisions made in advance" regarding how to approach and succeed in either a given market situation or in creating new markets. All three types of strategy must be used in the right combination in every organization that seeks to achieve significance in a market and which seeks to become an authority in a given market sector.

There is much debate as to the relative value of "strategic planning" versus "strategic thinking." Strategic planning is the process where an organization:

- defines its vision and goals
- assesses its current position and abilities
- systematically pulls together knowledge and information about the external environment
- identifies and evaluates opportunities, activities and approaches that will promote its success
- develops a plan, according to a schedule, for implementing the activities most likely to succeed
- monitors the results of the activities
- revises the plan and activities to improve its chances of success.

Strategic thinking can be thought of as a more isolated event (as opposed to an ongoing organized process) where an individual or organization makes a decision about a certain direction or significant activity, taking into account the organization's vision and goals, its current reality, the environment and opportunities/challenges that the oganization faces. In reality, strategic thinking and strategic planning are two sides of the same basic coin and organizations which promote both at all levels of their organization are better positioned to develop and implement high-growth strategies than their counterparts who don't.

One business consultant used to give his clients 40 ideas for growing their organizations each and every quarter. The consultant has replaced this practice with giving his clients several *strategies* each quarter for growing their organizations. Why are several high-growth strategies better than 40 growth-oriented ideas?

Webster's Dictionary defines strategy as "a plan, method or series of maneuvers or strategems for obtaining a specific goal or result." Strategy begins with a clear idea of the specific goal or result that you want to produce. It starts with the "end." That is why the mission and vision statements for your organization are so critical. They are the beginning points toward development of a strategy, be it a survival strategy, a low-growth strategy or a high-growth strategy.

The creation, development and implementation of successful high-growth strategies for entrepreneurial organizations requires:

- a process
- a calendar
- significant research and learning by the individuals involved
- a communication system that supports inputs from every quarter of the organization and delivers outputs and direction from the leadership with clarity and precision.

The communication system requires not only a common language, but also common assumptions and a culture in the organization that promotes, *even demands* – the free flow of honest, accurate information in all directions within the organization and between the organization and its external environment.

A communication system based on integrity, where the motto, "The truth is good enough," must be instilled in every organization that seeks to implement and sustain high-growth strategies. The efficiencies that are created and the commitment generated within an organization (and between an organization, its members and its external relations) by being able to rely absolutely on everyone in the organization explaining things accurately are the strongest selling points for organizations to tell the truth in every transaction and interaction. The huge decrease in stock prices of Cendant and other corporations when it is announced that the accuracy of their financial reports is under serious question shows that Wall Street will severely punish corporations and their investors when it appears that inaccurate financial reports have been published. In addition, the high-growth strategies of the Olympic Games may be in some jeopardy due to the scandals associated with the awarding of the 2002 winter Olympics to Salt Lake City. Although no one can measure the "stock price" of government, we can measure the cost in tens of millions of dollars in government expenditures and billions of dollars of human time, effort, TV and media exposure as the price the US paid for the "untruths" of President Clinton. High-growth strategies require not only an open communication system within your organization, but also honest, accurate, reliable communication throughout the organization.

Can there be a high-growth strategy without a *calendar*, i.e. a timetable? We doubt it. A new word is cropping up in the business and organizational development literature. That word is "calendarizing." We like the old word "schedule." Webster's Dictionary defines "schedule" as "a plan of procedure, usually written, for a proposed objective, esp. with reference to the sequence of and time allotted for each item or operation necessary to its completion." *Schedules are fundamental organizing principles.* Ask yourself what is the fundamental organizing principle of any high-growth professional sport? It is the "schedule." Without the schedule, there is no professional sport of any economic significance. The NBA and the basketball players union both learned this lesson at the strike-delayed start of the 1998–1999 season. No schedule. No business. No sport.

Mission statements and vision statements do not contain schedules generally, although it is advisable to put a "by when" into your mission statement and vision statement. The processes of developing a strategy and implementing it must be driven by a schedule. At ASTD, the strategic planning system comprised 27 people, and included outside consultants, numerous committees, background papers, review time frames, meeting time frames, decision deadlines and other key milestones set in a schedule nearly one full year in advance of the final completion date.

The coordination of all of the elements of a strategic plan, for even the smallest organizations, requires a schedule of events prepared in advance to guide the process. At MicroStrategy, there are quarterly strategic planning events lasting two days. These strategy sessions, involving over a dozen people, take place away from the office, and are followed by a schedule for disseminating the information and decisions generated at the sessions. MicroStrategy develops annual strategic plans with quarterly in-depth reviews. ASTD undergoes its detailed strategic planning process every two or three years with a goal of setting two-year budgets to replace the current one-year budgeting cycle.

Effective strategic planning is important to all organizations, large and small, that seek high growth. In small non-profits such as the Joy of Sports Foundation, Inc., one or two people can prepare the basic strategy documents in a few hours or a few days. In larger organizations, such as MicroStrategy and ASTD, the process is more complex. In every organization the elements of a strategic plan, including marketing, recruiting, financial administration, technology, alliances, customer service, budget and other key elements must be coordinated. The process of coordinating each of these elements is called *managing* the "strategic planning process." In each organization, regardless of the size, one person or committee must be responsible for managing the strategic planning process. The recognition of this fact has led to the creation, in many organizations, of the position of "V.P. for Strategy," and in-house staff and consultants who occupy this function are, on good days, called "strategic visionaries."

Strategic planning is dynamic – it changes all the time. It collects input from many sources on regular and ad hoc bases. A strategic plan is a living, breathing document based on the best information available at the time. The days of a five-year strategic plan being cast in stone are over. Even strategic plans that have a one-year focus must be flexible. Probably few at America OnLine in 1997 would have thought that in 1998 it would purchase Netscape and SunMicro Systems. The opportunity was envisioned, strategic plans were quickly assembled, financing was arranged, negotiations were held and the plan was implemented. Did the Microsoft antitrust trial change the landscape of the industry during late 1998 to such an extent that such a merger between AOL, Netscape and Sun became not only possible, but also an excellent strategic move? We do not know what role the antitrust trial played in America OnLine, Netscape and SunMicro Systems' thinking, but we do know that if it did play a role, the strategic planners at each of these three organizations reacted quickly to an ever-changing business environment well before the trial was over and any dust settled on the future role of Microsoft in the computer software and Internet industry.

Since the strategic planning process is dynamic, most organizations would not be well served by a strategic planning process that takes an entire year before implementation begins. In addition, organizations can no longer rely on a strategic planning process that is conducted once every three years. This model, previously employed by ASTD, renders an organization less able to collect and analyze information on a continuous basis, and therefore less able to react to opportunities in the marketplace that show up quickly and may pass just as quickly.

The new-found dynamism of strategic planning has spawned the creation and expansion of several monthly publications that are useful to aid an organization in its ability to undertake strategic thinking and strategic planning processes. Monthly publications such as *Fast Company, Inc. Magazine,* and Booze, Allen & Hamilton's *Strategy and Business, Harvard Business Review* and organizations such as the Strategic Leadership Forum, the American Management Association, the American Society of Association Executives and many others provide monthly publications and reports, or have web pages or have interactive CD-ROM strategic planning products to aid a company or non-profit organization with strategic planning. We recommend that your organization custom-makes your strategic planning process in order to generate a process that pays off dividends from the first day it begins the process. Phase one of the strategic planning process – creating the context for high-growth strategies – can, in and of itself, be one of the most important activities your organization has ever undertaken. And it is only the beginning.

Phase two: a closer look at the objectives of growth for your organization

From the book the *Art of War* by Sun Tsu, we learn that the direct approach is not always the best approach. We also learn that any strategy must take into account the external environment (economic, political, market, demographic, etc.) and the internal environment (including the human factors within your organization, its culture, values, stakeholders and mind-set) in which the strategy is crafted. Every strategic plan must have clear and well-defined objectives. Ultimately, the goal of every strategic plan is to achieve all that you set out to accomplish in your organization's mission statement and to do so following the values included in your organization's vision statement. However, at the outset, strategic planning at the ground floor level must focus on exactly what short-term or near-term objective or objectives you are attempting to achieve in your market or markets. Again, we start at the end. What does high-growth mean to your organization in detail? Generally there are three types of objectives that organizations pursue that they label "high-growth."

The first type of growth objective is often defined as financial success or bottom line success in terms of output or market expansion (see the example below).

GROWTH =

- more revenues
- more sales
- more profit
- more shareholder value
- more economic value added
- more cash flow
- more customers
- more members
- more people served

- more assets
- more publicity
- more impact on policy
- more students/teachers/courses
- more books in print
- more markets served
- more potential customers (prospects), etc.

This is often termed short-run "financial advantage." Every category is measurable. However, it is important to note that the strategy to increase sales may not always be the best strategy to increase profits. One strategy that will be discussed in detail later, "outsourcing," where your organization relies on the assets of another organization to fill a supply or resource need, may conflict with your organization's strategy to build a larger asset base. Developing a high-growth strategy requires fine tuning and prioritizing among the objectives your organization is seeking to achieve. Organizations often want to achieve many objectives simultaneously. Once strategies are developed to achieve each objective, it will be seen that many of the strategies are complementary. However, where they are not complementary, priorities will need to be established as to which strategy should be pursued over another. An essential component of a successful process for managing the creation and implementation of high-growth strategies is knowing how to sequence the various strategies into an integrated, holistic strategy management process.

> An essential component of a successful process for managing the creation and implementation of high-growth strategies is knowing how to sequence the various strategies into an integrated, holistic strategy management process.

A second type of growth objective is more competitive in nature. The term "competitive advantage" can be viewed in many ways, as shown by the example below.

Creating and analyzing high-growth strategies from a "competitive" vantage point requires you to gather data on your competitors and compare your results either to your competitors' or compare them against your organization's own past performance or your projected performance. Again, measurement is required.

COMPETITIVE ADVANTAGE =	
• better customer/member service than others	• increase in market share
• improved customer service (better than your organization is now doing)	• distinguish/differentiate your organization from competitors, etc.

The process called "benchmarking" is documenting a starting point for comparison and collecting data and information so that when you compare results after the implementation of a strategy, a fair comparison can be made. With the Internet and the explosion of data-tracking software programs, ideas such as measuring many key variables in your business environment (using a "balanced scorecard" or some other approach in tracking the "metrics" of your organization) are now feasible. In addition, with the greater availability of data through the use of computers, new data warehousing and data mining techniques, it is possible to measure where your organization is now and re-measure where it is in the future using comparable data. A good wrinkle in using competitive advantage as an objective of your high-growth strategies is that if your organization is already doing a great job being the market leader (or town leader or block leader), your organization can always and must always compete against itself. In fact, our consulting practices have discovered that market-leading organizations almost always compete against their past successes, using them as a benchmark rather than relying on direct comparisons with competitors.

A third type of growth objective is what we call "capacity building," or "developing organizational capability." This new focus is especially relevant to the non-profit sector which historically has been more about doing good deeds than about building organizations that have the capacity to continue to do good deeds after the big grant or contribution runs out. This objective is also critical in the for-profit sector, as companies must focus on becoming global in scope and determine daily whether to take on new opportunities based on their capacity to perform the activities necessary to succeed in the new endeavor. With the current strong emphasis on "strategic partnering," mergers and acquisitions, an organization's ability to develop and implement strategies designed to increase its capacity may well become more important than its ability to create profits in the short run. Examples of growth objectives in the area of "capacity building" include those shown below.

CAPACITY BUILDING =

- increasing the quality/training/education of the organization's workforce
- improved equipment
- use of technology and facilities
- expansion/improvement of the board of directors
- expanding the organization's geographical presence (or footprint)

- investing in knowledge management systems, organization retreats and cultural events
- creating and implementing an organizational contribution strategy
- acquiring assets
- investing in strategic planning systems, etc.

Capacity building requires honest capacity assessment. Creating and attempting to implement a strategic plan that cannot be successfully implemented because there are insufficient resources or stakeholder support, overloads your organization's ability to change or violates the unstated culture of your organization, will cause significant employee discord. In addition, it will threaten the viability of future strategic planning efforts and the organization itself. Assessing an organization's present capacity requires honest feedback and communication across every level of the organization. It also requires a clear determination within an organization as to who is committed to helping build up the capacity of the organization and who is committed (sometimes covertly) to keeping the organization from increasing its capacity. Strategic planners must constantly make assessments and carefully monitor the ability of an organization to grow, learn, take risks and step into the unknown world of high growth.

The payoffs from successful capacity building are two-fold. First, your organization can achieve and sustain higher growth with a stronger foundation. Second, your organization, once a sufficient organizational capacity is developed, will not be willing to settle for anything less than high-growth. The importance of this second payoff cannot be overestimated.

Entering phase three: beginning to develop "the plan"

Phase three begins with:

- selecting the person, team or teams to lead the development of the strategic plan and its components
- deciding the time frame or frames the strategic plan will cover (this can be as short or as long as an organization wishes)

- identifying a schedule for the plan, including all major meetings, review periods, decision points, implementation phase-in dates, etc
- determining the budget or resources to expend on the plan, and software to be used
- determining how the plan and background papers, if any, will be distributed and reviewed
- setting a *learning* agenda and a *research* agenda
- determining how the plan and background papers will be reviewed by persons in the organization (or outsiders), modified through review and discussion and ultimately adopted (voted on)
- selecting the person or group responsible for overseeing the initial implementation of the actions called for in the plan
- selecting the person or group responsible for monitoring the results of the plan and outside environmental factors which will result in modifications to the plan after the initial adoption of the plan takes hold
- developing an ongoing strategic planning system that continuously works for your organization.

This entire process can take less than an hour or several days, depending on the size and decision-making processes of your organization.

Undertaking these activities will result in *organizational breakthrough* for your organization. Even if you are a small company or non-profit, identifying these roles and who will perform them will help improve your organization's capacity. In addition, in undertaking these steps, it may be advisable to seek the assistance of others on a paid or voluntary basis who may be outside of your organization and have an objective set of eyes and ears to help with this process and the next part of the process, creating the strategic plan.

Completing phase three: creating the strategic plan and crafting strategies

While crafting a great strategy is an art form, we develop in this book a methodology for crafting strategies and managing the strategic planning process that will promote the creation and successful implementation of realistic, executable high-growth strategies that are right for your organization. There are seven steps to your high-growth strategic plan. They can be accomplished with pen and paper, with dedicated software and through involvement of many people or just a few. We recommend the inclusion of more of the people in your organization rather than less and starting with pen and paper (or simple word processing and spreadsheets) unless your organization is clear about the best software to use. We do not recommend putting off the strategic planning process for months or even weeks looking for the "perfect" strategic planning software. The steps in the process are outlined below.

Seven steps to a strategic plan

Step 1: identify where your organization is today and how it got there

Identify your high-growth objective in terms of its rationale (compelling reason) and in numerical terms. Describe the gap that exists between where your organization is today and where it intends to go.

For example, if one of your high priority objectives is to be a ten billion dollar company in annual sales (a goal of MicroStrategy), identify where you are today and how you got there. For some goals, this process might be difficult to quantify with great precision, and if this is the case, use broad brush estimates if necessary. For example, if one of your high priority objectives is to be the recognized world leader in the knowledge development and dissemination aspects of the training industry (the goal of ASTD), then you need to know where you stand today in relation to that objective. While there are an infinite number of ways to quantify the goal "recognized world leader" one can select such indicators as:

- how many ASTD members or conference attendees are from countries other than the US
- how many organizations/individuals purchase ASTD materials from outside of the US
- how many speeches have ASTD employees given overseas in the past year
- how many offices does ASTD have outside of the US, etc.

Step 2: identify what has worked and what has not worked

At this stage, you should assess what has been successful (and what has failed) in your organization's past in its effort to reach previously articulated objectives. If the objective is new, identify what efforts have been successful in your organization's past that will contribute to success in reaching this objective.

For example, in 1994 MicroStrategy shifted its emphasis from being a software/database-oriented consulting company to a company that sells products first and consulting services second. This not only boosted revenues in the short run, it made high-growth possible, especially as the labor market was becoming tighter and tighter and MicroStrategy's ability to hire large numbers of technically trained employees was reaching limits. Selling software products is not limited in its growth potential to the extent that providing cutting edge, technologically oriented consulting services is limited in its growth potential, since providing consulting services is constrained by the limited number of trained workers currently available in this area.

ASTD has had great success in putting on educational and networking conferences nationally and internationally. In 1998, nearly 10,000 people attended the ASTD conference in San Francisco. ASTD, recognizing that conferences require years to build up in terms of quality and numbers of attendees (and are generally unprofitable during this period), decided to purchase an organization that already had multimedia education and training conferences. ASTD's goal in purchasing these conferences was to be able to skip the development stage, boost revenues and immediately provide an additional service that many of its members regarded highly.

Step 3: create new approaches to achieving your objectives

When finding new ways of achieving your objectives, you should consider both the external environment, and your current and potential resources and constraints. This may include challenging both the *industry mind-set* (this is discussed later in this book) as well as your organization's mind-set.

For example, MicroStrategy, in its early years, used another company's product as a component part of its own product (such as a car company might buy a stereo system from another company) and paid a licensing fee. When Microsoft's product "Visual Basic" came out, MicroStrategy ceased to use the other company's product and changed its product line to accommodate this new technology. This change forced MicroStrategy to stop service to users of MacIntosh computing sytems and set the company off on a far different course from its previous strategic plan.

Similarly, ASTD decided to spend hundreds of thousands of dollars annually on its website beginning in 1997 and to embrace the new technology in its efforts to reach more people worldwide. This shift in resources to a web-based knowledge management system, and a web-based customer service and information system represented a new approach designed to promote improvements in customer services and enhance the likelihood of ASTD becoming the world's leading non-profit association in the training industry.

New approaches must take into account your organization's constraints, which may include capital constraints, knowledge constraints, employee attitude constraints and other limitations that exist within any organization at any given time. Clearly identifying these constraints early in the process will give your organization both the time and inclination to address these constraints, craft more appropriate high-growth strategic plans, recruit additional resources and tackle serious, and often not discussed, organizational practices that serve as barriers to high growth.

Step 4: develop an implementation plan

This means developing a tactic around each high-growth strategy which, after careful consideration, allows your organization to predict the financial costs, timeframe, human resources needed, potential benefits and payoff and probability of success of each strategic initiative.

One organization, the small Parent Student Teacher's Association of a Maryland high school, had an approach to raise money that included collecting dues ($10 per member) and selling fruit. In 1998 (at the urging of one of the authors) the organization adopted two strategies that it had never undertaken before which challenged the mind set of the organization. The first strategy was to have different levels of membership ranging from $10 to $250. This strategy conflicted with the egalitarian philosophy of the organization, but was accepted when the higher-level contributors were given additional products and services that were not designed to give them greater access or influence within the organization. The strategy of providing a precise level of additional services and products for the higher-paying members allowed for a careful estimation of the additional cost of this strategy. This high-growth strategy resulted in over a 100 percent increase in dues collections in its first year with few additional costs. The second new strategy introduced by one of the authors was to have a car dealership donate a car to raffle off at a fund raising event. The donation of the car led to the successful development a first ever "auction" type event of the school that further builds the organizational capacity of the PTSA.

These strategies open the way for high school PTSA's throughout the country to change their mindset about raising funds, about "tiering" their membership categories while remaining a democratic, egalitarian organization and fostering win-win relationships with businesses that can benefit from investing their goods and services in a rewarding marketing effort. For each of the strategies employed, the step 4 implementation plan was both straightforward and evolving. Having the car donated led to an auction, which the school had never undertaken before. The learning that has occurred from the implementation of this event and the new "tiering" of the membership system will lead to further improvements, further refinements and new strategies to continue to promote the high growth that has begun in the 1998–1999 school season at Blair High School. In addition to financially oriented high-growth strategies, the PTSA (also at the urging of one of the authors) began efforts to improve the quality of education at the school. Reverend Jesse Jackson was invited and spoke to a large crowd at the school and efforts were started to have the highly respected organization, Quality

Education for Minorities, Inc. undertake a large scale study of the educational practices at the school. These strategies were designed to build the organizational capacity in ways that do not directly turn into dollars, but serve to increase the quality of both the PTSA and the school that it serves. Eventually the results of these strategies, if successful, will be measurable.

Step 5: compare each high-growth strategy

How do you compare alternative high-growth strategies and choose the best one or ones? How many high-growth strategies can or should your organization attempt to undertake at the same time? Which easier, less complex, or less straining high-growth strategy or strategies will create the increase in organizational capacity that will make other future or long-range high-growth strategies more likely to be successful? This process requires "guided judgment" which is an art. However, there are certain criteria which will help your organization guide itself in making these evaluations and selecting and sequencing your potential high-growth strategies in the best order. The following questions should be addressed.

- How robust or sturdy is this high-growth strategy?
- How compatible is it with our organization's capacity and culture?
- Will this strategy require changing customer behavior to a great extent or will it require only minor modifications in customer behavior to be successful?
- Do we have the right people, skills and resources to implement this strategy and implement it well, making it a source of pride to our organization?
- How much support will it have from our stakeholders?
- How big is the payoff and for how long?
- How much will it cost?
- How can this strategy become a systems-wide or organization-wide approach to growth?
- How will it affect the organization's reputation?
- What effect will it have on employee satisfaction?
- How feasible is the strategy technologically and logistically?
- How will implementation of this high-growth strategy contribute to increasing the organization's capacity and culture and its receptiveness to future high growth?

These are questions that no one person or even one department in an organization can answer fully. Unless your organization is large, using outside resources may be necessary to address many of these questions. From the beginning of the strategic planning process, and especially here in step 5 where guided judgment is required, it is important to tap into the collective wisdom of all of the people associated with your organization. At this stage, where you are comparing options for high-growth, tapping into this collective wisdom is critical not only to achieving the right decision, but also to learning how each person in your organization perceives the difficulties and potential of each of the strategies under consideration. One of the authors in a consulting assignment recommended that a 20-year-old, non-profit educational organization, which raised most of its revenues from student fees to create an "endowment" and embark on a fundraising drive, focusing first on individual donors and then progressing to companies and foundations. Much to the surprise of the author, at a board of directors meeting where this proposal was discussed, the chairman of the board asked, "Have you investigated all of the risks that are involved if our organ-

> **From the beginning of the strategic planning process, it is important to tap into the collective wisdom of all of the people associated with your organization.**

ization had more money?" Even though the board voted 15 to 0 to endorse the endowment concept, not one board member ever did anything to help the fundraising effort and it failed during its first several months to raise significant funds and was abandoned. Clearly, this strategic initiative did not have the active support of stakeholders or officers of the organization, was inconsistent with the cultural view that "more money for our organization is very risky," and the implementation plan which relied on fundraising events was neither sturdy nor robust enough to withstand a very slow start. Including the board of directors as "voters" was clearly insufficient to sustain this strategy. The success of this strategy required board members and officers to become active participants in the strategy, not just observers and voters. Without their active participation, this strategy failed one of the key questions identified above, "Do we have the right people, skills and resources to implement this strategy and implement it well, making it a source of pride to our organization?" An honest assessment of the capacity of the organization early in the strategic planning process can go far in avoiding failed strategies that deplete the organization's resources and capacity rather than lead the organization toward high-growth.

Step 6: adopt and implement

While this step may seem straightforward, our consulting experience shows that many organizations cannot tell you on what date they adopted a strategy and began implementation. A strategy becomes a living, breathing "organism" within your organization. Knowing the date a particular strategy "began implementation," tracking the pace of implementation, documenting the cost and effort that went into the implementation, and measuring the effectiveness or success of implementation are all necessary steps to successful implementation of high-growth strategies. Our experience further shows that these steps are often missing when an organization tries to figure out what went wrong with a strategy that seemed to have promise when it was on the drawing board. "Benchmarking" involves an organization's efforts to create data at the beginning of the strategic planning process to allow it to measure change and progress over time resulting from a particular strategy. We find that the whole field of benchmarking – potentially a very useful approach to organizational success – is hampered because most organizations do not adequately collect data on key factors before the strategy is implemented. There is often no document that adequately describes the strategy, when its implementation began, the real cost of the strategy or tracks the changes that resulted in bottom line success and enhanced organizational capacity as a result of adopting and implementing the new strategy. In fact, many organizations do not even track how well the actual implementation of the strategy compares to the strategy that was developed in the first place. The role of monitoring the plan and making necessary revisions to it, based on what the monitors discover, is the final and possibly the most important step in the entire strategic planning process.

Step 7: monitor and revise

Both the external environment ("the rugged landscape") and the internal environment of your organization ("the really rugged landscape") can play havoc on strategic plans. Either the internal or external environment is misread (or ignored) in the planning stage, or it changes during implementation in ways that could not have been forseen. The environment can stop the strategic plan in its tracks or may cause the strategic plan to be implemented in a way that the designers did not envision. In either event, the strategic plan will miss its mark. In addition, a strategic plan can be implemented perfectly and not create the customer response or high growth that was expected or predicted for the plan. Often organizations ignore or never fully understand the effects the internal organization, external market, or economic environment has on the implementation of the plan, or why there has been a falloff from the expected results when the implementation activities themselves go according to the plan. This is especially true if the people who are responsible for implementing the strategic plan are also the people responsible for monitoring and revising it. In small organizations, it may seem difficult to have someone or an outside group monitor the implementation and suggest revisions in the strategy who is not also responsible for the implementation of the plan. It is not difficult at all. The board of directors, consultants, volunteers or others can play this role and through technology, it is becoming easier even for the smallest organization to allo-cate the responsibility for monitoring a plan to someone different than the person or group implementing the plan. A simple "checks and balances" example will show how to accomplish this important allocation of tasks in a one person company.

There is a small company called Richardson Personal Training (RPT). This fitness-oriented company often provides 1–3 years of personal fitness training to individuals and groups at their homes, at business locations and in health clubs. RPT assists in:

- assessing a person's current fitness level and reviewing the person or group's fitness and health history
- identifying a person's fitness and health objectives
- quantifying these objectives
- developing exercises and strategies to assist the person in reaching his or her goals
- teaching and training the individual on how to perform the exercises, often using free weights and large numbers of different exercises
- scheduling the exercises
- supervising the implementation of the plan through personal, one-on-one, visits and training sessions.

The average customer usually purchases this intensive fitness training for 1–3 years. What happens after that? Usually, the individual trainee then is left on his or her own to *implement* the physical fitness regimen, *monitor* the imple-mentation and its results and *revise the implementation* to meet the targets and objectives they have set for themselves in the current period. RPT, with the assistance of one of the authors, identified the problem that inevitably occurs where the same person is given the responsibilty for implementing, monitor-ing and revising the implementation of a strategy and expanded RPT's business model to make sure that a different person is responsible for imple-menting the new strategy (that is, doing the exercises) from the person who is responsible for monitoring the implementation (the coach).

Part of RPT's new virtual business model, aided by the Internet, is that RPT will monitor the implementation of your fitness training program on a regular, periodic basis for a very small annual fee. It will monitor your implementation of your strategic plan (exercise regimen) via phone, fax and e-mail, and works with clients in this way to ensure proper implemen-tation of the plan and to revise the fitness program when weight and other data show that a change is necessary to produce the desired results. Under this virtual business model, RPT extends the "customer life" of the client considerably. This increases business revenues to RPT and allows for high growth, since RPT is able to monitor hundreds, if not thousands of customers using this approach, but could only service a small number of customers with one-on-one personal training. More importantly, this business model promotes the long-term success of the client, promotes greater customer referrals, challenges the industry mindset of how to do "personal training," is very low cost for both the client and the company, and can expand greatly with the personnel available to RPT. Simply put, RPT has the capacity to be 10 or even 100 times more profitable by adding this business model to its service offerings than it was capable of becoming under the traditional personal trainer industry mindset. The new RPT program specifically targets customer value creation in a big way at low cost, since it is surely worth a significant amount to feel better, be healthier and to extend your life by 5 years and your active life by 8 years as research shows is the result of proper, regular exercise.

Similarly, when one person or section within an organization is responsible for both the implementation and the monitoring of a strategic plan, there are no checks and balances system and no "objective eyes," as Andy Grove says, in determining if the plan is being carried out in the best possible manner. The use of paid or volunteer advisers, as discussed in Chapter 3 (see "Councils of Masters/advisory boards"), can produce not only the desired division of labor but also bring wisdom and insight to the monitoring and revision process that could never surface from the person in the trenches trying to make the plan "happen."

The point is, even if you are the smallest business or non-profit organization, a one person shop, separating out the implementation of a strategy from monitoring and suggesting revisions to the strategy or plan is not only possible, it is easy and inexpensive to do. The rewards from separating the personnel involved in step 6 (Adopt and Implement), and step 7 (Monitor and Revise), can be huge. Finding the right person or group to monitor the implementation of your high-growth strategy and suggest revisions is easy, practical and essential in insuring the successful implementation of the high-growth strategy.

Promoting the success of phase three: implementation of your strategic plan

As discussed earlier, high-growth strategies require change. Change requires people successfully doing something new and different. It also requires that this new implementation process be managed and directed. We acknowledge that, all other things being equal, any strategic planning process will work a little better if the planners and implementers (employees) have more talent, more resources, greater adaptive capacity and are luckier.

The business press is filled with articles on how difficult it is to recruit and keep high quality talent. One recent magazine article even stressed how companies should hire people who answer "Yes" convincingly to the question "Do you feel you are lucky!" This may be pushing it.

MicroStrategy moved its corporate headquarters from Delaware to northern Virginia since it believed that the Washington, D.C. area to be a "hotter" location and having a "hot" location was essential in recruiting high quality employees. One company has developed a strategy of identifying people who would make great employees or managers and letting them know *more than a year in advance* that when an opening comes up they will contact them about becoming an employee. This strategy keeps everyone in the organization constantly looking for talent far in advance of the actual need to have the talent on board, builds up tremendous good will among those told they might be offered a job in a year or two and sends a signal out to the community that the company is on a long-term growth path. In addition, many organizations, in their efforts to hire additional workers, now employ outsourcing techniques such as having temporary employment companies provide names of acceptable recruits. For years, companies have paid bonuses to current employees who recommend persons to join the organization when the job applicant is hired and stays on the job for a minimum period of time. All of these tactics can be employed by organizations as part of their high-growth strategies.

Another strategy that will assist a company in being able to recruit and keep talented employees is having a good strategic planning process that involves employees in every stage of the process. Our research has shown that great strategic planning systems bring out the very best in employees, in board members, in consultants, in managers, in customers and in the quality of products that are produced. Great strategic planning systems *leverage* talent. They may even *elevate* talent. Poor or non-existent strategic planning systems destroy and hinder talent and often send talent off to another organization. Great strategic planning systems empower employees to develop and communicate their best ideas for improving the organization, foster communication within the organization and require that employees, managers and even board members keep their eyes open to deficiencies in the internal landscape and changes in the external competitive landscape faced by the organization.

Non-profit organizations and educational institutions often rely significantly on volunteers. In fact, many for-profit companies now use volunteers who seek to improve their employability skills, seek a non-pressure work environment or who volunteer for any number of other reasons. The American Association of Retired Persons (AARP), a non-profit organization, has over 32 million members. AARP estimates that it has over 500,000 volunteers on an annual basis, many of whom devote 40 hours or more a week to volunteer activities. ASTD has thousands of volunteers who organize and staff local chapters, participate as members of working groups, committees and even serve on its board of directors. Our research with organizations which use volunteers shows clearly that volunteers want to be part of a strategic plan, they want their organizations to think about the future and ask them for help in creating the future. Often, the volunteers are the front line for the organization, the part of the organization that deals on a daily basis with the customers or persons actually served by the organization. In one instance, an organization, EMMAUS in Washington, D.C., which provides a full range of social, nutritional and health-related social services to the elderly, was debating at its board of directors' level how much to grow and how to grow. After soliciting input through surveys of its volunteers regarding the unmet need for the services it provides to the elderly community (GAP analysis), the board of directors solidly endorsed a high-growth strategy that included purchasing a building that would house not only EMMAUS's administrative staff, but also the staff of other organizations serving its target population, the elderly.

For far too long, volunteers and even board members of organizations have been asked to solve last week's problems and/or raise money to pay for things that should have been done last year. In a non-profit organization or in a business, this is a prescription for burnout. There is simply little energy to be gained from only being asked to solve problems that have plagued organizations for years. Energy and talent (and these two "phenonena" are related) are generated and supported by asking volunteers, board members and staff for their wisdom in what the organization should do,

> **For many organizations, much growth can be obtained from a better deployment of the personnel your organization has and the personnel that it will bring on board in the future.**

how it should do it better and how they can participate in creating the future of the organization.

Recently, the use of the human resources available to an organization has received little attention compared to the huge body of literature and money spent on "high technology." Yet for many organizations, where employees and volunteers are not regularly perfoming at high levels, much growth can be obtained from a better deployment of the personnel your organization has and the personnel that it will bring on board in the future. It is no accident that we use the terms "emloyees" and "volunteers" in the same breath. While we use the term "volunteers" in the traditional sense to mean non-paid persons who assist organizations on an ad hoc basis, a much broader definition of the term "volunteer" is appropriate to the future study of human resource managemient, organizational development and strategic planning.

Everyone – employees, managers, board members, stockholders, stakeholders, consultants, vendors, suppliers, customers, co-workers, students, teachers, janitors, contractors – associated with your company, organization or educational institution is a volunteer. They could leave tomorrow or even today. They may suffer some adverse economic consequences, but they are affiliated with your organization in a voluntary status! You cannot force them to stay. The basic implication of this overlooked fact is enormous for managing successful strategic planning within for-profit companies, non-profit organizations and educational institutions. One of the goals of strategic planning must be to create an environment where your "volunteers" (also known as your "employees") want to stay and, in fact, encourage others they know to join in your organization's efforts. It is no accident that one of the fastest-growing recruitment strategies is paying current employees to identify and suggest new recruits for the organization to hire.

Charles Handy, the great British business guru, suggests transforming the concept "employees" into the concept "members," and creating "membership" organizations. Robert Reich, in a 1998 article in the magazine *Fast Company,* talks about the need for businesses to have a "social glue" that binds the workers to the company. His article discusses stock options (employee ownership) and the importance of social and educational events for a company's employees and customers as key parts of a company's high-growth strategy.

MicroStrategy has several week-long events for its employees, all at company expense. It has a "friends and family" week where the employees and their families are treated to an all expenses paid vacation in the Washington, D.C. area. It has a company sponsored cruise each year. It has a week-long "university" where employees come together to attend classes and learn about the future development of their industry. And it has a week-long event called the "DSS World Conference" where employees, customers and strategic partners come together for educational courses, business meetings, attending keynote speeches and socializing. The importance of these events cannot be underestimated. They form the social glue necessary to keep employees (and volunteers) operating at high levels. They promote learning and communication. They promote employee satisfaction and even more importantly, they meet former Secretary of Labor Reich's concern that organizations create meaning for their employees beyond the earning of a wage. A key recruitment and retention policy is essential to any high-growth strategy and, as Reich and others suggest, organizations must make work and worklife fun and meaningful in order to attract and keep good talent and to keep employees productive.

We would go one step further. If an organization can create meaning for everyone associated with it, it will not only *attract* talent, it will also *create talent and energy* in ways that are not available to those organizations that fail to make the grade in this regard. For some people, meaning is derived predomininantly by the value the employee and the organization produce in terms of goods and services to others. For some people, meaning is derived predominantly by the value the employee and organization produce in the economic marketplace. For others, meaning is derived predominantly by the value they receive from the training, education, learning and self-improvement they realize from working with the organization. The leaders of ASTD see the current boom in the training market as coming from both the need for more training due to the faster pace of change in the market-place and the new role that organizations are playing in meeting the need for meaning at all levels for their employees.

Treating everyone associated with your organization as a "volunteer" is a transforming change. Our research indicates that such a change will improve the culture of your organization, change the way your managers relate to their subordinates and vice versa, change the way your employees work and produce value and will increase the probability that your organization can develop, implement and sustain high-growth strategies.

Conclusion

Strategic planning is a pivotal process in organizations. It is the central activity that promotes the organization in getting from where it is now to the position where it wants to be at some established point in the future. Strategic planning defines an organization's capabilities and why it is so important for the organization, the market and the world for the organization to achieve its high-growth goals. Strategic planning must be externally focused (to capture a market) and internally focused to insure that the organization's employees and systems will thrive along the way. Strategic planning must take into account both quantitative aspects (how big is the expected financial return and cost factors of the strategy), as well as qualitative factors (how will this strategy affect the relationship your organization has with the external environment and how will it affect the relationship the organization's employees, strategic partners and customers have with the organization).

Strategy, strategic anticipation, strategic thinking and strategic planning constitute the fuel in the world's entrepreneurial engines. Entrepreneurial engines exist in the non-profit world and the government sector as well as the for-profit world. In fact, entrepreneurial engines exist in the communist or socialist world just as in the capitalist world. Strategy is what guides people and organizations toward not only creating more efficient and successful organizations, but also toward creating new knowledge and products, improving the distribution of products and knowledge and improving the human condition as we know it and would like it to be.

The foundation for strategy is an accurate picture of the present situation. Strategy helps your organization paint the picture of the future it wants in a way that promotes progress toward achieving that future. Strategy then helps decide what to do to achieve that future, then links what to do with how to do it. It creates and sustains organizational breakthrough. *Strategy*, in one instance, built a solid, hard working 22 member board of directors when a new company just started out with almost no financial capital and one small client. Even though the company had severe financial constraints, faced entrenched competitors who had over 140,000 employees and sought to grow without significantly tapping the financial markets in its early stages, the small company had a mission and vision, great products and services, a clear strategy regarding how to penetrate its multibillion dollar market and a human resource strategy that consistently attracted great talent even when it did not have sufficient business revenue to employ this talent. This strategy led to the organization being able to compete effectively against organizations that were hundreds of times larger and expand into several cities in its first two years of operations.

Strategy makes competitors allies and wins elections. Strategy brings people together to work in a framework that taps into their knowledge in a mutually enriching manner. Strategy gives meaning to often empty phrases like "customer service" and "employee empowerment." It turns chaos into order and organizes organizations. Strategy changes industry and organizational mind-sets. Strategy separates winning, high-growth organizations from those that equate mere survival with success.

This book provides you with a starter set of tools to put in your strategic toolkit and a framework in which to use these tools. New strategic tools are being created every day. After reading this book, whether you ever thought of yourself as a strategic planner or not, you will realize that if your organization uses these tools, or creates variations of them, it can dramatically increase the probability of reaching its high-growth objectives. Welcome to the rebirth of strategic planning – one of the fastest growing aspects of business improvement and organizational enhancement available today.

2

High-growth strategies – what are the tools?

- Introduction

- Physics and high-growth strategies for entrepreneurial organizations

- The implications of physics for strategic planning

- Strategic tools made simple – 12 strategic tools
  - Tool 1:   gap analysis
  - Tool 2:   root cause and defining moments analysis
  - Tool 3:   competitive analysis
  - Tool 4:   flexibility/innovation analysis
  - Tool 5:   PEST analysis – political, economic, social and technological forces
  - Tool 6:   growth drivers
  - Tool 7:   Porter's five competitive forces plus Grundy's "industry mindset"
  - Tool 8:   scenario planning and visualization
  - Tool 9:   SWOT analysis
  - Tool 10: stair analysis: assessing the overall strategic health of an organization
  - Tool 11: economic value added, GE grid and attractiveness/implementation difficulty grid
  - Tool 12: implementation forces analysis

- Conclusion

Energy is the ability to do work.

Contemporary College Physics, Text Book

Introduction

The tools used in strategic planning were all made up by inventive, creative people trying to solve a problem or improve a situation. The goal of this chapter is to give you a set of recognized tools and new, user-friendly business strategy tools to assist you in becoming a craftsperson so that you can develop your own tools to fit the needs of your organization. Just like a household toolkit, these techniques should not be used all at once, but chosen skillfully for each application.

Strategic planning is the process of generating strategic *outputs* (results) including decisions, priorities and programs of actions. Strategic thinking is the reflective learning that accompanies the strategic planning process. Both strategic planning and strategic thinking represent means to achieve your goals, they are never ends in themselves. None of the tools cited above is very helpful if you or your organization do not know the objectives you are trying to achieve with the tool. Therefore, the effectiveness of any strategic planning tool is a function of how solidly you or your organization has formulated its objectives, created alignment in support of its objectives and communicated its objectives so the behaviors needed to achieve the objectives can be identified, developed and implemented in a successful, organized manner.

In addition, the tools cited above will not do much good unless you have an "object" to hammer or a "plant" to spritz. Strategies, without some plan or basis to generate the resources necessary to implement the plan, are only dreams. This is a book about high-growth strategies, not about making up a huge wish list and just waiting or hoping for your wishes to be fulfilled.

The good news is that a great strategy, when put into action, often generates its own resources. Stand around a construction site long enough as a carpenter's helper with a hammer and someone will probably give you nails. But they might also take the hammer away from you. Once you get a nice spritzer from your family as a birthday gift, it becomes more likely that someone will give you a nice plant or you will go and buy yourself another plant. High-growth strategies are *enrolling* in nature. They make possible, sometimes even probable, what could not have been accomplished without strategic planning or strategic thinking. High-growth strategies are designed to generate, enroll, leverage, and even create resources as they improve an organization's ability to achieve its goals.

Certainly to some extent, high-growth strategies are dependent on the industry or sector involved. Some industries and some sectors will not grow as fast as others at certain points in history. Today the Internet sector is booming and natural resources are not. High-growth strategies for these two different sectors will certainly be different to some extent. In the Internet sector "going public" and raising venture capital are key components of high-growth strategies. In the natural resources areas, these strategies are still common as high-cost exploration requires capital to be raised, often in the billions of dollars. Regardless of the sector your organization fits in and regardless of its stage of growth, there are a dozen key strategic tools that are universal in nature and applicability. Of course, it will be harder for a small home health care company in 1999 to reach double digit growth with the recent withdrawal of much government funding for this area than it will be for an Internet company to reach this level of growth with the costs of computers plummeting and the invention of new, easy ways to access the Internet. Industries and sectors themselves make a difference to some extent in an organization's ability to achieve and sustain high growth. However, they are often not determinative as the US economic landscape is full of companies that have grown substantially when their economic sectors did not grow much at all.

Recently, business books have looked to ecology, biology, chaos theory, psychology and other sciences to shed light on business practices. We have chosen the field of physics since it gives us great insight into the business strategic planning process. The application of physics to strategic planning will work equally well with for-profit companies, non-profit organizations and educational institutions.

Physics and high-growth strategies for entrepreneurial organizations

What has physics got to do with high-growth strategies? The answer is "everything." Physicists talk about force, energy, work, objects, mass and acceleration. Strategic planners, CEOs, board members and the "yous and mees" of this world talk about costs, revenues, strategies, plans, change agents, leadership, high performance, organizations, customers, profit, loss and growth. The translation between physics and strategic planning is simple and elegant because at a base level, physicists and strategic planners, businessmen and women, heads and employees of non-profit organizations and educational institutions are all *talking about the same thing, the same processes.* Let's start with some simple definitions from physics and it will become clear how we bridge the gap between the laws of physics and the rules of commerce.

Combining definitions from physics and business literature as shown below gives us a framework for applying some of the basic laws of physics to the laws of commerce.

Work = the action or force that moves mattter (something) or causes a change.

Energy = the ability to do work. There are two types – potential energy (stored and capable of being converted to do work under the right circumstances) and kinetic energy (energy in motion).

Objects = the things moved or changed by energy and work. These can be rocks, light or non-profit organizations, businesses, educational institutions, individuals or teams.

Mass = a body of coherent matter. This could be any physical matter and could also apply as a description of the systems, the economic size of the organization, its culture, assets, liabilities and operating activities.

Acceleration = the rate of increase or decrease in velocity (speed). This could also be the change in "growth levels" (if positive) or "declines" (if negative). For our purposes strategic planners can equate acceleration with growth (increase in movement toward your objective).

Force = mass × acceleration. Force is applied energy. For strategic planners, we can say that it takes a force of *100 units* to generate the work (success) equal to getting a mass of 10 units to increase its speed by 10 units.

Gravity = the attractive force that keeps mass (objects) from moving about freely.

With these rough definitions, now we are able to create our first formula:

Force = Strategy + Implementation
(assuming a constant, frictionless environment)

Now we will apply one of the best known laws in all of physics to the world of commerce.

Newton's First Law. When no force is applied to an object, it either remains at rest or continues its motion with constant speed in a straight line.

The trick to understanding how Newton's First Law applies to business or high-growth strategies is knowing that there is *always force putting downward pressure* on your organization and on your strategy. In physics that force is gravity. In economics that force is the cost, in terms of money and resources, competition and the real and perceived limits of energy (the ability to do work).

Two other laws in physics now come to mind. Newton's Second Law says that when force is applied to an object, the motion of the object (direction and magnitude) changes in direct relation (proportion) to the direction and magnitude of the force.

According to the First Law of Thermodynamics, you cannot get more energy out of a system than you put into it, in all forms. (Energy is the ability to do work.)

The key elements in physics most relevant to high-growth strategies is represented by the formula:

$$f = m \times a$$
$$(Force = mass \times acceleration)$$

Now, let's redefine strategy and the strategic planning process in terms of the formula:

Strategy and the strategic planning process is the governance of the formula
$f = m \times a.$

Strategy is the governance and planned application of force to act on a mass to create acceleration or a change in direction to produce a desired result (high growth).

Stated in more detail:

Strategy is the governance (creative element – derived from insight, knowledge, experience, wisdom) and planned application (derived from "knowhow," scenario planning, research and applied learning) of force (action) to act on a mass (a situation, organization) to create acceleration or a change in direction to produce a desired result.

One other area of physics is also important. Heisenberg's "Uncertainty Principle" states that the more that you try to measure a particle's location and velocity, the less you can know about where it actually is. The implication of this principle is that uncertainty to some degree is inherent in organizations. The greater focus you have on knowing exactly what everyone is doing in your organization, the less everyone in the organization is able to carry out the duties and responsibilities necessary to achieve success in your high-growth strategies. The tension between careful monitoring of the creation and implementation of a high-growth strategy and the empowering of the managers and employees to use their good judgment to direct and carry out strategic plans requires that strategic planners develop "strategic imagination" and "strategic anticipation" skills. These skills are required because strategic planning must be *predictive* in nature, predicting the most likely response by both the internal and external market and economic environments to the behaviors introduced by the strategic plan. *Strategic imagination* is critical, since there are many possible behavioral and market-oriented responses that can result from any aspect of change brought about by the strategic plan. Strategic imagination will allow the organization to anticipate, understand and appropriately respond to a much broader set of behaviors than would be the case without proper strategic imagination applied from the outset in the strategic planning process.

The implications of physics for strategic planning

From physics, we can generalize that *mass* is what you have. It is your organization and all that it encompasses such as yourself, your people, your sales/revenues/costs and it is your environment including your economic, social, technological, competitive and supportive enviroment. *Acceleration* is the movement toward the goal. So, given our formula, $f = m \times a$, *(force equal mass × acceleration)*, *force* must be the key factor in getting your mass to achieve your objective.

The *force*, which we defined earlier as "*strategy + implementation*" must be equal to the task of getting your organization to the goal. Therefore, there must be a great strategy to achieve a great objective within a set timeframe.

This analysis based on the fundamental laws of physics, is important for two reasons. It simplifies the world into three elements. Americans like things in threes. Three strikes you're out, three downs you punt, three beers (and sometimes less) and you are over the legal driving limit and three cheers is usually the right number in most settings.

Can life be that simple? *Strategy + implementation = your organization accelerating toward its objectives*. In theory, yes, it can.

In commerce, there are few stated and generally accepted "laws" that guide the organizations seeking to achieve and sustain high growth. The laws of physics can shed considerable light on how to look at strategy and how to use the strategic toolkit provided below. These tools can be used on a daily basis by employees at all levels of the organization. Many of the tools presented below are those taught in MBA courses across the world. Several, including the "defining moments" analysis and the "flexibility/innovation" analysis, have been developed by the authors and are not yet commonly taught in MBA courses.

The purpose of providing these strategic tools is two fold. First, they are off-the-shelf analytical tools. Second, and more importantly, they may be the springboard for your organization to create its own custom-made tools to analyze your current situation and to help you craft high-growth strategies. In fact in a front-page article in the *Wall Street Journal* (31 December 1998), it was reported that more and more companies were designing their own MBA type programs with business schools. The article cited research by Kwartler Communications, Inc., a company that tracks business school programs. The article suggested that companies can benefit in two ways from designing their own company-specific MBA programs. First, it can teach the companies' employees the narrow range of courses and analytical tools that are best suited for that company. Second, by sending its employees to learn together a specific curriculum developed especially for them, such programs can help promote and foster the exact type of learning and culture that the corporation seeks to have.

Similarly, by applying and modifying these MBA type tools, your organization can achieve the dual goals of tailoring business strategy tools to your own environment and promoting an organizational culture that supports strategic planning and strategic thinking as centerpieces of your business design. In using these strategic tools, there must be a balance between the amount of organizational resources you spend in applying the tools and the amount of resources that your organization has left to implement the strategies that result from applying these tools. In order to use these tools effectively, there must be "a proper budget" (as an Australian colleague once put it) devoted to learning these tools, applying them and monitoring the implementation of the strategic outputs created. No off-the-shelf answer can be developed that applies to every organization regarding how much of its annual budget should be devoted to strategic planning. However, it is important to note that, for organizations that have never engaged in systematic strategic planning, the investment in time and money in this process may be significant. However, the payoffs from doing so could include not only a good strategic plan and high-growth, but also the achievement of strategic alignment, a more highly educated workforce, better decision-making structures and an organization more responsive to high-growth opportunities, and more sensitive to previously hidden barriers to achieving and sustaining high-growth.

> **No off-the-shelf answer can be developed that applies to every organization regarding how much of its annual budget should be devoted to strategic planning.**

Below are the tools we provide to your organization to deploy today in its quest for high-growth. They are organized in the following manner. We begin with a simple tool, the "GAP analysis," and then present the "root cause" analysis and our own "defining moments" analysis. We start with these tools because they require an organization to dig down deep and look carefully into the nature of the organization, how it reached its current position and where it wants to go.

Tool 3, "competitive analysis" requires your organization to begin to look systematically outside of itself at who its competitors are, what they are doing from which your organization can learn, what they are doing that your organization can do better and where they are clearly superior or inferior to your organization. ASTD uses a very thorough study of its competitors to help it determine not only how to improve its internal operations and external activities but also to determine which other organizations ASTD might want to form strategic alliances with. The next tool, the "flexibility/innovation" analysis, allows your organization to question openly and systematically what it is willing and capable of changing in order to promote high growth. The fifth tool, the "PEST" (political, economic, social and technological) analysis assists your organization in analyzing the external and internal environments in order to assess the desirability and feasibilty of high-growth goals and strategies.

The sixth tool, "growth drivers," is designed to make an organization look very deeply into the true reasons why it expects its market or market share can grow and to analyze carefully how the organization can take the best advantage of the things in society (attitudes, shifting consumer preferences, economics, etc.) that will help fuel its high-growth strategy. The seventh tool, "Porter's five competitive forces plus Grundy's industry mindset," will sharpen your growth drivers analysis and help your organization efficiently analyze information about its external environment.

Tool 8, "scenario planning and visualization" will allow your organization to craft different, insightful versions of the future based on your findings from the first seven tools. The ninth tool, "SWOT analysis" is an overview type of tool that will allow your organization to take into account the information derived from the eight tools previously identified and allow you – in summary form – to craft a strong, clear and precise picture of the strengths, weaknesses, opportunities and threats to your organization and its high-growth strategies. The tenth tool is the "STAIR analysis" which is a strategic health test for your organization.

Tool 11 is "economic value added" and the "growth earnings grid" which allow your organization to refine your economic models to improve the economic results of your high-growth strategies. These models are presented in summary form and can be made very mathematical upon further study. The twelfth tool is the "implementation forces analysis" which allows your organization to begin to understand and dissect the "rugged landscape" or external environment that your organization faces in implementing high-growth strategies. A thirteenth tool, "stakeholder analysis" is discussed in Chapter 3. This is useful not only for identifying and crafting high-growth strategies, but can also be used to help organizations *achieve organizational breakthrough and increase their capacity and capabilities.* Entire books have been written about each of these tools. We have provided an overview of these tools in a manner that can be applied today in most organizations.

Strategic tools made simple – 12 strategic tools

Tool 1: gap analysis

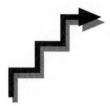

Fig. 2 Gap analysis

A gap analysis has three parts:

- identify who your organization is, where it is, and how it got there
- identify where your organization wants to go
- determine by when your organization intends to get there.

How does an organization determine "who it is" and "where it is" and "how it got there?" While the answer is simple, the task is not. In order to do this, an organization must openly and systematically ask questions about itself. It must ask others outside of the organization, record the information/answers, communicate the answers to others to check them out and write down a summary of what the organization has learned in the process. Several starter questions include, "What is the history of this organization?" "What kind of business are we in and how did we get into this business?" "Are we now and have we been a proactive organization or a reactive organization?" "Have we been and are we now a high-growth organization?" "What is our financial performance?" "What kind of relationship have we had in the past and do we have now with our employees, board members, vendors, customers?" And so on.

We recommend that an organization picks 10–20 great questions that are important to it and solicits short answers from as many (or as few) people as it desires. The questions will change to some extent depending on the type of organization involved. The role of the strategic planner regarding this tool is to ask the right questions that focus the organization's ability to define itself as accurately as possible.

As you ask where your organization is regarding a number of areas, then for these same areas ask the question, "Where does our organization want to go?" because it is the gap between where the organization is and where it wants to go that you want to identify. Then ask the question for each area, "By when does the organization intend to close this gap?"

ASTD's gap analysis, which it labeled the "Breakthrough Opportunities Analysis," revealed that it was not participating sufficiently in the international training market, it was not servicing customers and gaining customers (members) up to its potential and it was not capturing a high enough percentage of the market for training-related knowledge-based products.

ASTD's gap analysis, or "breakthrough opportunities analysis" builds on impressive growth over the past four years. Membership has doubled to nearly 70,000. Customer service has improved through the use of its extensive website and through centralizing customer inquiries to ensure consistent treatment for all members. In addition to the "breakthrough opportunities analysis," ASTD under the section "gap analysis" performed a "breakthrough needs analysis", where it identified what it needed to accomplish to realize the opportunities that it had identified.

MicroStrategy, Inc., with its goal of being a $10 billion (sales per year) company, clearly has defined the economic gap that it intends to close. Current revenues are in the $100 millon range. MicroStrategy has also identified a gap in the current ability of organizations and individuals to access technology and data. MicroStrategy intends to close that gap. Currently, technology and data are available primarily through computers. While there are laptops and palm-held devices, MicroStrategy is developing products that utilize the cellular phone to deliver usable data, thus opening up data and information to millions of additional users who can access and deploy technology many more times each day when they are on the road and away from a computer. MicroStrategy's gap analysis propels it to develop new products and approaches on a constant basis.

Tool 2: root cause and defining moments analysis

Root cause analysis, also called the fishbone analysis, is a quick and easy way of going behind a surface-level definition of a problem or opportunity. It seeks to break down every opportunity or problem into its component parts for analysis. This analytical model focuses an organization to address the question of "why" in a manner that tests key assumptions. For example, when an organization considers increasing training for its employees, it is easy to be glib about how training is good, more training is better, and how training is expected to lead to greater productivity. In fact the "value" of training is often taken for granted and certainly rarely measured with any precision (a problem that ASTD is working hard to resolve). Therefore, a fishbone analysis of whether to embark on a training program might look as shown in Figure 3 below.

Defining moments analysis

A new analytical tool which is also designed to get to the "why" questions that must underlie every high-growth strategy is the "defining moments" analysis. This analytical approach has been designed by the authors and is modeled after the "critical incident technique" in social science research developed by the American Institutes for Research. It is also patterned after the case studies presented in Professor Joseph Badaracco's book, *Defining Moments*. More than any other analytical technique used by organizations, this analytical tool will assist an organization in determining "who it is" in a manner that can assist in creating and promoting a high-growth stategy. Below, we suggest one method (among many possible methods) organizations can use to perform a "defining moments" analysis.

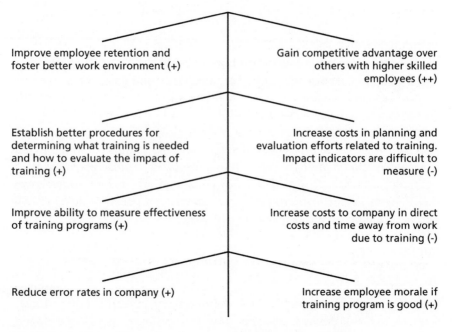

Fig. 3 Evaluation of the attractiveness of training opportunity

Preferably in a group setting, review the history of your organization and list several "defining moments," moments or decisions that changed the organization dramatically, that reflect its true character and set the stage for its current situation. Such moments can be deemed positive or negative. They may include situations when an organization consciously changed the way it did business, launched a new product, entered into a new market, hired or fired a CEO or made other important personnel changes. It may also include situations when it decided to pursue or separate from a particular customer, joint venture partner or when it decided to embrace or not embrace a new technology. It may include situations when the company took a stand on an issue that was based on a princple and not in the best, short-run financial interests of the organization. Analyze those moments, looking for the values they reflected, the objectives the organization was seeking to achieve at the time and the results that were generated from those moments. You can use this simple, straightforward analytical tool to springboard to a very important and rarely asked question in business and organizational life. "What future defining moments do you see on the horizon or want to bring about for your organization?"

When you ask that question in earnest, in a group setting, we recommend that you hold on to your seats and tempers and take good notes when that discussion occurs among your employees, your management, board of directors, customers and stakeholders. This type of discussion will certainly encourage members of your organization to speak with passion about the future they want to see for the organization.

MicroStrategy's defining moments came when it decided to shift to a products-based company from a services or consulting-based company. Often a defining moment comes about when an organization decides not to do what it has done in the past. The key to a defining moment is that everyone in the organization should become fully informed of the magnitude of the moment and the true implications of that moment on the future of the organization. The defining moments analysis, being both a historical process as well as a future-oriented process, will reveal information about the true willingness of the organization to take risk, to see itself as the master architect of its past and as the designer of its future. With new technologies allowing organizations to have virtual meetings with hundreds or even thousands participating and contributing, the defining moments analysis need not be simply a "soft" or qualitative approach to understanding your organization's true character. It can also serve as a means to

> **A defining moments analysis can serve to educate persons associated with your organization and gain their participation and contribution to shaping the organization's future.**

collect "hard" or quantitative data from many sources and provide a rich database of perspectives on defining moments from all of those associated in any way with your organization. For example, your organization can gain important information from past and present employees, customers, vendors and members of the board of directors. In addition, a defining moments analysis can serve to educate persons associated with your organization and gain their participation and contribution to shaping the organization's future.

Tool 3: competitive analysis

> **"Competition is an opportunity."**
> *The ASTD Strategic Planning Book – 1998*

Everyone, every business, every non-profit organization, every school has competitors. Organizations must be both intelligent (capable of learning) and knowledgable (informed) about competitors. The key questions to ask are as follows.

- Who are and have been your competitors? (Think very broadly.)
- What and how are they doing now and have done in the past several years?
- What do you think they will do in the next several years?
- How have they changed/improved/declined in the past several years?
- How do you think they will change/improve/decline in the next several years?
- How have they helped or hurt the organization in the past?
- How do you expect them to help or hurt your organization in the next several years?

The sources of this information are everywhere including the telephone, the newspapers, the public libraries, your board members and by simply asking your competitors the questions directly. Harvey McKay's business books stress the importance of knowing your competition intimately. Organizations are not islands. To know where an organization is in relation to its competitors is important, even critical, for an organization to be able to understand its environment. This means knowing your competitors, the economic landscape and how future events are likely to shape your organization and organizations with which you compete.

The goal of carrying out a competitive analysis is to identify your competitive advantages (and figure out a way to build on them) and your competitive disadvantages (and figure out a way to minimize them or their impact on your organization). Competitive advantage is defined as "adding more value to your target customers/members/students than your competitors and at a competitive cost."

Value is a tricky concept. First, value can be either real or perceived. An "increase in value" can be the result of increasing the quality or utility of a product or service or by producing and delivering the same quality or utility at a lower cost, a faster rate or with greater convenience to the customer/member or student. Second, value can never be separated completely from cost. Organizations must often undertake to keep their cost structure in line with an industry cost structure that is forever changing. For example, in 1998 not only has the Internet cut costs of distributing products, but the "old line" automotive industry has also made great progress in cutting costs in manufacturing.

The result of a competitive analysis can be put in a diagram form, like an atom. At the core of the atom are the strongest, most sturdy, hardest to imitate competitive advantages. After identifying your organization's strongest competitive advantages, list some of its less sturdy advantages. In the atom diagram shown below, these advantages are (and act like) electrons swirling around the core. These "advantages" could easily disappear since competitors can equal them in either a short time or without expending substantial resources. An organization's relatively "weak" advantage could still represent an area where the company or non-profit organization is doing great work.

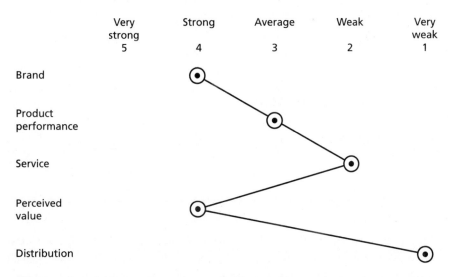

(Note: you should try to profile yourself against at least one strong or potentially strong competitor)

Fig. 4 The "Atom"

For example, one of MicroStrategy's strongest competitive advantages is its recruiting of excellent employees ("stars") and its employee retention ability. MicroStrategy has grown from 150 employees to 950 over a period of three years. It has developed and is successfully implementing a world class human resource system including a great hiring strategy (talent recruitment), spending enormous sums on training (called "boot camp"), on events (cruises, educational activities, and conferences) and developing a culture that makes it very comfortable for any employee to make any request of and any statement to any other employee, even the President. One of MicroStrategy's other advantages is a great advantage, but in 1999, we would not call it a "core advantage." MicroStrategy has approximately $40 million in the bank as the result of a very successful Initial Public Offering of stock in the company in mid-1998. In the fall of 1998 its stock price has regularly been 2–4 times its initial offering price. Given the ability of other high tech companies to raise substantial amounts of capital and to have strong stock price showings, this advantage is more like an electron rather than a core advantage, since other companies can duplicate it. We would, on the other hand, acknowledge that having $40 million in the bank is a significant advantage for a company over less capital rich competitors.

ASTD, on the other hand, has as its core strength a longstanding, nation-wide network of local chapters, a great publishing track record, highly successful conferences and an excellent research department. Although it serves its members well with quick response and thorough support, other competitors could match ASTD on its general customer support functions. ASTD identified 88 competitors in its strategic planning book, "The Red Book." In the ASTD strategic planning process each competitor is listed by name, address, phone number, number of employees, name of senior executive, and a description of what the organization does. This type of complete analysis allows ASTD to determine which competitors to seek strategic alliances with, and which ones pose the greatest competitive threat to its future plans.

With regard to CocaCola®, or any soft drink brand, one of the core competitive advantages is the symbol and packaging for its product. While in Brownsville, Texas one of the authors observed what appeared to be a Coke® can, with the same type of lettering, colors and overall 'look,' but with the writing in Spanish. This can was not a "Coke®" can and did not contain the Coke® product. Rumor had it that sales of Coke® declined significantly before these cans were taken off of the market. We have heard estimates of tens of thousand of corporate logo violations annually and are aware of strong organizational efforts to police intellectual property rights. The entire body of intellectual property law is designed to allow trademarks, copyrights and patented information to become *core strengths and major assets* of a business, non-profit organization or educational institution. Without these laws, the advantage given by "branding" would be very small and would fly away from an organization as easily as electrons fly away from the nucleus of an atom. One new strategy of organizations is to conduct an intellectual property audit and appoint a senior officer as "V.P. for Intellectual Property." Identifying the intellectual property assets of an organization, maximizing the value of the intellectual property of an organization and policing the Internet and traditional venues of commerce for violations of an organization's intellectual property rights will certainly become a more heavily used high-growth strategy for entrepreneurial organizations in the future. Intellectual property has the distinct advantages of distinguishing your organization and its products from every other organization, creating loyalty within the organization (employees and investors) and outside of the organization (customers, vendors and the media) and having a shelf life that can last hundreds of years with the value increasing over time rather than suffering from diminishing marginal returns. Therefore, part of any competitive analysis must be an analysis of how your organization's currently protected (and soon to be protected) intellectual property stacks up against the competition and how your organization is promoting and exploiting the value of its intellectual property.

Significant and longstanding competitive advantage generally needs to come from a number of sources (better price and service, for example) to be sustainable. Also, an organization must have some large-scale advantage related to its core strengths or competencies in order for that advantage to serve as the key launchpad for development of a high-growth strategy. Securing and policing intellectual property protection for logos, inventions and other intangible assets can be expensive. However, it is often this protection that catapaults a growth strategy into a high-growth strategy through the greatly heightened value achieved through the protection. A general rule of thumb regarding intellectual property is "If you do not want your competitor to use what you have, protect it with a copyright, trademark or patent in as many markets as you plan to compete in in the future."

It is equally important to analyze an organization's competitive disadvantages in order to avoid strategic disasters. An entire book could be written just on the topic of competitive disadvantages since they play such a pivotal role in limiting or short-circuiting an organization's efforts at creating high-growth strategies. A few sources of competitive disadvantage include:

- poor geographical location
- lack of market share
- high cost relative to competitors

- less money, resources, talent, or intellectual capital than competitors
- weaker transportation and distribution systems
- outmoded manufacturing facilities
- less effective, insightful, productive research and development (R&D) programs
- weaker reputation and less publicity/brand name appeal
- less developed organizational infrastructures
- less skilled or trained workers
- inferior management or board of directors
- weaker supply chain management systems
- weaker use of technology
- weak CEO
- limited access to capital.

While thinking about an organization's competitive disadvantages, it is important to get beyond standard measures and categories and analyze both why your organization has these disadvantages and how to craft strategies that can either improve your organization significantly in this area or otherwise limit the adverse impact they have on your organization's growth potential. For example, you may find that your organization has a number of competitive disadvantages, including that it is less willing than its competitors to:

- take risks
- make good, quick decisions
- change and innovate
- invest in training, employee development and new technology
- modify its business models
- seek strategic alliances or enter into joint ventures
- make its suppliers its partners
- get to know and to listen to its customers
- accept less profit per sale in order to expand sales.

All of the areas listed above may be the root causes of your organization's competitive disadvantage and must be dealt with in order to strengthen your organization's ability to compete effectively.

One CEO we interviewed informed us that an organization cannot be strong in any of the areas of marketing, employee recruitment and retention, finance, technology, administration, product development, public relations or organizational development unless the CEO was himself or herself personally strong and well trained in each of these areas. His view is that a thorough "competitive analysis" must include a careful study of the strengths and weaknesses of the competitor's CEO. When this company identifies a competitor CEO's weaknesss, it begins to suspect that the entire organization will be fundamentally weak in that area of business. This company then develops its competitive strategy to focus on the area of weakness of the CEO of its competitor.

Prabhu Guptara, Group Director, Organisational Learning & Transformation, Union Bank of Switzerland and Chairman of Advance, Management Training, Ltd. has developed a similar theme over the past 20 years, arguing that no CEO today of any organization of any reasonable size can function properly without a clear understanding of and hands on capability in the area of computer technology. The multi-faceted position of CEO today clearly requires a broad-based set of skills. Organizations whose CEO has a limited, specialized base of skills and knowledge often face a serious competitive disadvantage when competing with organizations with more broadly trained and skilled CEO's.

Evidently, what one person believes is a competitive disadvantage, another person may believe is a competitive advantage. However, clarity must be sought in determining whether a particular fact is either advantageous or disadvantageous for the strategy that you wish to undertake. If, after careful analysis, there is doubt, ambiguity or disagreement regarding a particular item, write up the item in both the list of advantages and the list of disadvantages and analyze it from each perspective. Of course, whether the glass is half full or half empty often depends on whether one is pouring or drinking!

For example, Boston Chicken (which became Boston Market) and its financial debacle in 1998 presents an interesting situation where what clearly looked like a competitive advantage, turned out to be a disastrous competitive disadvantage. Boston Market was designed to capture the "home meal replacement market." Offering carryout and onsite buffet-style service, Boston Market built hundreds of outlets, often near Blockbusters video stores. We are told that Boston Market restaurants were located close to Blockbusters videostores for three reasons. First, Blockbusters developed their location strategy based on detailed analyses of large scale demographic data to determine what locations would be geographically close to their anticipated customers. Second, some Blockbuster management were hired by Boston Market. Third, Boston Market anticipated that the same types of customers who would purchase from Blockbusters would buy from them.

Boston Market developed a hugely profitable dinner business and for a while was a darling of Wall Street. Its strategic planners thought that since it had great locations, it could upgrade its less profitable lunch business and take advantage of available staff, resources, reputation and location to use lunch business to increase its bottom line. At first, after the upgrading of its lunch menu, all went as planned and the company had excellent lunch sales. Then, it noticed its dinner sales, which were much more lucrative, started falling off. One employee informed us that instead of families coming to Boston Market for dinner and spending well over $25.00 for a family of four, only one member of the family came to Boston Market for lunch and usually spent less than $6.00. It came as a huge surprise that upgrading the lunch business could "cannibalize" the dinner business to such a great extent. While the authors are unaware of how much this situation contributed to Boston Market's falling, it does provide a great example of how a strategic plan must take into account external, environmental factors such as "cannibalization" as hidden threats to a high-growth strategy.

For those of you who think your organization or business does not have competitors, the authors strongly suggest to you that you *do* have competitors. The De Beers diamond company has an expansive view of its competitors. In a recent advertising campaign, diamonds are prominently displayed and the caption reads, "New Kitchen... Next Year." However, if you still do not think your organization has even one competitor in the world, you can still use a form of a competitive analysis that will be useful. Compare your organization against itself (its past and expected future), or against some ideal or benchmark (numerical goal) that you give your organization. Apply the same techniques in the analysis and compete against "yourself" as you constantly look for outside competitors.

Tool 4: flexibility/innovation analysis

Another new strategic planning tool developed by the authors quickly analyzes the ability and willingness of a company, non-profit organization or educational institution to be flexible in its operations and to innovate. Innovation is the ability to do new things. Flexibility is the ability to do existing things differently.

This analytical tool builds on the work of Daryl Conner who promotes the idea that, as the speed of change increases in the marketplace, organizations must become more "nimble." Our approach is a qualitative approach that safely allows organizations to question the outer limits of the amount of change, innovation and flexibility that they are willing to attempt. There are two different aspects of this type of analysis that require special mention. The process is designed to:

- identify what an organization is willing to change and
- provide insight into what an organization can change in the short run.

While strategic planners may often assume that every behavior within an organization is changeable overnight, our research and the research of others shows that many organizations are simply not capable of changing their activities, systems, outlook, culture, behaviors very quickly at all. All persons who seek to advise and to lead organizations must keep close tabs on how adaptable the organization in question really is. For some organizations, when change comes too fast, the resistance that employees and others create soundly defeats the goals of strategic plans. The ability to measure an organization's flexibility and innovation capacity or its adaptive capacity is still in its infancy. The process that we offer (as described below) is a first step to opening the door to greater understanding of this most important metric. Underlying our development of the flexibility/innovation analytical device provided below is the understanding that flexibility and innovation are two of the most important sources of competitive advantage in the marketplace today.

Measuring ability to change, innovation and flexibility

List the organization's major activities and break down each activity into its component parts. For example, one author has experience with a non-profit educational institution that sells after-school, "hands on" science programs for elementary school children. The organization, often through PTAs, hires the teachers and sends the prepared science kits to each teacher that covers 8 1-hour after-school sessions. When asked about the sizes of the classes where the science program was taught, the organization said that the largest class was 11 students and the smallest was 7. Realizing there must be a huge market for class sizes larger than eleven students and fewer than 7, we sought to understand why the class sizes were so narrowly ranged in the number of students. The answer was to be found in the organization's business model. The organization sold the science kits in packages of 12 completed sets. One of the kits was for the teacher, so the maximum class size was 11. Since the teacher had to pay for all 12 kits, the teacher lost money if fewer than 7 children were enrolled in the class. In spite of the fact that the organization was turning away many students (because if only 6 children signed up, the class was cancelled and if more than 11 signed up, children were turned away) the organization refused to change the way it boxed its science kits. In fact, two of the areas where the kits could be sold quite readily was to the 1.3 million US children who are schooled at home, and in the classrooms of schools where 20–30 students could have used these lessons to supplement their standard science curriculum. Since we anticipate that the number of home schooled children will grow rapidly in the US, selling the kits to home schooled children appeared to be a natural high-growth strategy. Similarly, since the organization had not sold any kits for use in elementary schools, this market also presented a huge opportunity for high-growth. The organization, however, decided during the short time one of the authors worked with it that it was either unable or unwilling to change its system of selling 12 kits per box, was unwilling to sell to home schooled children (because the teacher for the home schooled child had not received the organization's required training) and was unwilling to allow its kits to be used in regular elementary school classrooms.

This organization's experience in standing rigidly by its business model provides a key insight into how to identify key elements of your organization's business design or business model and to break down your economic activity into component parts. After gathering a substantial list of business activities, systems and procedures that make up your organization's stated or implied business model, discuss each activity from the point of view of how willing and how capable your organization is to be flexible and innovative on this activity.

If you want to quantify this practice, you can rate each activity for flexibility/willingness to innovate on a scale of 1–10 (with 10 being the most flexible). Regarding many areas of your organization's operations, a score of less than five could spell doom to your organization and be a source of competitive disadvantage if your competitor is willing to be more flexible in this area.

This analytical tool makes strategic planning potentially very revolutionary. You can get into as much detail as you like in breaking down your operations (such as, "how exactly do we buy paper clips?") or you can stick with the major activities of your organization (such as, "how do we make decisions around here?"). This process questions everything. You may wish to consider how flexible/willing to innovate your organization is in:

- changing office locations
- instituting telecommuting policies
- allowing employees at all levels to form strategic planning teams
- being willing to take risk
- entering into strategic partnering/joint venture arrangements
- modifying your business model to promote high growth
- discontinuing work habits/work procedures that employees do not like
- investing in and using state-of-the-art technology
- doing business in a foreign country
- changing salary levels and benefit levels to reward certain types of behavior not previously rewarded
- introducing new products/services
- treating customers in a new way
- treating employees in a new way
- raising capital through new means and sharing ownership
- changing the way the board of directors is selected, evaluated and turned over.

While change is not necessarily good, without innovation and flexibility there can rarely be a sustainable high-growth strategy. From Michael Maccoby's book, *Why Work: Motivating the New Workforce*, we learn that the "expert type manager," the one that learned the "right" way to do things, became very good at it (with credentials to prove it) and wants to keep running things the way the expert "knows" is right, is no longer the ideal type of manager for many, if not most business-oriented situations. Maccoby presents a compelling case that the 1990s and beyond belong to the "innovator type manager" who is less interested in getting things done correctly the old way and more interested in getting the desired objective accomplished any way that works, that is cost-efficient, is legal, ethical and does not harm employees or consumers.

Another example. Some years ago one of the authors conducted an "entrepreneurial management program" for selected Marks & Spencer (M & S) managers. M & S has had great success over the past several decades but had poor financial results in 1998. It is currently seeking to become a world retailing giant. However, not many years ago, M & S refused to accept any credit or debit cards other than its own. On the flexibility/ innovation grid score, on this one M&S gets a "0." M&S has now changed that policy. The major lesson of the late 1990s is that high-growth strategies must be "customer-centric." Every high-growth strategy must focus on making it easier for the customer/client/student to obtain, pay for and benefit from the services and products of the organization.

> **The major lesson of the late 1990's is that high-growth strategies must be "customer-centric." Every high-growth strategy must focus on making it easier for the customer/client/student to obtain, pay for and benefit from the services and products of the organization.**

Organizations must not only be entrepreneurial and customer-centric in their operations, they must be entrepreneurial in their *culture* and in the manner in which they treat their employees. An example came up during the M&S entrepreneurial management program when the managers who were taking the program began to see how "anti-entrepreneurial" M&S was at that time. The senior manager who had arranged the entire program and secured funding for it (the advocate) was confronted by other managers who said that M&S was not entrepreneurial. In response, the senior manager turned to the consultant and said, "I told you we weren't entrepreneurial. Look at me, because of my style, I have not been promoted!" The failure years ago to reward an entrepreneurial manager at M&S sent a clear signal throughout the organization of the type of behavior that would not be rewarded. Trying to achieve strategic change in many organizations can be like turning a supertanker. The physics of the supertanker are an equal match, in lacking flexibility and innovation to an organizational culture that prefers plodding along at a steady pace, making no sharp turns and resisting severely efforts internally for it to change course or reverse directions suddenly.

Examples of flexibility and innovation are also common. Today ASTD and many other organizations allow conference attendees to register through the Internet. While Merrill Lynch lays off 3,400 stockbrokers who deliver stock brokerage services using the old, expensive stockbroker model, Charles Schwab (eschwab), etrade and other companies that have embraced direct on-line brokerage services are experiencing tremendous growth. On-line mortgage lending, on-line airplane ticket purchasing via auctions and similarly innovative, customer-friendly innovations represent the results of well-thought-out high-growth strategies. The expansion of Amazon.com into music, toys and other retail markets is an excellent example of innovating a solid business design and being flexible enough to take advantage of opportunities quickly as they appear.

Tool 5: PEST analysis – political, economic, social and technological forces

This analytical tool is called the PEST analysis and focuses on the need to analyze both the external and internal environments whenever doing strategic planning or strategic thinking. We begin our explanation of the PEST analysis looking at the external environment faced by an entrepreneurial organization.

P – political forces
E – economic forces
S – social forces
T – technological forces

The external environment is always changing. In fact, in the last five years the impact of technology has become so high in the US and the impact of politics on the day-to-day business climate is now so low, we considered reversing the traditional acronym from PEST to TESP.

This qualitative analytical tool is straightforward and can be performed at either a basic level, or in great depth and detail. Every serious strategic plan should list the external and internal political, economic, social and technological factors that it expects to play a part in promoting or working against an organization reaching its desired objective.

Looking externally at the environment in a systematic manner can have a strong impact on the future direction of an entrepreneurial organization in terms of product development, service delivery area and scope, formation of strategic alliances, and the physical location of one or more offices or sites of the organization. For example, MicroStrategy, a technology company, relocated from Delaware (where it was originally located due to its initial relationship with DuPont) to the northern Virginia, Washington, D.C. area in the 1990s because it determined that it needed to be in a "great social and economic location" to be able to attract the best technology-oriented students and employees, who might not want to live in Delaware. Some very insightful companies in the US, that rely on government contracts or are sensitive to government regulation, have gained great benefit by being located in the State of Mississippi because of Mississippi's very senior and powerful Congressional delegation. External economic factors are always a major factor in an entrepreneurial organization. However, since the US has ridden a growth wave for most of the past two decades, often single site organizations see little need to pay close attention to these external economic factors. Now that economic growth in the US is surging much more in some areas than others, and clusters of economic resources are gathering in selected geographic locations in the US and throughout the world, entrepreneurial organizations – now more than ever – must pay very careful attention to where they locate their main and branch offices. While this seems to be a contradiction, with the Internet making the world smaller and connecting more and more entrepreneurial organizations daily, regardless of geographic location, our research shows that making location decisions based on a careful analysis of the local economic climate is growing in importance rather than declining.

Keeping up to date on other economic and social trends has become more important, as trends are moving more swiftly, due to rapid technological change, than in the previous economic times. For example, in 1999 some non-profit organizations (as well as for-profit businesses) are starting to see a significant decline in net revenues from direct mail solicitations and catalogs. Although industry data are hard to gather on a weekly basis, especially in the non-profit industry, it appears that the future of the direct mail fund-raising industry and the mail order, catalog type of business that has flourished in the 80s and 90s may be in some jeopardy as e-mail and the Internet sweep the technology marketplace. It was insightful that on the day in December 1998 when Delia's (a clothing and accessories company exclusively directed toward teenage girls that had relied heavily on mail order, catalog sales) announced that it had entered into a strategic alliance with the Internet company, Yahoo, to sell its products in a virtual store format, the stock price of Delia's went up 67%. Non-profits relying on direct mail fund-raising solicitation will need to determine how to use the economic opportunities of the Internet for fund-raising as the direct mail industry becomes less and less successful in this regard. Ironically, non-profits may be well served through extensive websites that include video clips, virtual tours of non-profit operations and projects, "live" testimonials and other advanced website applications as the website can give people a greater "touch" and "feel" for the non-profit than conventional direct mail solicitation. We certainly expect that, even for the million dollar websites like ASTD (which is not used for fund-raising, but is used as an educational tool, a sales and marketing tool, and a means to create a "virtual community"), the per person cost of maintaining and updating the website on a daily basis will be less than direct mail costs.

Politics and the quality of government services still plays a large role in attracting businesses and large non-profit organizations. The District of Columbia in the fall of 1998 had an election for mayor who instituted new economic growth plans immediately. While this is positive for the District of Columbia, many technological, economic, political and social factors strongly favor the surrounding jurisdictions of Maryland and Virginia to be the location of choice for businesses and non-profit organizations in the future. These factors include better technological infrastructure and much better public schools in the suburbs. The failure of the District of Columbia and many other urban jurisdictions to improve their schools is a strong negative factor keeping families with children from moving into the nation's capital and other major cities across the US. Organizations take into account economic and political factors, in addition to social factors such as quality of schools, crime rates, average commuting times and other factors, in making strategic decisions regarding where to locate and where to do business.

Regarding the internal political, economic, social and technological factors, entrepreneurial organizations that want to embark on high-growth strategies must pay careful attention to how these factors come into play. Chapter 3 discusses the role of a "stakeholder analysis" since a stakeholder analysis, per se, is not a key high-growth strategy. However, growth strategies are only as effective as the level of political support they generate and sustain over time. And politics applies to a two-person organization as much, if not more, than to a 1,000 or 100,000 person organization. The best approach to analyzing the political forces within an organization is to group the key players (the voters or stakeholders) into one of four categories as described below.

- *Decision maker* – the one who ultimately decides.
- *Sponsor* – a key designer, architect or potential financial supporter of the high-growth strategy.

- *Advocate* – a supporter who would welcome the opportunity to work on the particular high-growth strategy at issue and who would bet some or all of his or her bonus, organizational prestige and capital on the high-growth strategy.
- *Potential blockers* – persons or groups with something to lose from the high-growth strategy or who have expressed some opposition to the strategy and who could only reluctantly be won over to support it.

Identifying the expected roles or "predisposition" of each key person in an organization as early as possible in the strategic planning process will not be easy, which may be why this important approach is so often overlooked in the strategic planning process. The costs of failing to undertake an analysis of the political forces within your entrepreneurial organization can deal a serious blow to a high-growth strategy. Legend has it that at board of directors' meeting at PEPCO, the local electric power utility for the Washington, D.C. area, a senior manager made a presentation to the board requesting half a million dollars for a project. Five board members were present and as soon as the manager finished his presentation, the chairman asked each member to vote on the project. Each of the first four members voted "No" and then the fifth member of the board, the chairman, said, "I vote yes, the project is approved!"

Analyzing the social forces within an entrepreneurial organization may be new territory for some strategic planners. What we can say about this area is that high-growth strategies are not based on flow charts, spreadsheets, new sales or marketing programs or analytical tools alone. One insurance company analyzed the factors that were correlated with the failure of a client to renew insurance after the initial period ended and found, much to its surprise, that if there was a big difference in the ages of the insurance agent and the client, there was a much higher than expected rate of non-renewal of insurance. We include in the social factors within your organization, what sociologists, organizational development specialists and now business people refer to as the "culture" of the organization. Being able to understand your entrepreneurial organization's culture and being able to predict how it will evolve over time in response to the implementation of high-growth strategies is now a critical role for strategic planners, CEOs, top management and consultants.

Analyzing the technological forces within an organization is more than preparing a strategic plan for the next level or next period of technological improvement for your entrepreneurial organization. A technology plan is critical, especially now in the age of organization-wide enterprise resource planning, and the development of a knowledge management system will go far to make or break an organization. One accounting firm which did not have a knowledge management system nor any organized way to identify all of the skills and experience of its 90-member accounting staff, submitted a bid on a government contract without including the resume of a relatively new accountant at the organization who had very strong credentials and expertise in exactly the area required by the contract. This firm would greatly benefit from adopting a knowledge management system that would allow it to identify the key areas of experience and expertise of all of its staff in seconds.

A major, and often overlooked, part of analyzing the technological challenges which your organization faces, is analyzing how the people will react and be able to absorb technological change. No area of strategic planning requires more attention than the "people side of the equation", especially in plans to upgrade the technology used by your employees. The purchase of smart, competent technologies alone is not enough to guarantee success – there must be a plan to bring those who are going to use the technology up to speed on the new processes. This usually requires substantial training, process planning, and sufficient lead time to allow for periods of slow absorption.

In the early 1970s, before the Three Mile Island debacle, one of the authors had the opportunity to have frank discussions with a person who was a leader in the nuclear power industry and who was very familiar with the operations of Three Mile Island. At that time, there was total confidence among many nuclear engineers and project managers that a safe nuclear power plant could be built. However, upon deep probing we found a real concern in this engineer that the *people side*, the daily management of the nuclear power plants, was not as fail-safe as the design, planning or construction side. In Three Mile Island, human error played a great role in the disaster. The phrase "human error" is always a potent factor in entrepreneurial organizations, whether it is a Three Mile Island disaster or a Barings Bank disaster. Therefore, when analyzing the technological forces within your organization and developing a strategic technology plan, focus not only on current technological sophistication and needed improvements, but also on how receptive employees are to embracing and mastering the proposed technology. It will be important to determine in advance what your organization can do to enhance the employees' (or supply side vendor or other affected party) willingness and ability to succeed using the new technology.

All of these factors can be put on the table quite quickly and early in the strategic planning process. Most organizations will conduct this analysis using internal staff, but some may require outside consultants who can use diagnostic tools, surveys, groupware and other devices to gather and analyze information quickly to help an organization to get a handle on these forces quickly and efficiently. Finally, with regard to these forces, once the organization gathers the data, the data may only be accurate for a short period of time as things change within the organization. Each organization must assess for itself how often to collect and analyze this information in order to stay current about its internal operations.

Tool 6: growth drivers

The growth driver analytical tool is based on a qualitative version of "force field" analysis, where you look at the prevailing forces in your industry segment, in your organization and in the overall economic and social landscape. These forces are identified and their strength (high, medium, low – for example) is assessed. What drives a market? What drives the growth internally in an organization? What drives your customers to your door to buy your goods or services at the prices you set? What will drive your future customers?.

What holds back a market or causes a market to decline? What retards growth internally in an organization? What limits the size of the total market of customers and buyers both now and in the future? What limits your present and future market share? We call these "growth brakes." Below we provide a simple example of several growth drivers and growth brakes regarding Internet-related sales of goods and services.

This analytic tool (as the others) is just as valuable for any non-profit organization or educational institution as for a for-profit company. What will drive future contributions, grants, entrepreneurial revenues for your non-profit organization? What will drive applications up (in terms of quantity and quality of students) to your school? What will drive your successful recruitment of new faculty, employees, your CEO, board members, vendors and suppliers?

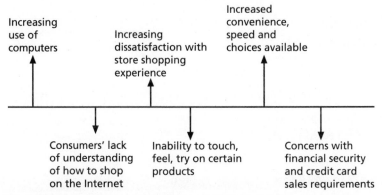

Fig. 5 Growth drivers and brakes on Internet sales

Another way of looking at growth drivers is to look at them as "motivating" or "hygiene factors" that define the key factors which really inspire a customer to purchase your products or services or contribute to or volunteer for your organization. On the flip side are the growth brakes – the factors that demotivate or contaminate a customer's desire for the value offered by your service, product or organization. Growth drivers analysis is important in differentiating your organization's products and services, avoiding competitive disadvantage, and in helping to determine resource allocation in product and service development and distribution.

Looking directly at the question of what drives your market is critical in strategic planning and strategic thinking. For example, we are all buyers and sellers and must analyze growth drivers and growth brakes from both a buyer's perspective and a seller's perspective. As a senior member of ASTD has said, in every meeting regarding a business transaction, it is critical to know whether you are buying or selling. (Of course, often there is a little of both going on from both sides of the table at the same time.)

Businesses buy from their supply chain and sell to customers. Schools buy faculty (and through scholarships buy students). They generally sell to students and their parents. Non-profit organizations sell their ideas, policy positions, causes, platforms, research agendas and services to the needy or to a buying public, which buys with contributions, volunteer efforts and so on.

While it is an art to discover what drives a market, new data warehousing and data mining techniques pioneered by MicroStrategy and others are turning it into more of a science. Using the old pencil and paper approach, there are several important guides to uncovering growth drivers. Typical external growth drivers include:

- service innovation
- technology innovation
- increased learning/acceptance/awareness of a product/idea/business model
- price reductions
- product improvements
- safety or security improvements
- scarcity of substitutes
- changing perception of time (driving the convenience factor in industries)
- changing fashion.

External growth brakes include:

- shortages of skilled labor
- shortages of low-priced alternatives to high-priced supply chain elements
- lack of capital or high interest rates, etc.

Typical internal growth drivers include:

- growth-oriented CEO or chairperson of the board
- organization culture that demands being number one or two in an industry
- excellent training, human capital development philosophy.

Typical internal growth brakes include:

- lack of growth planning and strategic planning
- lack of vision
- lack of mechanisms to enter into and exit from strategic partnering relationships
- lack of capital

Analyzing growth drivers and growth brakes can highlight some future opportunities or limits that are not revealed with other analytical tools. It is an important device which can be used for "strategic benchmarking" as an organization can look externally and internally to understand more fully the current motivators of customers and employees, and how these motivators (and detractors) can change over time.

> **Growth drivers can help an organization to understand more fully the current motivators of customers and employees.**

Tool 7: Porter's five competitive forces plus Grundy's "industry mindset"

Michael Porter has developed a useful framework for analyzing a company's immediate and future competitive environment from the customers' point of view. Porter is known for his generic strategies (cost leadership, differentation and focus) which have guided many strategic planners for years. His five competitive forces are as follows.

- *Entrants* of other companies, non-profits, schools (including for-profit schools).
- *Substitutes* – better, cheaper products, alternative products that reduce demand for your services, NPO's agenda.
- *Buyer power* (i.e. of customers) – reduction of loyalty, increase in group purchasing, buyers becoming sellers to compete with buyers.
- *Supplier power* – when supplies of one or more elements in the supply chain diminish and the price goes up, or when a supplier has such a large share that it can dictate the terms of the deal.
- *Competitive rivalry* (between existing players) – which may result in price wars, mergers, acquisitions, etc.

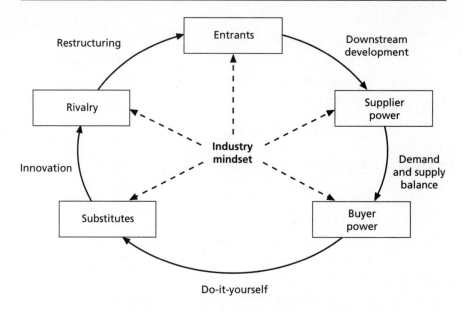

Note: the 'big six' competitive forces is a refinement of Michael Porter's five competitive forces (*Competitive Strategy*, Porter E.M., The Free Press, Macmillan, 1980).

Fig. 6 The "big six" competitive forces

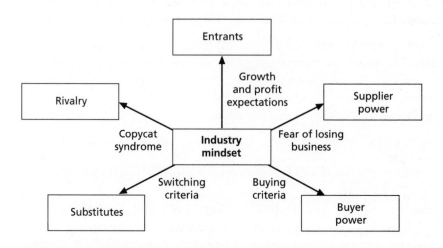

Fig. 7 The impact of industry mindset – the sixth force

In a previous book by Tony Grundy, *Breakthrough Strategies for Growth: Delivering Sustainable Corporate Expansion,* an additional, important competitive force has been identified and explored. It is *industry mindset.*

Industry mindset applies both in the for-profit and the non-profit sectors and refers to the perceptions, expectations and assumptions about the competitive environment, the level of financial returns and the factors critical for success in the industry. Industry mindset is, at one level, easy to discern by reading trade press and going to conferences. For example, the industry mindset in the computer industry is that people expect the speed of personal computers to double every 18 months. This leads many people to replace computers every two years, or more often. In the 1950s and 1960s US cars were so badly made that many people replaced their cars every 2–3 years as they fell apart. Now, improvements in the automobile industry are such that replacement of cars within two years because of poor craftsmanship or design is rare, and car owners are holding on to their cars for much longer periods of time. In addition, with the improvement of automobile manufacturing, the industry and customer mindset pertaining to used cars and long-term leased cars has changed in a positive direction quite dramatically.

In the computer industry, there is a competitive mindset that if your organization is not gaining market share, it will die. This mindset clearly sets the stage for the goal of every computer technology organization to increase its market share. History has shown that many of those computer companies which are not increasing their market share are becoming targets for acquisition by companies that are.

Analyzing the Porter competitive forces and the industry mindset allows you and your organization to delve into such issues as differentiation and cost leadership, and to analyze the future from the customer's point of view.

Tool 8: Scenario planning and visualization

Scenario planning and visualization are actually different tools, but we are combining them since they fit together so well. Scenario planning, as used extensively by Royal Dutch Shell and other major corporations (as well as every little league baseball coach and family gardener), is the simple to sophisticated use of "what if" questions to develop a set of futuristic pictures and planned behaviors designed to achieve an objective. The more "what if" questions one can ask, answer and organize, the more sophisticated the analysis. Diagrams, flow charts, computer simulation, computerized mapping and the old "pencil and paper" can be used in scenario planning, and can assist your organization in seeing and planning for differing versions of the expected future.

Scenario planning sets out several different comprehensive pictures of the future relevant to your organization and its strategic plan. It looks at the future like a video, taking one frame or time period at a time, with each time period building on the results of the previous time period, and a story line that moves the scenario through each time period. Scenarios are greatly affected over time by key transitional events that are envisioned by the planner that combine to create a predicted future pattern of events. Since key transitional events are difficult to predict with any certainty, often an organization will construct three scenarios of the future (optimistic, neutral and pessimistic) and then assess probabilities to each of the scenarios actually being closest to being accurate. The value of scenario planning is that it allows organizations to create strategic plans consistent with each of the potential scenarios and allows them to leverage some value out of their view or views of the future. Scenarios have, in the past, been the result of brainstorming sessions, usually involving a small team or two small teams working in parallel fashion to identify first the key issues/drivers that are of most concern to the organization and its future, and then to take these key issues/drivers and plot out how they will play out in the future. The process is intricate, but not necessarily difficult since everyone has some view of how the future will look, based on their own rudimentary form of scenario planning. In order for scenarios to be of some benefit to businesses, the scenario builders must take into account the interrelationships of many unpredictable factors such as technology, government policies, personal attitudes, economic and political trends, and lifestyle changes. They must also consider changes in relative economic costs and personal values in areas that can affect an organization's future and the future economic viability of its products and services. Computer technology could enable you to include inputs from large numbers of people from your organization to contribute to the scenarios that are developed about the future.

Visualization is the "seeing" of an event before it actually occurs. Jack Nicklaus said that he had never hit a golf shot without first visualizing exactly how and where he wanted the ball to go. (That's why he is such a slow player, especially on the green where he sees in his mind the ball roll along a line into the cup before he actually putts the ball.) One great composer, when asked if he had ever heard his greatest symphony played perfectly said "Yes, when I composed it." Walt Disney is given great credit for his visualization skills. Visualization in business has been prompted by computer graphics and some argue that visual modes of thinking are now becoming more and more popular due to the influence of television and computers. The authors welcome the myriad books touting visualization, "scientific visualization," environmental scanning and suggesting that "foresight" is the goal of strategic planning and strategic thinking. Through rigorous scenario planning, putting things down on paper in novel, pictur-esque ways and through being willing to innovate with computers, 3-D graphics and data mining tools, the reader can go far along this recom-mended path to "seeing" the objectives of the organization and the best ways of getting there.

Tool 9: SWOT analysis

S = Strengths
W= Weaknesses
O = Opportunties
T = Threats

The SWOT analysis is possibly the most common business analytical tool. We have put it near the end of the list of analytical tools since it incorporates many of the other, narrower, analytical tools. In addition, we placed it far down the list of tools because we want to correct the misperception that doing a SWOT analysis alone is doing strategic analysis – it is not. It is simply an inventory device or assessment device that alone will never pro-duce a clear high-growth strategy, nor will it tell your organization with any great certainty or precision the potential for success of any high-growth strategy being considered. In addition, we place it near the bottom of the list of analytical tools because we would like to correct the practice of many entrepreneurial organizations of relying too extensively on this analytical tool. Our research shows that organizations that use this tool as their first "tool of choice" or use it as their only analysis tool, at best, do not collect or analyze a sufficient amount of information to create and implement the best high-growth strategies available to their organization and, at worst, court disaster. Employing other analytical tools before performing a SWOT analysis will improve the chances of developing robust, successful high-growth strategies.

From the organization's point of view, a SWOT analytical device seems straightforward. If your organization will perform a competitive analysis, flexibility/innovation analysis, a gap analysis and PEST analysis, you will already have much of the information needed for this analysis. This analy-sis does help an organization look carefully at *opportunities* and *threats* that may not become apparent through the use of the other tools.

How does an organization identify opportunities and threats in a systematic way? First, for something to be a legitimate opportunity it must have sufficient political support within an organization and pass the stakeholder analysis (discussed below) with flying colors. Second, it must fit within the overall framework of the organization, its culture and values. The right strategy/idea/opportunity in the hands of the wrong organization can wreak great havoc. Third, the high-growth strategy and the opportunity that it seeks to capture or the threat it seeks to thwart must be described in such a clear and precise manner that insiders and outsiders understand the goals and objectives and modify their behavior accordingly. It is most important that some clear measure of success be defined when seeking to capture an opportunity. Lag times between implementation of a particular strategy and successful results coming back to the organization should be carefully thought out. For example, does your product have a six-minute sales cycle or a six-month sales cycle? We are not saying that the results of every high-growth strategy must be quantitive. What we are saying is that every high-growth strategy must, in advance of implementation, articulate what "success" will look like, either numerically or otherwise. The value of the high-growth strategy must ultimately depend on one's ability to "see" some results from the activity both during the planning stage and when the real results come in.

Two things must happen in order to "see" results in non-quantifiable situations. First, you need to look in the right places and be proactive in soliciting information through surveys, questionnaires or just asking about to determine if anyone noticed the changes, results or improvements you sought through the high-growth strategy. Second, in order to do this, an entrepreneurial organization must be keenly aware of the results it is seeking with the strategy.

One of the benefits of a SWOT analysis is that it promotes the free flow of information. In addition, it is relatively easy to create scenarios and do scenario planning that highlight opportunities and threats to the organization. Sometimes, however, identifying threats to your organization is more difficult, and it often takes an outsider to have what Andy Grove calls "an objective set of eyes." There are several important reasons why it is hard to ascertain threats to your organization or to your strategy. First, information regarding "threats" often does not flow up to management quickly for two reasons:

- sometimes management is perceived not to want to hear about threats
- often people in the organization fear that the bad news will not be received kindly by others, to put it mildly.

Again, referring to Marks & Spencer, a British analyst once stated:

People just don't say anything. No one will speak against the Chair, because they say it shouldn't be done. You can just see people's faces changing (when you say critical things). People just don't believe you, when you say something bad about Marks & Spencer, so you just don't bother.

The best way to identify threats to a strategy or more general threats to an organization's well-being is to list all of the things that are going wrong, or that could easily go wrong, and then identify their implications. Then consider whether they are great or minor barriers to success. Are they the result of some pervasive problem or idiosyncratic? How do you plan around these threats or set up contingency plans to deal with the threats? How costly is it to implement the contingency plans? Will the organization be able to identify the threat early enough to avoid major problems by using early detection systems?

The concept of *robustness* is central to understanding a fundamental principle of strategic planning and strategic thinking. A robust plan is one that can stand up and succeed, even if many of the assumptions upon which the plan is based turn out to be wrong or if the implementation of the plan does not meet expectations. For example, let's say that a person wanted to develop a strategic plan that would lead to revenues of $1 million in the year 2000 even if her computers crashed due to the "Millennium bug" or even if she died in the middle of the year. Well, buying a $1 million life insurance policy payable to her company will assure that her company will have at least $1 million in revenue if she dies. Dealing with other problems, such as reaching the $1 million revenue mark even if the millennium bug seriously interrupts her business, might be much harder and expensive to plan around for this company.

Threats can be internally derived (employee dissatisfaction, product failure), supply chain derived (UPS goes out on strike and your organization has no backup plan to get your time sensitive products to market), or totally externally driven via economic or political factors.

Tool 10: stair analysis: assessing the overall strategic health of an organization

The tools explained in this book are designed to assist a person or strategic planning group to gain insight, in order to make better economically oriented decisions. From insights a strategic planner must craft a strategy. After the creation of a great high-growth strategy, the most important next steps are:

- excellent implementation
- careful diagnosis of how the strategy implementation is progressing in terms of the planned activities and planned results
- revision of the strategy to take into account new learning, a new understanding of the environment and a better appreciation of what type of strategy will work best.

A summary analytical device that is useful for entrepreneurial organizations is the STAIR analysis. The mathematically inclined may see that the success of a strategic plan is a function of $S \times T \times A \times I \times R$, but applying this analytical rigor or quantifying on a percentage scale is not necessary to get the full value of this device.

STAIR is a straightforward strategic examination tool that can be used both early or late in the planning process, and can be used for macro strategies such as the future direction of the company and micro strategies such as moving the annual "Christmas" party to late January, a new trend recommended by the authors for a whole host of cash flow and other reasons. There is the upward STAIR and the downward STAIR.

The upward STAIR focuses on:

S = a simple, clear and coherent strategy
T = good timing
A = advantages created both internally and externally
I = implementation capability
R = appropriate and sufficient resources.

The downward STAIR focuses on:

S = simplistic and superficial
T = temporary and tactical
A = actively resisted (either internally or externally)
I = impractical
R = unduly risky or the risk has not been carefully evaluated.

While there is no formula for weighting these aspects of your plan, one device is to give your organization a rating on each scale of 1–10 (low to high) or give each item a percentage (maximum 100 percent). For the upward scale, if your number falls below 7 or 70 percent, you should go back to the drawing board. For the downward scale, the higher your number, the more you need to worry and no general rule of thumb can be developed.

Tool 11: economic value added, GE grid and attractiveness/implementation difficulty grid

Strategic planning tools must take into account cost and financial data. Since profits or earnings (typically defined as revenues less costs) can grow dramatically per unit with increases in the number of units sold, it is important for strategic planners to be aware of the organization's ability to capture this "economies of scale" information in evaluating any high-growth strategy. Revenues are usually fairly easy to measure. However, costs are not.

In any organization, strategic planners must wrestle with revenues and costs regardless of how they are defined. For larger organizations, we present a brief synopsis of a new way of measuring costs known as "EVA."

While it is beyond the scope of this book to discuss all of the theories and practices in the field of "cost accounting," one insightful way of looking at cost is described by Al Ehrbar in his recent book *EVA*. Based on the work of financial economists Miller and Modigliani, businesses are now using a new measure of economic results to replace the "inaccurate" terms "profit" and "earnings." EVA or *economic value added* is a measure of the value of a company which alters standard accounting terms such as "profits" and "costs." EVA analysis requires that companies take into account the cost of all sources of capital, including the capital that is given by shareholders, in calculating the return on operations. "Economic value added" equals net operating profits less the percentage cost of capital times the total capital used in the activity.

$$EVA = NOPAT - C\%(TC)$$

This economic measurement system seeks to capture the concept of "opportunity cost" and seeks to reward those elements that produce economic value added. While there is no simple device created today to apply the EVA concept to small organizations or non-profits, every organization can use the idea to undertake a three step process of figuring out whether its assets (its capital, whether donated, or equity or debt in nature) is producing value for that organization.

First, look at all of your organization's assets (and assets that you expect to purchase or are contemplating purchasing) and identify their full cost. Second, identify the financial return or contribution to the organization that the asset makes presently or could make if it were sold or used differently. Third, calculate whether the asset is a net financial drain or positive economic value adding component of your organization. This analysis may lead your organization to think more carefully and analytically about the true value of its assets and may lead to efforts to fill your organization with a higher percentage of assets that add economic value to your organization.

EVA also stresses that compensation should be closely aligned to the value that employees and managers add to the organization. There is certainly a movement afoot to reduce base compensation and increase variable (bonus) compensation for many managers and employees.

The GE grid and Grundy's attractivenesss/implementation difficulty (AID) analysis are also important in determining how attractive a particular market opportunity may be. Market attractiveness can be investigated carefully when one combines a PEST analysis, analysis of Porter's five competitive forces and applying a GE grid.

General Electric developed the GE grid as a means of determining what markets to enter during its high-growth acquisitive stage and how to evaluate the current markets it was serving. A GE grid is a chart that shows the total market attractiveness of a particular high-growth strategy in comparison to the relative competitive position that one has in the market.

The GE grid enables an organization to:

- position an existing business, having analyzed its total market attractiveness and competitive position
- compare with other organizations in the same market
- evaluate new economic opportunities
- reposition a business to improve its competitive position
- challenge the adequacy of investment needed to achieve a profitable position on the grid
- compare your organization's position with other competitors.

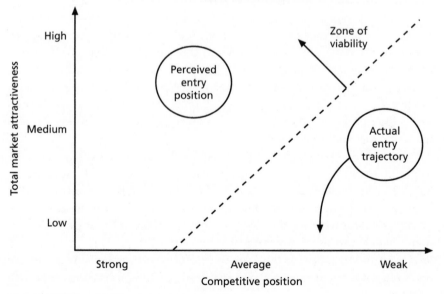

Fig. 8 Mapping market entry strategies

GE has had the publicly stated position that its business units would be either number one or two in a given market or it would get out of the market. The reason for this position is clear, as shown by the huge rewards given to the number one company in a market, whether it is America OnLine, Amazon.com or CocaCola® and the far lesser returns for number two. The chart below gives a pictoral, manager-friendly view of the GE grid, and entrepreneurial organizations can find themselves on the chart. This chart shows that if the total market attractiveness is high, even a weak competitive position in a marketplace can prove financially rewarding.

Organizations seeking a high-growth strategy through entering into a completely new market usually face a low competitive position. However, the ability of amazon.com to extend itself due to its technological advantage into music, toys and other generic retail items with a strong initial competitive showing shows that today moving from one type of retail business to another may be easier than in the past due to the seamless fluidity that the Internet provides across markets.

Organizations seeking high-growth today face the question of which high-growth strategy is most likely to pay off the most in the long run. There are significant accounting issues that are beyond the scope of this book as to whether a *net present value analysis of expected earnings* (using one expected earning figure for each high-growth strategy) is an adequate basis

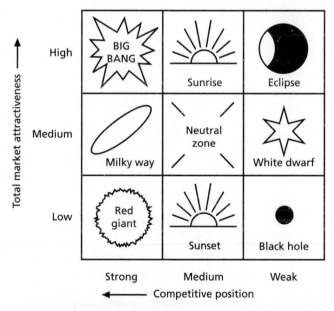

Fig. 9 Relabelling the GE grid

for making choices between various high-growth strategies, or whether an organization must develop a range of expected values (outcomes) for each high-growth strategy and then calculate the average net present value for the entire range of expected values anticipated. One of the authors – in collaboration with Hewlett-Packard – has developed a graphical approach called the attractiveness/implementation difficulty grid which brings to the surface a large number of issues including forcing an organization to describe all of the reasons and economic analysis supporting why a high-growth strategy is attractive and at the same time paying careful attention to the difficulties that it will incur in the implementation.

The key questions to ask in developing this "AID Grid" are listed below.

- How does the overall attractiveness of the high-growth strategy (net benefits – costs) appear?
- To what extent are these benefits tangible versus less tangible, and can the less tangible be made more targeted and specific?
- Has your organization really thought through all of the costs, especially the indirect costs and the costs of change?
- How difficult is it to get this high-growth strategy approved by all key stakeholders?
- How difficult is it to get this high-growth strategy implemented, monitored, evaluated and revised as new information becomes available?

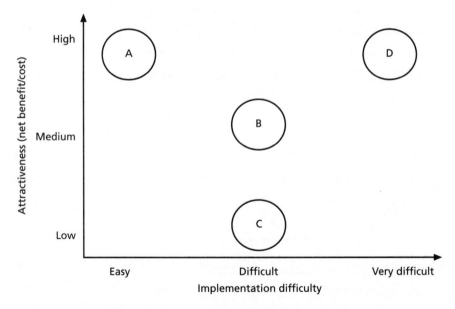

Fig. 10 An illustrative portfolio of projects – the attractiveness and implementation grid

- To what extent is the high-growth strategy vulnerable to changes in either the internal organizational environment or external economic environment?
- What can your organization do to secure either higher attractiveness or easier implementation, or both?

Combining EVA with the GE grid and the AID grid will give your organization a strong analytical framework for rigorously testing and comparing various high-growth strategies in order to select the best strategy for your organization.

Tool 12: implementation forces analysis

The goal of any strategy is the successful implementation of that strategy. Every organization must analyze the enabling and the constraining forces that will come to bear in helping or hampering the implementation of a strategy. Without looking at these forces, strategic planning is left with a naked cost-benefit type of analysis that sheds too little light on the probabilities associated with actually implementing the strategy as designed or planned. In addition, failing to take into account implementation forces may leave your organization with very unrealistic estimates of the specific costs of implementing the high-growth strategy and the expected benefits from the strategy.

> The goal of any strategy is the successful implementation of that strategy. Every organization must analyze the enabling and the constraining forces that will come to bear in helping or hampering the implementation of a strategy.

Looking internally, ASTD listed six areas where it evaluates positive and negative forces which will affect the ability of the organization to implement its strategy successfully. They are:

- leadership and management of the strategy
- communication and employee support of the strategy
- performance measurement
- structure of ASTD in support of the strategy
- systems and processes capable of implementing the strategy
- financial and other resources availability/constraints.

Looking externally, organizations must focus on such items as:

- customer and product acceptance
- supply chain capability
- success of strategic partnerships
- understanding and predicting future trends.

The best way to represent these forces is pictorially.

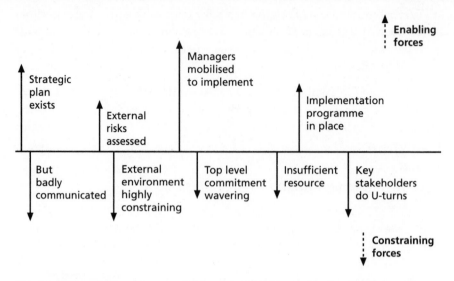

Fig. 11 IMF analysis of Dowty Communications strategic development plan for the early 1990s

Conclusion

The 12 strategic planning and analysis tools discussed in this chapter can start to work for your company, non-profit organization or educational institution immediately. These tools focus on helping the organization develop its capacity to implement high-growth strategies. In addition, they focus on assisting the organization in developing, selecting and implementing the best high-growth strategies from all of the options identified. Chapter 3 focuses on the theme "achieving organizational breakthrough." Through our research and work with over 100 organizations over the past 25 years, we have observed and developed high-growth strategies that can improve the capacity and success of your organization.

The tools described so far can be used individually or together. With the careful delegation of assignments and with the advent of computerized networking, intranets and the web, organizations can spread out the use of these analytical tools among different employees and different teams of employees and managers. In fact, many organizations would be well served to have many, if not all, of their employees learn some of these analytical tools and for each employee and manager to apply at least one tool to the organization in an effort to identify a potentially successful high-growth strategy.

These tools can be useful at the strategic level in guiding entire organizations toward their future. In addition, some of these tools can easily be adapted to promote improvements in the productivity of the division, team or employee.

One observer has commented that 80% of what an organization will *need to know* to survive and grow over the next five years will come from *outside of its industry*. We have selected physics to shed light on what strategy really is. Organizations and environments are "mass." Growth is acceleration. Force is what makes mass accelerate. And strategy is what governs force. Clearly, every organization in pursuit of high-growth strategies will need to learn from the high tech, information, marketing and training industries as these industries are transformed themselves by technology over the next several years. All high-growth strategies will depend to some extent on weaving new knowledge created in these industries into the daily operations of your organization.

These analytical tools are as applicable to non-profit organizations that have a budget of $5,000 per year as they are to educational institutions with billions of dollars in endowments, and to companies of all sizes. These tools will become a part of your organization's culture and common language by sharing them with each and every employee (member). Strategy is no longer exclusively the province of those with an MBA and others with graduate degrees. We have tried to explain these strategic tools in simple, straightforward terms. We have modified some of them to fit the needs of everyday organizations as we see them.

They are building blocks, not stumbling blocks. The tools should be used with several important guidelines in mind. First, they will produce different results for different people in your organization. Do not expect agreement by everyone – it is therefore important to manage differences of opinions as they arise. Second, these tools can be undertaken and employed with pencil and paper for five minutes each or can be used with terrabyte size databases taking months to complete. The use of the tools must be consistent with the resources available and the real needs of your organization. We have presented these analytical tools in a simple, practical format so that your organization will avoid paralysis by analysis. High growth today requires decisions and action, fast decisions and faster action.

Finally, we hope you will not only use the tools presented but also improvise and create your own tools. We invite you to write to us to share your newly developed analytical tools.

Achieving organizational breakthrough

- Introduction

- Stakeholder analysis

- The Internet

- Human capital, intellectual capital, and attitude capital

- Knowledge management – the management of knowledges

- The role of teams and virtual teams

- Values-driven growth model

- New selection process and paradigm for boards of directors

- Councils of Masters/advisory boards

- Spinoffs/spinouts

- Outsourcing and new labor force practices – contract employees

- Consolidation and roll ups

- Profit zone analysis

- Globalization

- Conclusion

Do not look to improve your business. Look to reinvent it.

Deborah McMahon, *Mercer Management Consulting*

Introduction

This chapter identifies breakthrough strategies that can improve the organizational capacity of your business, non-profit organization or educational institution. Although there is no one size that fits all, there are some common themes that come close to being "silver bullets."

The first key point that we want to make is that strategic planning and strategic thinking must focus on capacity/capability building as much as it focuses on the specific goals and objectives that most often come to mind including increasing sales, profits, customer satisfaction, grant funding, numbers of students or size of endowment. The second key point is that organizations are "people." They are formed by people, they grow usually by adding people as employees or customers or both, and they serve people. For organizations to transform, change, reinvent themselves or merely try to improve themselves, they will do it through the people that populate the ranks of their employees, their management, their suppliers and their customers.

We are now in the age where some businesses are beginning to automate to such a great extent through web-based technologies, robotics and other approaches that the vision of businesses running to a great extent on "autopilot" is no longer total fantasy. Through data mining and data warehousing techniques, enterprise resource planning software, robotics and sophisticated decision-making formula, such issues as inventory control (purchasing and stocking), manufacturing process and many management decisions can be now be made by computers. In spite of this "autopilot trend," achieving organizational breakthrough today still requires individual breakthrough by the people who populate your organization.

Any effort to improve or expand the organizational capacity or capability of a company, non-profit or educational institution must begin with a great sensitivity to the people in the organization. We begin our analysis with a "stakeholder analysis" approach that is designed to focus attention on the political views of the members of the organization. No change, improvement, merger, acquisition or reinvention will ever be successful without sufficient support from stakeholders. Although one can never be sure why the new CEO of Grant Thornton who came from outside of the organization only lasted three months in 1998, one can be sure that he either never had or quickly lost stakeholder support.

Strategic planning and strategic thinking ride the fine line between pushing the edge of what can be accomplished within a given timeframe and wishful thinking. Beginning our focus with a stakeholder analysis will show that "strategic alignment" is one of the early, critical steps to accomplish in the strategic planning process. Throughout the course of our research for this book we found several consulting firms and new softwares that focus on achieving "strategic alignment." In addition, a key focus of any strategic planning process must be the careful execution and implementation of the plan. The key to implementation of any strategic plan is the people who will implement it. Are they ready, trained, supportive, understanding of the need for the change and the basic design for implementation? The people who will implement the plan are always to be considered one of the key stakeholder groups regarding the plan. In our stakeholder analysis, we focus on other groups as well, but if the employees of an organization do not believe a strategic plan will work, *then it will not work*. This is what we call an *implementation reality*.

The key elements to success of a strategic plan are as follows.
Strategy
- Is there a simple and clear objective?
- Is the plan coherent?
- Does the plan fully address the key implementation issues?
- Is the schedule reasonable?

Structure
- Are the roles of key implementors clear and well communicated?
- Do the implementors have the proper resources and power to achieve results?
- Is the plan properly coordinated among different actors and divisions which need to be involved?
- Does the implementation team have sufficient leadership and communication infrastructure?

Skills, Culture and Commitment
- Are the implementors properly trained and do they have sufficient skills?
- Has the culture of the organization been taken into account and transformed if necessary to implement strategies that require substantial change in behaviors?
- Is there sufficient commitment to the objective and the plan to promote success?
- Will the strategy implementation be monitored properly?
- Will the strategy implementation process be sensitive to changes in the environment (both internal and external) to know when to make shifts to achieve the stated goal?

In fact, we know that strategies require certain "realities" in order for them to succeed. The term "organizational alignment" refers to the successful mobilization of all elements of an organization simultaneously in support of a strategic plan. The importance of this "unity" as a former owner of a home health care company in Mustang, Oklahoma calls it, is growing and many organizations are now hiring orchestra leaders as consultants to assist them in this area due to their recognized ability to create unity and alignment among professional musicians and between the musicians and their customers, the audience.

In addition to stakeholder analysis, this chapter addresses the following key areas in the field of achieving organizational breakthrough:

- the Internet
- human capital
- knowledge management
- the role of teams and virtual teams
- values-driven growth models
- new paradigm for boards of directors
- Councils of Masters/advisers
- spinoffs/spinouts
- outsourcing
- consolidation and roll ups
- profit zone analysis
- globalization

Many books have been written on these topics. In this chapter, we do not aim to review this entire body of literature. Instead, we provide you with our own organizational breakthrough tools and practical suggestions that we have discovered from our experience that you can apply today in your organization.

Stakeholder analysis

The days of "one man rules" are dying fast. Some suggest the days of "one woman rules" are coming fast. Most likely the future will be characterized by a middle ground where *enlightened leadership* will be leadership that actively takes into account the positions of many groups within an organization. Organizations need support of front-line workers who determine the exact level of customer satisfaction that is achieved. Management needs to know what the front-line workers are learning from customers on a daily basis. Companies need to know who the stakeholders are in every situation.

For example, Child Trends, Inc., is a non-profit organization that analyzes data on the well-being of children and youth. With a budget of nearly $3 million from government funds, foundations and publication revenues, the organization prepares papers for key Congressional Committees and policy makers in the US at the federal level. When asked who the "stakeholders" were for their organization, we were told that the 100 leading federal policy makers were the key stakeholders for the organization. Our own analysis of their research findings shows that the true "stakeholders" for their organization are the 50 million people in the US who either have children, are children or who are likely to very interested in the well-being of children. An organization with 100 stakeholders will have a completely different business model and different breakthrough potential than an organization with 50 million stakeholders. Just ask the people at the American Association of Retired Persons (AARP), which has 32 million members with over 500,000 persons volunteering on a regular basis. There is an organization that knows who its "stakeholders" are – and it is not the 100 leading policy makers on issues affecting the senior population in the US.

Stakeholder analysis is the systematic identification of key stakeholders and appraisal of their influence and posture towards implementation of a high-growth strategy. This form of "organizational radar" is necessary at the early stages in developing high-growth strategies, in order to avoid wasting strategic planning resources on a high-growth strategy which key stakeholders will not support. Stakeholder analysis is also very helpful in reformulating and improving high-growth strategies in order to win the approval of key stakeholders who have objections to part of the strategy. Defining the key stakeholders as broadly as possible will open up not only broad areas of potentially high-growth strategies, but also new approaches to rapidly expanding the capacity and capability of your organization.

> **Stakeholders are those interested in and capable of significantly contributing to (or creating barriers to) your organization implementing high-growth strategies and improving its organizational capacity.**

Organizations usually define their stakeholders as owners – people occupying powerful positions within the organization, or people with the power to affect the organization's costs and revenues significantly. Stakeholders may be internal or external. This narrow, stifling view of stakeholders may have been appropriate before the world became linked, or at least linkable, via the Internet. It is now less appropriate.

Defining who the key stakeholders are is an art. But we do know that most mistakes are made by defining stakeholders too narrowly. Usually stakeholders are defined by their power within the organization. We expand the term stakeholders to include people who are currently outside of your organization who could become an important part of your business model if your organization achieved breakthrough growth. Stakeholders are those interested in and capable of significantly contributing to (or creating barriers to) your organization implementing high-growth strategies and improving its organizational capacity.

Another example comes to mind of how a progressive organization defined its stakeholders far too narrowly. Upon the proper identification of the broader range of its actual stakeholders, it reversed a key policy and embarked on a very successful high-growth strategy. For several years, Starbucks refused to serve drinks with skim milk and non-fat milk, as Howard Schultz believed the company should only sell coffee with whole milk. Schultz was reported to have said that products with skim or non-fat milk could not be "Starbucks products." Presumably, he was trying to keep his company's products consistent with those whole milk coffee products he experienced in Italy and upon which he modeled his company. By refusing to sell skim and non-fat milk in his products, he may have been faithful to the tradition upon which the "Starbucks product" was based, but he ignored the important stakeholder, the person who wanted the Starbucks' experience, but did not want the taste, fat or calories of whole milk. Finally, someone in the organization spoke up often enough and loudly enough for these stakeholders (which turned out to be hundreds of thousands of potential customers and possibly the shareholders who wanted to capture the increased earnings from these additional sales) to change not only the way Starbucks served coffee, but also how it defined itself as a business.

Stakeholders, especially those within the organization, do have immediate political power. They must have an opportunity to have their views heard at every stage in the process. Employees are clearly stakeholders. One airline in the US did not consult its employees on an issue that adversely affected the employees and soon thereafter customer luggage mysteriously began to be rerouted to the wrong city to the great dismay of customers – and you thought they "lost your baggage" through incompetence!

The stakeholder analysis will tell you early on which stakeholders will need to have their issues addressed before strategic alignment takes hold. In addition, by weighting the relative influence of each stakeholder or stakeholder group, an organization could go far in gaining insight into making the right judgment calls. In the Starbucks example, the relative influence of hundreds of thousands of potential customers for skim or non-fat products should easily have outweighed the lone voice of one man, Howard Schultz, voting with the past in mind rather than engaging in breakthrough thinking. If Starbucks at that time before skim and non-fat milk products had sought to reinvent itself to expand its customer base, rather than sticking to its traditional product line, it might have had an easier time in giving consumers what they wanted. Today Starbucks sells ice cream and other products, and is clearly a company capable of listening to all of its major stakeholders.

Stakeholder analysis requires "learning." Often, organizations have never defined "stakeholders" more broadly than owners, board members, key customers, suppliers and top management. Defining stakeholders to include large blocks of potentially profitable customers or large blocks of persons in need of the services or products that your organization offers could lead to breakthrough growth. For example, often when organizations, especially non-profits, gather data and information showing just how many people need their services, they get energized, raise funds, expand the number of volunteers, gear up their strategic planning processes and seek to expand to meet the need for their services.

A deeper form of stakeholder analysis is called the *stakeholder agenda analysis*. This type of analysis takes each stakeholder, one at a time, and probes deeply as to why this particular stakeholder is either supportive of the high-growth strategy or against it. This detailed analysis is now

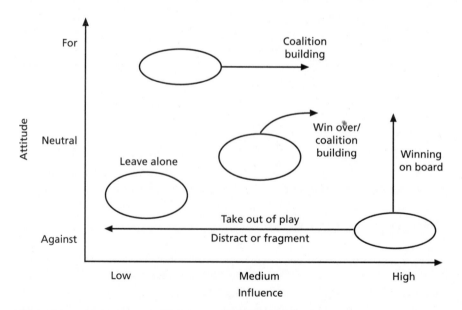

Note: This tool is based on earlier versions by Piercey (1989)

Fig. 12 Stakeholder analysis

becoming more critical as our workplaces are becoming more culturally and internationally diverse, and a higher level of understanding of the values, predispositions, attitudes and personalities of key stakeholders is becoming more important to success in the economic marketplace. This form of "high touch" analysis is qualitative in nature and subject to being only as good as the person performing the analysis. However, its value can not be underestimated in getting an organization from the conceptual stage of "we want high-growth" through successful implementation.

A third stakeholder analysis technique called *stakeholder prioritization* completes the stakeholder analysis triad. One of the authors developed this technique while working with Domino Printing Sciences, an international technology company based in Cambridge, UK. The process rank orders the stakeholders in terms of the importance they have or influence they have in getting their way within the organization. Use of this simple device creates a navigational device through the political minefields of the organization and provides key insight to strategic planners in the development and promotional aspects of the strategic planning process for high-growth strategies.

The Internet

No book about strategic planning and business could be complete without a discussion of the Internet. We offer several key insights about it. In 1999, new business models were perfected that have guaranteed that the "Internet sector" will grow faster than all of the other sectors of the US or any other developed economy for the forseeable future. The first reason for this growth is speed. The Internet travels at the speed of light. Second, as will be shown below, the Internet can dramatically cut costs. Third, the Internet allows for levels of customer service and product customization that were never possible before. Fourth the Internet eliminates geographical, political, physical and other "borders" that have kept human beings apart from each other and the products and services they want since the beginning of time.

The new Internet business model puts at the consumer's fingertips products and services that were often difficult to obtain under the old business model. It is clear that the Internet will eliminate many jobs. One could hardly help but notice when Merrill Lynch laid off 3,400 employees in 1998 and eSchwab was hiring. On-line stock trading, on-line purchasing of cars, computers, mortgage financing, credit card lines of credit, airline tickets, books, music, clothes, and an endless list of other products is now taken for granted. This shift in "instant shopping" is such a paradigm shift that it will cause a surge in the demand by people to end the long lines that we experience everywhere from the grocery store to driver's license renewal.

We can easily foresee the day when most people will renew their driver's license and obtain many government services on-line rather than standing in line for hours.

The story of Amazon.com, mentioned earlier, is telling. First, the economics. Barnes and Noble, its major old line competitor is a very well-run company and has beautiful stores that are a true pleasure to visit. Barnes and Noble spends approximately $1.50 in capital in order to generate $1.00 in profits (1998 figures). On the other hand, Amazon.com spends less than a penny in capital expenditures to generate a $100 in profit. How does Amazon.com do it? First of all, the company gets your money from the on-line order well before it has to pay for the books or other items that you order. (This is called the "float.") Second, it has little inventory in the form of books or other assets required to process your order. This model of doing business is almost infinitely profitable when one calculates return on capital. Third, Amazon.com collects, stores and utilizes customer data in a way that can never be matched without the Internet. Whenever someone orders a book, Amazon.com asks if the customer would like to be told of future books in that category. So,when a book arrives in your designated field, Amazon.com recommends the book to you. In addition it surveys customers and gathers data on books that people like and ones they do not like. Amazon.com also publishes book reviews that people send it right along side of the title of the book, creating a very friendly, high touch, informative business environment. Similarly, "E-bay", the on-line auction company, also gains the benefit of a long float with funds deposited by customers. In early 1999 this float became so large for "E-bay" that it was reported that the owners were going to start their own bank.

Suppliers and vendors through the Internet can trace their customers' usage of their products and spot immediately when sales are falling off or taking off. Problems of not having enough stock to meet demand or having it at the wrong store can more quickly be addressed through the use of Internet-based sharing of data between suppliers and retail stores. In fact, in 1999 it has become clear that many segments of the economic marketplace will undergo a profound shift toward Internet-based approaches to doing business. A new word – "etailing" – may be replacing the word "retailing" in many sectors of the economy.

The Internet allows companies to organize in a fundamentally different way. Telecommuting, forming strategic alliances and teaming relationships with people across the globe will be a much more common part of the business and non-profit organization landscape. Companies will have a great incentive to open offices in far-off places in different time zones to capture the advantages of the 24-hour office. Someone can begin a project in New York and at leaving time save the work on a computer file. Then, instantly a person in Paris can open that computer file via the web and begin working right where the other person left off, only to be replaced eight hours later by someone in Tokyo or Austraila. Computers will be able to translate from one language to another automatically and language barriers will be significantly lessened. The authors are fully aware that there are over 5,000 languages and this barrier will not be overcome throughout the world by the time of publishing this book. The Internet will be a force that will drive a tremendous "consolidation" in the field of language with English, in all likelihood, becoming the unofficial language of the world of commerce by the year 2005, if not sooner.

We also recognize that there are many places throughout the world without a stable enough supply of electricity or a sufficiently stable communication system to support a widespread use of the Internet. However, just as it was an incentive to Coca-Cola® to clean up water systems so that they could produce Coke in developing lands, it will be an incentive to huge financial interests to push for electricity and stable communication systems to allow them to expand their Internet-related businesses into developing and emerging countries. Welcome to the new steam engine, the telephone and the new railroad all rolled into one.

The Internet allows people not only to work where they want to but also when they want to. Conferences are a huge business and will continue to be. However, new forms of conference over the Internet allow people to "attend" sessions when they want to, conduct dialogues via chat rooms and listservers, and even allow people to "give" presentations via video-conferencing without ever attending the conference. The ubiquitous use of e-mail, groupware, videoconferencing and other forms of software that allow groups to interact in efficient and productive ways will give a real business advantage to the Internet-wise organization. In fact, with the explosion of distance learning, some predict college campuses will lose significant population in the US over the next two decades as on-line educational programs proliferate.

While it has been clear for years that the Internet allows for the more rapid dissemination of information, only in 1998/99 did it become clear what impact the Internet will have on our ability to measure and improve human capital, and on the production, dissemination and management of knowledge both within organizations and between organizations.

Human capital, intellectual capital, and attitude capital

One breakthrough economic strategy that appears to be a silver bullet today for organizations is improving the human capital of their employees and management. *Human capital is a person's ability, plus knowledge and experience, that empowers him or her to perform a certain task or tasks.* Now that many people and companies have approximately the same access to capital, the same types of organizational structures, the same market data, the same number of workers, etc, human capital can become the deciding factor in achieving high-growth strategies. The world economy is far less industrial today – in the past most jobs were repetitive and physically demanding. Now, as the world moves even beyond the information age to the knowledge era in the developed countries, there is a new emphasis on education and training for the workforce. For years, investments in training have been limited by our inability to measure the impact of training on the improved capacity of the trainee, on the change in behavior of the trainee, the trainee's productivity and on the trainee's contribution to the profitability or growth of the organization. Now, through the work of ASTD, Scandia Air Lines and many other companies, common measurement tools (called "benchmarks" and "metrics") are being developed that give organizations important feedback – showing to what extent training and education works, and how it impacts the organization's ability to generate profits, improve service, heighten customer satisfaction and meet the needs of those served by the organization.

Efforts to improve the human capital of those involved in your organization will cost less in the future. We predict the costs of education and training will drop significantly over the next decade due to the new delivery systems being put into place to make broad scale dissemination possible at a relatively low cost per trainee. Delivery of training and education will take new Internet-related forms, and our ability to customize education and training products to match the learning skills and preferences of students of all ages will also greatly increase. The era of "mass customization" in the field of education and training will result in the world, and your organization, having access to a much more efficient, workplace-oriented educational system. Government-run and traditional parochial schools are likely to lag in their ability and willingness to adopt the mass customization approaches that will drive the adult education and training market in the next decade.

Companies have had their own "universities" for years These schools were originally designed to meet the needs of the company for better trained and educated workers. They were "cost" centers. As we approach the year 2000, companies are rethinking the role of their "universities" and making them "profit centers" where they will accept students from outside of the company for a fee. (In fact, they charge a "fee" to the departments within the company that send their employees to them.) This shift from a cost center to a profit center is an organizational breakthrough. Our expanded emphasis on human capital improvement over the next decade will fuel a huge growth in for-profit educational activities and for-profit educational companies. We are already witnessing some training companies going "public", and capital flow is moving into this industry that was formerly fragmented, not very profitable and whose companies remained very small for a long perod.

There will be great organizational breakthroughs made possible by increasing the human capital of employees. Layers of supervision will vanish and workers' wages could and should increase with their increased human capital. As will be shown below, workers will be able to build on each company's database of knowledge, and will be able to obtain answers to questions instantly on-line, from people all over the world who can now "hear" or "see" their questions posted via the Internet or answer with on-line help systems.

While we acknowledge that this web-based, human-capital-focused, high tech scenario does not apply to some low tech industries and low tech workers, it is important to note that low tech organizations such as grocery stores must prepare now for the day when ordering the groceries over the Internet will be affordable for most consumers in developed countries.

Knowledge management – the management of knowledges

There is a clear distinction between information and knowledge. Information consists of data and elements. Knowledge is a synthesis and distillation of that information using thought, insight and wisdom to combine the information in such a way as to produce something that is of far greater importance. We think of information as the flour, chocolate chips, sugar, nuts and other ingredients that are used to make chocolate chip cookies. Knowledge, that's the recipe for the great chocolate chip cookie (that often costs nearly a dollar retail!) In 1976 one of the authors using an on-line data base, ERIC, was able to locate 55 articles on how university presidents were selected in the US. The research time was just two minutes at the University of Texas. Typing in the words "University & President & selection or process", the articles appeared on the computer screen and were printed overnight. Several days later, after reviewing these papers and interviewing the major stakeholders at UT, this author working with a fellow graduate student Wayne Roberts, wrote a paper on how the University of Texas

> **There is a clear distinction between information and knowledge. Information consists of data and elements. Knowledge is a synthesis and distillation of that information using thought, insight and wisdom to combine the information in such a way as to produce something that is of far greater importance.**

President was selected in 1976 and should be selected in the future. Today this research capability now exists regarding tens of thousands of databases and hundreds of thousands of topic areas.

Before the Internet, the only knowledge generally available from data bases was "published" data. Today, companies write a report in the morning on a particular topic or event and it becomes available to its 50,000, 100,000 or even 200,000 employees and their clients instantly through the company's web-based knowledge management system. Knowledge management systems create a huge competitive advantage for organizations who can create, own and rapidly disseminate privately generated or collected knowledge. Often, large organizations – by having the advantage of having many knowledge creators working simultaneously – can compile this new knowledge at a rate far greater than their smaller competitors. The Internet and knowledge management systems now give size a great competitive advantage.

However, the small organizations are not left out. Access to information and knowledge by individuals and small organizations is far greater today via the Internet than ever before. The ability of the small organizations to perform breakthrough work and to achieve high-growth strategies is actually heightened by their enormous power to access knowledge on a scale that is unprecedented, at a speed that was not imaginable in the mid-1990s and at a very low cost.

Finally, the Internet has proven to be a great source of accurate information and worthwhile knowledge. While not everything on the Internet is accurate, and Internet fraud is likely to increase, it is surprising how accurate the business-related information on the web is. With so much knowledge available so quickly, people will spend more time transforming the knowledge that they gain into the wisdom that they need to create and implement successful high-growth strategies. Massive business projects are starting to come in ahead of schedule and below budget. Information, knowledge and wisdom will speed across borders and no government can stop it for long. In 1998, the new Chancellor of Germany spoke at the Bundestag and declared that students must be taught the Internet. The Internet, unlike many other goods, is becoming a *right*, and companies like MicroStrategy want to be seen as being so essential in the marketplace that it is viewed as being just as important as a "utility" company such as the gas, water, electricity and telephone services we have come to depend on.

The role of teams and virtual teams

Achieving organizational breakthrough requires strategies that produce value over time. They must be planned or chaos occurs. They must be driven by a clear objective. Older forms of organizations such as hierarchy and bureaucracy involved a form of "top down" organizational dynamics. The leader told others what to do. They did it, usually. Today, we not only have teams of people co-located in space (geography), but we also have people in teams who are located far apart. What we have learned about teams from the work of Jessica Lipnack and Jeffrey Stamps, *Virtual Teams*, and others, is that teams, especially virtual teams, require a clear purpose, well-defined links and the careful selection of people who are the right people for the team.

We have always had teams of people who worked primarily in different locations and often for different companies. One good example is the board of directors. What is less common are teams of front-line employees from far apart getting together via technology to discuss ways to make the organization a more productive place or a better place to work.

Forming teams that are less hierarchical than departmentalized organization structures can have profound impacts. People – rather than working in one department – can belong to many teams that cross departments and even companies. It can make it difficult for accountants to allocate their costs among departments. This team approach can enliven a workforce by promoting diversity (e.g. someone from operations actually talking to someone in research on a regular basis) and distributes leadership in an organization more broadly and possibly in a more enlightened, egalitarian manner. Information is distributed in an organization more broadly. Breakthrough thinking is promoted by having teams form, produce and disband.

An organization that regularly forms and concludes the work of a team when a task is completed is less likely to become rigid and fail the innovative/flexibility analysis described above. There may be significant limits to the success of virtual teams, which require significant cost, time, effort and forward thinking to be successful. However, due to their flexibility and ability to capture and organize significant resources, virtual teams may be a silver bullet that promotes organizational breakthrough. Project management software is being developed that becomes a part of an organization's website or Intranet and which allows for persons in remote locations, including customers, to be able to access, track and put input into the schedules of activities in an ongoing project. Successful management of virtual teams will be a new hotbed of management publications in the coming years.

Values-driven growth model

"Growth drivers" analysis, described earlier in this book (see page 61), is an analytical tool that can provide great insight into customer behavior. Through brainstorming sessions, focus groups, customer surveys or other research instruments, organizations try to figure out the answers to a variety of important questions, such as:

- why the consumer chooses its products or services rather than those of its competitors
- why the consumer buys the product or service at all
- the conditions that would influence the consumer to purchase more or less of the product, and how much more or less.

These drivers are viewed as "external to the organization or company." Although a company may change the price, packaging, or bundling of a product or service, or institute a stronger marketing campaign, the consumer response is the "unit of analysis."

Now that significant product differentiation is becoming more difficult and market lead times shrink as competitors can often copy products quickly, organizations will have to turn *inward* for competitive advantage. Can a company sell more of its products, can a non-profit secure more revenue to serve more people, and can an educational institution attract more students and teachers and students and teachers of higher quality because of the values the company holds and their reputation for these values? This is an open question, but we expect that the answer may be "Yes."

Can an organization be more productive if it identifies its core values and secures alignment among all of its workers consistent with these values? The Microsoft trial of 1998 may shed light on the values that the company actually lives by. If Microsoft loses and the public perceives Microsoft as a "villain", this airing of these values may not play well. Competitors may find the door somewhat opened and begin to tout not only their products but their values as well.

To the extent that *values drive behavior*, the merger, acquisition and consolidation frenzy of the late 1990s can be seen in two distinct lights. First, these mergers, acquisitions and consolidations should produce the benefits of size, lower costs and combine complementary competencies. However, to the extent the real values of the workers or management of the combining entities are in conflict, the positive gains sought in the short run may be difficult to realize – it could take years and great expenditures for them ever to be realized. The difficulties of the Covey-Franklin Trust merger illustrate how different value structures and cultures between organizations can slow down the expected synergies and can result in stockholder value destruction rather than stockholder value enhancement, especially in the early stages.

The values of your organization must be made explicit if they are to become a significant part of a high-growth strategy. Organizations cannot rely on mere words chosen by a public relations firm and assume them as values for the organization. Determining the real values of your organization must be based on factual research data from employees and customers.

An organization's reputation for its values can go far in assisting it in developing high-growth strategies. One breakthrough strategy for organizations is to develop a "contribution strategy." A contribution strategy is a coherent policy of the organization to take significant and substantial action in support of charitable or educational institutions. For example, an organization's contribution strategy could be through a foundation created by the company or by direct company action. The company could donate time (through paying employees to perform "volunteer" efforts in the community), or it could donate money, products, cash, used equipment, buildings or other assets. It could even donate its relationship capital by hosting fundraisers where an organization's entire mailing list is invited by phone, fax, e-mail or snail mail. In the future, companies could also serve as training grounds for non-profit organizations and could assist them with their "business strategy," organizational development approaches and quality improvement programs.

While this book is written on the premise that the strategic tools that non-profit organizations should use are the same as those used by for-profit companies, the authors understand that many people either live in the "business" world *or* the "non-profit" world. Non-profit organizations know that they can achieve organizational breakthrough by emphasizing values and service. For-profit companies are just starting to learn this. For-profit companies achieve organizational breakthrough by building business models that can pass the rigorous scrutiny of a tough MBA professor while acting in a manner consistent with their values and mission. Non-profit organizations are just starting to learn this. This book helps bridge some of the unnecessary gap between non-profit organizations and for-profit businesses both in the way they "do business" and in the way they relate to each other.

Starbucks is an employer that strongly supports employee volunteerism. We think this policy is a high-growth strategy for Starbucks as it generates employee loyalty, retention and well-being, and probably contributes significantly to increase sales and reputation. We recommend that companies have a significant contribution policy because it is good business. After studying the strategic tools in this book and looking to the future when competitive advantage will often come from some source other than fancy marketing, low cost (cost leadership), a lack of substitutes or market leadership (first to market with a particular product), it is clear that a well thought out "contribution policy" can be a source of significant competitive advantage since it can achieve the following goals:

- consumer and employee loyalty and retention

- consumer attractiveness
- enhancement of human capital of employees
- contribute to the knowledge management structure of the organization
- promote working in teams and in shared leadership roles
- promote the networking ability of an organization
- secure entry to target markets.

The analysis shows that a contribution strategy could achieve many positive goals for an organization. Even non-profit organizations can benefit from having their own contribution strategy where they themselves contribute to, and have their employees contribute to, other organizations.

New selection process and paradigm for boards of directors

In large and small corporations, stockholders vote their shares to elect directors. Sort of. For non-profit organizations with members, members vote to elect directors. Sort of. Each year, several magazines "rate" the boards of directors of the various companies on numerous criteria. Our new paradigm respects the right of shareholders of corporations and members of non-profit organizations to vote for board members, but adds an important twist in determining what type of person should be on your organization's board of directors, and the type of work the members of your organization's board of directors should perform.

Our new paradigm starts from a premise that companies – and especially non-profit organizations – should rely on their boards for expertise, contacts, strategic advice and assistance in implementing critical activities. In the non-profit world, board members are often simply fundraising magnets. In the for-profit world, they are often merely friends of the CEO who will let him or her do as he or she pleases. Our research and work with hundreds or organizations shows that in many instances, boards of directors are one of most under-utilized human resources in commerce today.

The new paradigm, developed by Growth Strategies, Inc. is based on the belief that organizations and their leadership can identify where they need top-level assistance, and can gain that assistance through a board of directors where each member is selected due to a particular area of need of the company or non-profit organization. The approach is simple – the company, non-profit organization or educational institution would regularly determine (through brainstorming by key leadership or surveying all of the employees and even suppliers and customers and strategic partners) *what the areas of key improvement are that would benefit the organization*. The organization would then compile a list of key substantive areas where it needs assistance, including areas such as:

- technology
- employee compensation, recruitment and retention
- employee training and development
- capital acquisition or fundraising
- business planning and strategic planning
- financial management and accounting
- manufacturing process development and improvement
- labor relations
- intellectual property, science and new product development
- government relations and regulatory processes
- public relations
- advertising
- marketing
- organizational development
- health, safety and the environment
- geographical expansion and diversity
- race relations and multi-cultural competence
- transportation, etc.

After identifying high priority need for expertise, a board search committee would seek a person with high-level expertise in that field. That person, if willing, would be nominated for the board of directors and designated the "Board Member for _____" signifying his or her area of expertise. For example, one of the authors is currently the board member for strategy of the Washington Metro area chapter of the Strategic Leadership Forum (SLF). This chapter of the SLF uses a hybrid approach where some board members have specific areas of responsibility and others are members "at large" without a specific portfolio. We recommend that a board member with a specific area of designation pay special attention to his or her particular area of expertise and prepare monthly reports to the other members of the board in this area. This model has the extra advantage of allocating responsibility in a manner that would allow for a rigorous evaluation of each board member every year (similar to the annual appraisal system for employees).

More importantly, it would allow small companies and non-profits to attract exactly the talent they need, and would promote a team spirit of shared leadership at board level. We have seen this approach quickly double the size of small boards in non-profit organizations and are confident that this new paradigm is an infinitely better way to select boards than currently exists in 99 percent of the non-profit organizations (and maybe an equal percentage of companies). With the advent of the limited liability company – a hybrid between a corporation and a sole proprietorship or unincorporated association – many states have dropped the earlier requirement that a company have at least three board members. Cutting down on the number of board members to one person is inconsistent with the need in today's economy to form teams to accomplish significant economic objectives.

This new paradigm will work for any size organization. We have experience with instituting this type of board selection system in an organization whose revenue was $40,000 in the year when the system began, and watched the organization's programs improve and proliferate, with revenues increasing to $275,000 in the second full year after instituting the new board paradigm

The Internet, e-mail and other information technology allow boards of directors to be in daily communication and to see the progress daily in the organization via daily intranet reports or e-mail communication. The new technology will allow for greater board input into the operations and strategic planning of the organization. If the right board members are selected, their expertise will make a major contribution to the organization and is a strong source of competitive advantage over the organizations with either no effective board, or with a board of directors which must labor under the old paradigm.

Councils of Masters/advisory boards

Not every organization will have the ability to attract all of the board members in each area of expertise it desires due to limitations in the number of board members allowed by the bylaws (which are amendable) or for other reasons. One strategy that may be a silver bullet to aid organizations in achieving organizational breakthrough is to form a council of advisers on either a paid or unpaid basis. These "Councils of Masters" as we call them would have no decision-making responsibility, no policy-setting responsibility, and most likely, no legal liability for actions of the organizations as board members currently have. (The authors acknowledge that members of a Council of Masters cannot shield themselves totally from any legal liability, but under prevailing US federal and state laws, advisory board members may be far less likely to have legal liability than board members.)

A "Council of Masters" can operate as outside advisers to any size organization. To the extent the Council of Masters is comprised of senior citizens or youths, these councils could promote intergenerational learning. This concept is somewhat similar to the federal government program SCORE and the private, non-profit organization, National Executive Service Corps. Creating advisory boards or Councils of Masters can leverage great talent, expertise and experience and bring it into the organization at a very reasonable cost. Members of a Council of Masters, with their "objective eyes" might see that one aspect of the organization's activities either do not fit properly within the organization or could be done more efficiently or effectively outside of the organization. They may have a contact, the experience or knowledge to make the implementation of a high-growth strategy flow more easily or be less costly. They may also be the source of ideas that form the basis of high-growth strategies.

Spinoffs/spinouts

With the new wave of mergers and acquisitions, companies are "spinning out" or "spinning off" components of the company to employees who secure capital or otherwise buy part of the business away from the parent company. In fact, this trend has started in one form with the federal government giving the rights to private companies to exploit government funded scientific products in exchange for the government owning part of the company. This link between government departments such as the Department of Energy owning part of a company is a fascinating development and one which is beyond the scope of this book.

Every company or non-profit organization must determine and redetermine on a regular basis, "Exactly what business (market or markets) are we in?" For example, are Fed/Ex and UPS in the delivery business, the trucking business, the transportation business, the warehouse business, the product distribution business, the information technology business or possibly today, in the business planning business?

Opportunities may arise where both the company or non-profit organization and the receiving employees can benefit from a spinout. There may be cost savings and greater flexibility in the new company that will allow the parent company to serve its customers better through the new configuration. Certainly General Motors believes that spinning out its parts supplier, Delphi, will yield such results. GM announced that it would spin out Delphi and plans to sell stock in the company for $1.5 billion. Certainly, huge and immediate financial benefits can accrue to large companies as they spin out parts of their operations. Benefits can also accrue to small companies and non-profit organizations as well as large ones where small groups of employees take over one of the operations of the parent, start their own company and make their services available to other potential customers for their services.

Finally, spinouts and spinoffs can have serious labor relations impacts. Union agreements can be affected and if a spinout or spinoff is more economically efficient, jobs may be lost. The loss of jobs issue is diminishing in importance in the US as futurists predict labor shortages. However, this is not the case in developing countries with double digit unemployment rates.

Strategic planners must take into account that the people involved in the part of the organization that is spun out or spun off are stakeholders and their role in the process must be accounted for in the early stages of strategy development.

Outsourcing and new labor force practices – contract employees

There is no magic formula regarding when to "outsource" work. Outsourcing occurs when work is contracted out to another company to perform work that traditionally had been done within the normal company structure. Contract employees are persons who work on the site of a company or non-profit organization, but who are "employed" by another company and are "leased" out to the company where they work. Over the past ten years, this trend gained momentum with the use of part-time employees and now has mushroomed into a huge business. Outsourcing and the use of contract employees are two distinct, potentially high-growth strategies that can lead to organizational breakthrough in different ways.

Organizations can become fragmented over time. Organizations that produce products must have them delivered. Organizations that have employees must administer a payroll system, deduct taxes, manage retirement and health benefits, all of which lend themselves to great economies of scale. When they are small they may use their own delivery system to deliver products or keep track of payroll taxes, benefits and other "human resource functions" through employing someone within the organization to perform these functions. The cost per employee of managing a payroll and benefits system for small organizations is staggering. Outsourcing payroll and benefits has been a double-digit growth industry for years and will continue to grow as the process required by governments to handle taxes remains complicated with serious penalties for non-compliance.

With regard to delivering products, the same economic analysis applies. When a company is small it may deliver its own products at a great cost per product. As they grow, the capital costs of expanding a distribution system, a warehousing system, off-site inventory control and the potential management problems associated with such growth can drain a parent company. Outsourcing is beneficial economically when an organization can purchase the services it needs more cheaply than it can produce them. The benefits to the organization and management can reach breakthrough status for two important reasons. First, operations are streamlined and the company can refocus on what it can do best. Second, through outsourcing companies can create synergy with other companies and co-develop high-growth strategies with the organizations with whom they outsource. Organizations must carefully weigh the costs and benefits of outsourcing. The benefits include streamlined management, renewed focus on exactly the business your organization is in, and reducing the financial and managerial risk by not outsourcing that which is associated with owning and managing an enterprise and which is not related to your organization's core strengths and core values.

The use of "contract employees" has been controversial for many reasons during the 1990s but is becoming less controversial as the "industry" matures. The strategy of using contract employees is just as potentially beneficial to the small non-profit or educational institution as a Fortune 500 company.

The growth drivers behind the use of contract employees began when companies could shed the legal, payroll, benefits and other "human resource" responsibilities for employees. On occasion, workers lost benefits, including health care coverage. Now as the industry matures, the growth driver continues to come from a cost-reduction standpoint, but also comes from the ability of the contract employee companies to provide better health benefits, better retirement benefits and better payroll and human resource administration due to their superior buying power in the market. We are aware of a recent presentation by a company that started in the insurance industry. This company is expanding into the contract employee business and made a presentation to a group of 350 small non-profit organizations where the non-profits were told that the company would "hire" all of their employees, improve their benefits and not increase the cost of either the direct employee benefits or the administration of the human relations functions currently provided by each of the 350 non-profit organizations separately.

With the growth drivers now converging from the side of the original employer (lower cost, streamlining of the overhead of the organization and reduced managerial risk) as well as the employee side (improved benefits, especially health benefits where the best plans often require a group of 150 "employees" or more) we see the makings of achieving organizational breakthrough through improved strategic planning in this area. The fact that someone is technically employed by the XYZ company often becomes irrelevant to the employee, who continues to work daily without any change in his or her routines, responsibilities or any other discernable change in his or her relationship with the organization. The authors expect to see significant capital flow and strong returns in the contract employee market for the forseeable future.

Consolidation and roll ups

Consolidation, also called "roll ups" is a long-established business trend. However, it has taken up steam under the early success of Jonathan Ledecky with US Office Products, Inc. Although the company has fallen on hard times just a year after it appeared to be a great success, there still appears to be significant momentum in this approach. Industries currently being targeted for consolidation are car dealerships, building services, website design and management, printing and graphics, and printing services, among many others.

Consolidations take numerous small businesses and consolidate their ownership into one large corporation. The business strategy of roll ups is to pursue economies of scale while keeping the "ma and pa" storefront and local participation in the day-to-day management of the local stores. The initial success of US Office Products which rolled up over 200 office supply stores with over $100,000,000 million in sales was spectacular with a successful initial public offering at $25 per share. After early success the stock price went up to $125 per share only to fall recently to $5 per share.

There are many drivers that support the "roll up" or consolidation business process. First, local owners may have a strong desire to sell out for several reasons. As small businesses grow, the management headaches, capital requirements and limitations in not being able to be "full service" companies bear hard on owners. As these management difficulties grow, the desire for an owner to cash out or sellout for cash and stock in the buying corporation grows. Second, many businesses started soon after World War II. As the owners age and their children may not want or be able to carry on the business, selling the business is the only way for the owner to harvest the value of the company. Third, the new strategy of "buy and hire" is taking the place of the old strategy of "buy and fire." Previously, when a company was bought out by another company, it was usually a short amount of time until the old guard was replaced with the new company's management. Under the roll out or consolidation philosophy, the buying company keeps the previous owner as the manager of that location or that part of the business that he or she previously managed and generally keeps the employees. "Buy and hire" gives the previous owner the opportunity to continue to do much of what he or she was doing before the purchase with less of the onerous managerial responsibility the owner previously had, and reduces the costs of operating the business. For young owners who sell their companies to a roll out consolidator and for owners who are closer to retirement, it is a strong incentive to sell the company knowing that they have a job after the sale that looks much like the job they had before. In addition, owners of companies that sell their companies to consolidators often get performance payments based on the continued successful performance of their enterprises after they are sold to the consolidator.

One area where consolidation is taking place is in the printing, graphics and web design industries. US Web, Inc. has purchased over 35 companies using its stock (and possibly some cash) as the currency given to many owners of small web design and website management companies. The key to reaching agreement between the sellers of the small business and the owners of the buying business occurs in the valuation process of both the small business and the larger business. One company, Multi-Media Holdings, Inc. has rolled up eight printing, graphics and website companies over the past three years and has $5 million in the bank looking for more acquisition targets. Often it buys unprofitable companies out of bankruptcy or near bankruptcy. It may buy only the customer list, if all of the assets of the company to be bought are leased. Often when it buys a company, profitable or not, it leaves the company operations mostly intact at the original location and provides for that company a greater line of sales and marketing opportunities through integrating the services and products offered from its various locations. This gives the company the local look and feel, continuity of employees and customers, and allows it to move many of the customers up the scale in the products and services it offers. When it purchases an unprofitable company, it does not pay any cash. It pays for the company with its own stock which is not yet publicly traded. When it purchases a company that is profitable, it pays with some combination of cash and stock, usually 50–50.

How do roll out companies value the companies they buy? Often they will multiply the after tax earnings of the companies by between 3–6 times, depending on various factors including profitability of customers and other more intangible factors including some assessment of future profitability. If the stock of the consolidator is publicly traded, then it is easy to assess the value of the consolidators stock at the market price. However, if the stock is not yet publicly traded, how does a consolidator value its own stock? First, it may look to publicly traded companies that are in the same industry take their price to earnings ratios, and then discount them by 30 percent to come up with a value for its own stock. An alternative way is to assess the value of its own company is by setting a multiple of its gross revenues. In either case, the value of the company to be bought and the company doing the buying is negotiated. The result of this negotiation then forms the basis for the price paid, in stock and cash, for the company to be purchased.

> **The companies that go about consolidating industries, are creating currency with their own (often untradeable) stock and this currency is used to buy their competitors.**

The key element to consolidation is that companies with the vision and strategic plan to identify fragmented, growing markets that could benefit from economies of scale create perceived value in their own stock by their future plans and estimates of profitability through economies of scale and capturing an ever increasing share of the large growing market they are attempting to consolidate. In essence, the companies that go about consolidating industries, even if they do it only on a small scale of buying up a few other competitors per year, are creating currency with their own (often untradeable) stock and this currency is used to buy their competitors. The carrot being dangled in front of everyone is the fact that value of the consolidator's stock will increase through the increase in value by adding more and more companies to the fold.

This simplified view of consolidation shows that a company with a strategic plan to acquire other companies through the use of its own stock in combination with some cash, can often purchase many other companies using very little cash. This high-growth strategy can be very successful if the acquisitions in combination with the original business are profitable in their own right or can be made profitable under the new consolidated business plan. The consolidation strategy fails if the only way it becomes cash positive is to continue buying other businesses and capturing their revenue streams partly in exchange for stock of the consolidating company, since there is never any guarantee that the consolidator will be able to continue to purchase other companies.

Profit zone analysis

High-growth strategies in for-profit companies must be based on a clear understanding of the "profit zone" within a given industry. This phrase – made popular by Adrian J Slywotzky and David J Morrison in their book *The Profit Zone: How Strategic Business Design Will Lead You to Tomorrow's Profits* – identifies that within broad industry categories, some subparts of the industry are quite profitable while others are not. In the late 1980s and early 1990s when IBM focused on making and selling computer hardware, the profit margins were so low that the value of the company dropped from $80 billion to $20 billion in five years. Digital, Inc. suffered a similar fate focusing on the large mainframe computer market. The profit zone in this industry was in the "software" side of the market. Similarly, Coca-Cola® discovered that the profit zone was not in the syrup they made, but was in the bottling, the signage and the vending machine area. Coca-Cola® over the past decade consolidated its holdings by buying forward in the distribution chain to capture the profit zone. Similarly, IBM has consolidated operations by moving into the software and consulting side of the computer business. The creation of the Business Intelligence Division and The Knowledge Management Institute represent IBM's efforts to capture some of the rapidly growing market share of the large accounting/consulting firms and to capture some of the huge profits in the software industry.

MicroStrategy's decision to terminate its relationship with a supplier of a platform on which its software was based and consolidate its operations so that it produced its own platform was made even though the decision temporarily deprived it of many important customers who did not have equipment that could use MicroStrategy's new product. Although the decision was originally "painful" for MicroStrategy, it was the result of a clear strategy to capture the profit zone within the software industry and has proved to be the right decision.

Finding the profit zone within the profitable software industry and other industries is a daunting task in any particular industry and one for which consultants are paid huge sums. Business strategists, however, must take this type of analysis into account when assisting companies in developing high-growth business strategies, especially when high-growth is defined as "high profit" by the organization.

A similar analysis is applicable to educational institutions that focus not on profits to such a great extent, but focus on growth and gross revenues. In addition, as non-profit organizations seek to find ways to cover overheads that grants do not cover and to stabilize income through the thick and thin of grant awards, they will need to find services they can provide and products they can sell that constitute their entry into profit zones that surround them. Many non-profits provide training programs which are not profitable. However, there is a significant profit zone "next door" to the training program, and that is in the temporary and permanent placement business now inhabited by Manpower, Inc and other companies. We are personally aware of non-profits that want to assist their trainees in finding jobs on a regular basis, charging fees for this service and thereby capturing part of this profit zone that had previously been outside of their business model.

For many organizations selling some of the information they gather, such as mailing lists, books, sharing their popular website domain name, etc can prove to be profitable. Non-profit organizations who find for-profit organizations whose values are consistent with their own may form strategic alliances and leverage the organization's brand name and reputation when the non-profit organization assists in the marketing of the company's products. A good example of this is the American Society of Association Executives' endorsement of the Legg Mason Wood Walker investment firm's cash management products for non-profit organizations. This type of leveraging of a non-profit organization's asset (its name as an endorsement) requires a careful analysis of the value of the non-profit organization's assets to the for-profit world and must involve stakeholders early in the process to secure their input and approval. Recently, the American Medical Association had to stop a potentially lucrative endorsement program when there was a backlash by members who did not believe that the AMA should be endorsing products for a fee. One company – Avtel Communications – is currently developing an Internet service provider program that can be sold to members of non-profit organizations through the organizations themselves and which can take advantage of the organization's popular domain name.

In another example, the American Automobile Association (AAA) has started an interesting, socially useful and potentially remunerative expansion possibility. AAA, in 1999, will begin to offer driver education services in Maryland and charge for its driver's education programs. The leveraging of their AAA brand and the reputation for quality that AAA has achieved could provide a good basis for its strategy to expand into this market which is currently very fragmented and often viewed as providing a low quality service. In addition, with 42,000 deaths on American highways annually, AAA's driver education program has the potential to become very large indeed as improved driver education is obviously required in the US.

Globalization

The trend toward globalization has been extensively documented. In 1998, companies such as Whirlpool and hundreds of others introduced a global information system to assist them with operations and customer support. Almost every major manufacturer and large-scale business is moving to a global information system. With computer chips now able to track any item within 100 feet of its location and feed back information about its location every few minutes, soon containers of all kinds will be tracked routinely. The efficiencies and improvements available from this technology are enormous.

Relatively small and medium-sized organizations can now access the world of commerce and knowledge through the world wide web. The Internet and the information revolution give significant advantages to companies doing business across the globe. The impact on strategic planning of the globalization is significant because it expands the normal, one country, strategic planning process exponentially whenever a new country is added.

While governments have often had "export departments" or departments of commerce that have tried to encourage exports, these agencies are now being supplemented by direct company-to-company communication, and through organizations such as Equity International, Inc. and many others that specialize in the facilitation of trade and investment between the US and other markets. In fact, IC^2, the University of Texas high technology incubator, is now offering a service where it will assist companies with a globalization business plan.

Globalization is also being fueled by economies of scale, satellite and Internet technology that allows a company to communicate over far-ranging distances at the speed of light, language translation software, the success of the capitalist economic framework and many other growth drivers. While these new developments may give the impression that countries are without boundaries and that seemless entry into a foreign country is easy, experience shows that this is not the case. The list of new variables to add to the strategic planning process for a company starting operations in a foreign country is virtually endless and, almost always, outside consultants, knowledgeable about the new country and target area, are required to complete even a basic strategic business plan.

What is new at the turn of the century is that the creation and support of worldwide teams has never been easier or less costly. Companies must integrate their international strategic planning closely with their domestic strategic planning in order to promote both efficiency and effectiveness and take advantage of worldwide opportunities.

Conclusion

Achieving organizational breakthough and increasing organizational capacity will make the difference between "one time" success and long-term success. With employee turnover high and the speed of knowledge development activities making last month's database obsolete, organizations face a greater risk today that their organizational capacity will decrease rather than increase compared to that of their competitors if they do not actively invest in improving it. We have identified several high-growth strategies that can both produce short-term financial success and contribute significantly to improving the overall capacity or capability of an organization. With the emphasis on teams, organizational charts are dynamic in nature, job descriptions give way to job roles, and someone or group within the organization must keep the forces within the organization working together and building on success. That role falls neatly within the scope of a chief strategy officer (CSO). Strategic plans designed to promote organizational capacity must be both long-term (multi-year) and short-term (e.g. six weeks) to blend the need for stability with an organization's ability to be nimble and change with the changing circumstances.

While we have identified several ideas as silver bullets, in all honesty, they are actually "silver pellets." While providing these strategies, we emphasize the important role of every manager, employee, stakeholder (broadly defined), customer vendor and others in the strategic planning process. Strategic planning used to be the domain of the executive group or consultants huddling with the board and the CEO. Those days over – strategic planning systems that are fed by input from all levels of the organization will prove to be superior to the "top down" strategic plans that have gathered much dust in the past.

Money and resources

- Introduction
- Increasing dollars and resources available to an organization
- Recognizing value
- Raising money for companies
- Raising money and increasing revenues for educational institutions
- Raising money in the non-profit world
- Compensation of employees and equity participation
- Strategic partnering and the coming avalanche of mergers in the non-profit and educational worlds
- Mergers and acquisitions, strategic alliances, joint ventures (MASA-JVs)
- Strategic cost management
- Economic value added (EVA)
- Conclusion

The assets of the past can quickly become a liability. You must always be aware of the elements that are changing the competitive landscape in your business, and try to anticipate them before they happen.

Michael Dell, *Direct from Dell*, 1999

Introduction

Strategic planning and financial analysis should be closely integrated. This chapter bridges the gap in two areas. First, we discuss the role of strategic planning in increasing the dollars and other resources available to an organization. Second, we discuss the role of strategic planning in cost management.

Increasing dollars and resources available to an organization

Increased sales or regular contributions or grants are ways of fueling growth. However, high-growth strategies often require an infusion of money and resources as start-up activities take time to yield returns. In this chapter, more than in others, we make a distinction between for-profit companies and non-profit organizations. However, each side of the "aisle" can learn from the other. In the US there is more capital available than ever before. For small businesses, securing capital from private equity markets can be an inefficient process – often relying on "angels," wealthy individuals and small groups of wealthy individuals and families that allocate some of their assets to private equity investing. While the Internet is improving the investment outlook for small companies through "Direct Public Offerings," the recent book *Finding Your Wings* documents the labyrinth that small companies must go through in hopes of raising capital. Small companies often prepare a traditional business plan and then conduct extensive research to find the right angel or venture capital. After the "right" angel or venture capital fund has been located there is often a series of face-to-face meetings required for "due diligence" as the potential investor completes the investigation of the entrepreneur, the company and then potential profitability of the product or service offered by the company. Finally, there is a closing process where equity is handed over to the investor and funds are either given to or set aside for the entrepreneurial company.

The venture capital market funded over $10 billion in investment in 1997, but less than $1 billion went to start-ups. Government invested $63 billion and corporations invested $133 billion. Venture funds target certain high-growth industries and provide expansion capital at a high price in terms of the amount of control and ownership they extract for their capital. Venture funds look for "good managers." Venture capital will certainly increase as our economy grows and the total value of the stocks and bonds rises.

For larger companies, capital markets, while cyclical between crunch periods and fluid periods, are operating quite well. In fact, one official at Mobil Oil rightly suggested that it would be easier for his company to raise $5 billion than it would be for a small business to raise $5 million. Raising money through contributions in the non-profit world can also be quite difficult and is often based on a "who you know policy" rather than on a rigourous analysis of the non-profit's productivity level or the level of need in a particular area for the services provided by the non-profit.

Numerous books have started to appear suggesting that for-profit organizations have a duty to contribute to non-profits. However, in the late 1990s US corporations are giving a smaller percentage of their pre-tax earnings to non-profits than they did in the late 1980s. The term "social investing" is catching on, but it usually means companies making contributions to non-profits rather than investing for financial returns for the investor. In the conclusion to this chapter (see page 136) we explore the potential for greatly expanding a rarely used method of raising funds for non-profit organizations and educational institutions.

Recognizing value

Pricing models give businesses guidelines on how to set prices, taking into account cost of goods sold, comparisons with the prices of substitutes and other strategies to maximize value to the seller. In the information age, the cost of goods model is basically worthless in establishing the best price for a product. In situations where there are no good substitutes for the products that your company sells, these models are also worthless. Although it is beyond the scope of this book to explain pricing theory and models, one approach is worth mentioning that applies to everything from airplane tickets, to membership dues in the PTA, to software products. This pricing strategy is called "versioning" and involves a strategy whereby an organization takes one generic product and creates a "product pyramid" or series of differentiated products. For each product up the price ladder, there is some new or better "whistle" added. The range of prices for the various products is often large with the top price often being 5–10 times the price of the lowest model. Consumers then select themselves into one or more levels of the product pricing scheme. Tracking of consumer behavior to determine exactly why the consumer bought one level of product as opposed to another product is critical to allowing the organization to learn from its marketing. Often strategic planners link this approach with "market segmentation," an effort to figure out in advance what different groups of consumers will want to buy and what price they are willing to pay. Versioning can also apply to the same product but the change occurs regarding delivery time. Next-day service or delivery might cost 30 times the amount that receiving the service or delivery just two days later might cost.

Versioning allows for future flexibilty and changes in pricing structure without drastic changes in the product or service that is offered. Strategic planners must focus on the full range of market options available to the organizations they serve and versioning appears to be a sensible way to develop pricing models when traditional models do not work. MicroStrategy, Inc., during its first several years, set its prices for products based on its own view of the low end of what the market might bear in order to promote sales. New entrants into markets, as MicroStrategy, Inc. was a few years ago, are often at a disadvantage since they are seeking desparately to increase market share, find "early adopters" (anyone who will buy your product before most people will) and need sales revenues to fund operations. Increasing sales is certainly a high-growth strategy that is available to most organizations that sell products and services. However, creating new products, new services and finding other high-growth strategies with significant financial rewards must be critical elements of a broad-based high-growth strategy for your organization.

Strategic planning and financial or budgetary planning are two sides of the same coin in every organization. Many organizations fail to see that by linking the traditional strategic planning process with the budget process, significant wealth can be realized. Budgets focus on how real dollars have been spent and will be spent. Strategic planning focuses on leveraging the resources of the company for maximum competitive and financial advantage. While a patent may show up on a balance sheet as having "x" value, the budget process stops there since the patent, by itself, produces no value. The strategic planning process of any organization must devote considerable time to a process we call "value identification" in order to systematically extract the maximum value from every asset in the organization. Strategic planners must consider what in your organization or what about your organization is valuable? The second question strategic planners must ask is "How can that value be harvested?"

Is the story of how your company or organization grew valuable? Would writing a book on it be financially valuable in its own right or would an article on it be suitable for publication and provide a chance to enhance your organization's reputation? Would the book or article be valuable as part of the recruitment and culture creation process of your organization? Would it be valuable as part of your marketing plan? For these questions, we can define "value" as the immediate cash returns plus discounted future cash flows (for example, an advance from a publisher and royalties) less the cost of producing the story. We can also define it in non-quantitative, non-financial terms as increased reputation, employee or customer loyalty and other intangible, but very real factors that go into making an organization successful.

Some materials manufacturers in the US have now concluded that it is simply not economically feasible to attempt to bring a new material to market unless there is a $5 billion market for the finished goods that will use the material. The economic analysis and strategic planning is as follows. Assume that materials make up 10 percent of the cost of the finished good. This overall $5 billion market is now a $500,000 million market for materials. Assume that a company will be required to spend $50 million to acquire the material or create it from scratch by conducting thorough research and development. After $50 million is expended, this new material exists in only small quantities and scaling up to supply the market might cost $300 million in plant and equipment. Although expending $350 million to bring a product to market in a $500 million per year industry might look promising, look again. The company cannot expect to gain 100 percent of market share. So assuming that the company is very successful, it may gain 60 percent of the market share for several years while competitors learn to produce a similar product without violating its patent. 60 percent of the $500 million is $300 million and operating expenses to produce, distribute and market the new material can easily run to 80 percent of the final cost of the product. Thus, with a 20 percent profit margin, considered quite healthy in the materials industry, there is $60 million in annual profit for the company in the good years when it has a 60 percent market share, when the market is a $500 million market and everything is going right. In order to earn this $60 million profit, the company invested $350 million. The $60 million profit is reduced to $40 million after taxes and it will, assuming that the $350 million could have been invested by the company at 8 percent return or roughly $28 million per year profit, the company gets a mere $12 million annual return on its risky and arduous $350 million investment. A strategic planner calculating return on investment would be hard pressed to recommend to the company that it go ahead with the project based on these figures.

This simplistic example shows that "market" success in a half-billion-dollar market might not produce real or substantial profits. Strategic planners must focus not only on identifying great revenue enhancing activities, but also on identifying where huge revenues do not equate to "value" or a reasonable profit for the company.

Below are listed numerous sources of value that organizations rarely recognize, measure or attempt to harvest. Every organization will have a different list, so we recommend a brainstorming session or other informational feedback loop to bring in all of the ideas that employees, customers, vendors, board members, management and other stakeholders have regarding hidden value within your organization.

- Branding and packaging
- Excellent customer relations and strong ability to know your customer
- Strong, well-evaluated board of directors
- Excellent credit rating
- Human capital Intellectual capital (registered or not registered)
- Domain name
- Website
- Access to:
  - *Financial capital*
  - *Knowledge*
  - *TV, radio other media*
  - *Information of interest to large numbers of people*
- Reputation for honesty and integrity
- History of your current commitment to civic leadership
- History of government service or military service of employees
- Flexibility and "nimbleness" throughout the organization
- Diversity in your workforce
- Event planning capability on a large scale
- Ability to:
  - *broker knowledge*
  - *secure book contracts*
  - *create and sustain virtual teams*
  - *recruit successfully*
  - *find the profit zone*
  - *manage supply chains*
  - *manage and influence demand for product (customer influence)*
  - *form and exit strategic alliances*
  - *bridge generations at the workplace*
- Documentation of past successes
- Relationship with universities and government agencies
- Experience with foreign governments and in foreign countries
- Databases, mailing lists
- Systems to capture data
- Knowledge management systems
- State-of-the-art technology
- Strong employee involvement program in organization governance
- Networks and leadership roles within those networks

The list above only scratches the surface, identifying aspects of your organization that are valuable. This value can be harvested through developing high-growth strategies that are consistent with your organizations' core competencies and the compentencies that you want to develop in your organization.

The key to recognizing value is creativity. How much is "domain name" worth? One of the authors recently worked with a client who selected its domain name in 1991 and in 1997 switched the focus of its business. This change rendered the domain name worthless to the company. Since it was a catchy sounding domain name, it was put on the market and sold for $25,000. The company's investment in its domain name, including registration fees, was less than $400.

Strategic planning and strategic thinking must focus on the harvesting aspects of the business planning process. We suggest that an important step for strategic planners is becoming the agent within an organziation that identifies valuable, harvestable resources that have not been previously identified.

The process of identifying resources and harvesting the value from these resources can assist an organization in figuring out the business it is really in. For example, several years ago Disney and Jim Henson Productions started merger talks just before Jim Henson died. Everyone knew that Jim Henson was in the "character" business since he started his business to create "icons" for children to have as "friends." Disney was interested in the merger for many reasons. One of the main reasons that Disney was interested in the merger was because Disney is also in the "character" business. Basically, Disney creates a character and harvests that character's economic value through theme parks, movies, music and ancillary products which are character focused. For Disney, the entire business model begins with the *character*. In fact, possibly one of the reasons EuroDisney was not immediately successful was that someone at Disney thought it was in the theme park business. Without a cultural following in Europe for its characters, and without the characters having significant economic value in France, EuroDisney never had a chance to become a quick success in France. These factors, in addition to the relatively poor weather, the lack of a service culture similar to the culture of theme parks in the US and a host of other factors caused EuroDisney to lose huge amounts of money.

Raising money for companies

Capital does not flow in mysterious ways. It does occasionally follow a fad or trend over the cliff, but generally capital flows where someone has demonstrated, at least in theory, that by investing the capital in this endeavor the capital will be rewarded handsomely. Some venture capitalists will say that they invest in "people" and therefore the quality of the management team is the essential ingredient when investing in companies. Other venture capitalists will say that they invest in ideas, products, proven systems and market potential since if they do not like the people they invest in they just get rid of them anyway. The truth is that venture capitalists invest in industries or sectors that they believe are "hot".

Almost every organization that has made it to a multimillion dollar or even a multithousand dollar budget has a great rags to riches story and will tell you that the money they needed came just in the nick of time from the last source where there was any chance of getting a dime. And most every story probably has some truth in it because entrepreneurs feel comfortable spending all of their own money and all of anyone else's money until they prove they are right or go bust trying.

There are some general rules about raising money that every entrepreneur and every organization must follow whether seeking loans (debt) or capital (equity) or both. You (or your organization) must:

- invest your own money, time and effort in order to attract capital
- seek the money before you really need it
- shoulder a significant part of the risk
- give up a significant part of the ownership rights for large amounts of capital unless you have demonstrated a strong track record
- have a clear, simple business plan
- have a track record of success to secure the best deal
- have a solid vision and show great potential for the business
- have a good management team in place or willing to join in.

One case study for this book, MicroStrategy, Inc., had a very successful initial public offering. MicroStrategy, Inc. sold 4 million shares at $12 a share. Most of the shares were not voting shares. Therefore, company officials were able to keep 97 percent of the voting control of the company after selling well over 12 percent of the equity of the company. A key ingredient that allowed MicroStrategy, Inc. to be successful with this approach is its stand that it will never be acquired by another company. This view – held since the beginning by MicroStrategy principals – allowed investors to leave the voting power with the people who have given the impression that they will never leave the company.

Raising small amounts of money for businesses through debt has never been easier. With the proliferation of credit cards in the US and easy credit, small organizations, including non-profits, can often raise up to $100,000 in debt capital. In fact, the authors are aware of companies putting in excess of $250,000 in company purchases on certain credit cards. It has recently been reported that, in late 1998, 47 percent of all small businesses finance all or part of their businesses with credit cards and the amount of credit card debt for small businesses may equal the amount of debt owed by small businesses to banks through traditional loans. With the rebirth of "receivables" financing, companies, at a significant cost, are able to generate money through credit by selling their accounts receivables.

It is also important to note that many businesses today do not require the amount of capital that they would have required just ten years ago. The growth in home-based businesses, leasing equipment rather than buying it, and other economic efficiencies created through information technology allow companies to do more with less capital. Strategic planners must become thoroughly aware of ways that their organizations can accomplish strategies with a low capital investment.

Raising money and increasing revenues for educational institutions

Recent "capital campaigns" for universities are remarkable in their size. Companies have arisen in the consulting world that track high net worth individuals and analyze hundreds of their traits in order to allow "development" offices in non-profit organizations to identify potentially large potential contributors. Tax laws promote charitable giving, and educational institutions have been large receivers of such contributions. Computerized mapping allows these development offices to track regions of the country, and to identify clusters of givers and areas where contributions are low. This mapping software – in combination with the new information technology and data available to development offices – makes them ten times more powerful than they were ten years ago.

At all levels from K-12 to postgraduate education, new relationships between educational organizations, companies and government agencies are the wave of the future. Many businesses know that it is to their competitive advantage to have strong relationships with universities and are willing to pay for it. In addition, co-marketing relationships are occurring between businesses and educational organizations where the educational organizations receive a return for the value they add to the company. Usually this is in the form of some percentage of income derived from the client base offered to the company or some agreed "endorsement fee." Educational institutions are becoming more entrepreneurial, with fee-based extracurricular activities, fee-based certification systems, educational counseling, and similar income-producing services and products. In fact, possibly the newest wave on college campuses is the creation of "Centers for Entrepreneurship" such as the Dingman Center at the University of

Maryland. Such centers not only teach entrepreneurship, they create incubators for new businesses, take equity positions in businesses, serve as venture capital fund clearinghouses, networking organizations (for a fee) and attempt to create a cluster of for-profit economic activity on the college campus. The great business and non-profit organization guru, Peter Drucker has made it clear how important "clusters" of economic activity are to the success of many businesses. On many university campuses, the distinction between "town and gown" is disappearing, and businesses and the universities seek common goals.

Many educational institutions lack a clear strategic direction. In fact, many educational institutions, be they for-profit or non-profit cannot adequately define who their customers really are. For example, are students "customers" of a school or university? A good business model would show they are, but many educational institutions and even for-profit educational companies do not consider them "customers." For example, one consulting firm gives an annual one week management seminar. This seminar has taken place for 13 years and due to the intensive work, only a limited number of people can attend. The policy has been that only people who have not taken the seminar in the past can sign up for it. However, the seminar has changed over time with new knowledge infused into it each and every year. The question raised to one of the authors by the consulting firm was, "Should the consulting firm approach the client and suggest that they do the seminar two or three times a year and include people who have taken the seminar before?" The answer is not only "yes" but the very question requires us to pause and take a hard look at the education industry. The question, put in general terms, is: "Should the consulting firm or any educational institution focus on providing education and training services to people they have served in the past?"

> One area that we have seen lacking in the educational field is that many educational institutions lack a clear strategic direction. In fact, many educational institutions, be they for profit or not for profit cannot adequately define who their customers really are.

Put in this context, the answer is clearly yes. In fact, in normal business we call this "repeat customers" and few businesses can survive without them. Yet the business model of the education world is that someone can only be a customer for a limited, defined period of time. At the end of that time, we graduate (fire) the customer, and often the educational institution never seeks to provide services to the customer again. In the age of lifetime learning, the traditional education institution model is grossly inadequate from both the industry's standpoint and the standpoint of the customer.

Organizations with the business model of educate and graduate (fire the customer) are often "innovation challenged" *because* of their faulty business design. If you do not serve repeat customers, you do not have to change or innovate. And, you miss the "profit zone" because you only provide services when the students have little or no income. When these customers get their degree or certificate they start to make money, but the educational institution that provided the education has no way to capture some of the value it created for the individual except through "alumni" giving programs and usually elementary and secondary schools do a very poor job at alumni giving programs. While many colleges are instituting night programs and expanded programs for people with degrees, there is much room for expansion in this area.

With repeat customers, educational institutions will have many opportunities for substantially increased sales and revenues and will be required to expand their organizational capacity. The education industry would be well served to adopt the business models of the software industry and the models of companies like Amazon.com that build on networks and customer information systems. High-growth strategies in the educational industry designed to raise revenues, endowment, cash flow and even enhancing organizational capacity must begin to focus much more heavily on customer relationships, customer analysis and other customer-centric policies and programs. It is surprising that an industry that says that its product – education – is a lifelong endeavor, has not pursued a business model where it continues to serve the customer throughout his or her life. When it comes to private, for-profit companies that have created educational institutions, such as McDonald's University, Dell University, Motorola University, etc. these institutions are designing their curricula to serve *as the educational and training provider* for employees for as long as they are in the job. In fact, some of these corporate universities are starting to provide educational services to employees of other companies, even those of their competitors. Simply put, due to the failure of the business design of our traditional educational institutions, corporations with a much better business design are successfully capturing significant market share.

There are other indications that the traditional educational business model is so fundamentally flawed that the entire industry is ripe for a major upheaval. We already see a huge growth in the for-profit education and training industry and a splintering of the K-12 educational sector through the use of taxpayer-funded vouchers, charter schools, home schooling and private schools. Efforts to create a new business design in the education and training world are starting to pay off and in the next several years, many for-profit educational companies may "go public" and sell stock. In addition, since a great "profit zone" exists in the "linking up of educated and trained workers" to their first employer and linking up temporary and part-time workers with employers, it is surprising that more educational and training organizations do not attempt to capture some of that hugely profitable market. One of the authors has recently advised a non-profit organization that provides paralegal training programs to extend its services to providing part-time and temporary paralegals to law firms. These workers would be employees of the non-profit and be "leased" to law firms, just as any temporary staff agency works. Of course, the contract will provide that, should the law firm want to hire the employee on a permanent basis, a substantial fee would be paid to the non-profit over and above the hourly fee paid for the services of the paralegal. This profit zone has been there for years, but the educational business model would not allow the educational institutions to venture into this area that is such a logical extension of its business.

Strategic planners now can see clearly how the business design that has been used in the traditional educational world creates great "strategic risk" to the old line educational institutions. Mercer Management Consulting defines *strategic risk* as what occurs in organizations that do not change and innovate as quickly as the rest of their market. The economic impact of failing to keep up with "market paced" change is quick in the private sector and is becoming quicker in the public sector.

Education and training institutions that cannot identify their customers, cannot capture part of the educational profit zone and cannot innovate to keep up with the changes in educational technology and philosophy will lose market share. Taxpayers will see lower cost, higher productivity schools and educational models grow in number over time and will abandon the no innovation strategies found in many public school systems. High-growth strategies are available to all sectors of the educational system of this country. These high-growth strategies will not become obvious and cannot become successful until educational institutions discard their outdated business design and become entrepreneurial organizations.

Raising money in the non-profit world

Strategic planning, business planning, return on investment analysis, multi-year budget forecasts and long-range cash flow analysis are often foreign concepts to non-profit organizations, especially small and medium-sized non-profits. Only recently have performanced-based funding systems been established where foundations and organizations like United Way make funding decisions based on what the organization has accomplished in the past or plans to accomplish with the money. Evaluation systems are slowly being put into place in non-profits that emphasize organizational development, accountability and performance indicators.

There is a little-used method to fund non-profit organizations that has enormous potential to make non-profits behave more like businesses and might generate billions of dollars for the non-profit or independent sector. This method is for non-profits to issue bonds. The system has three simple premises.

- Social contribution (charity) will be replaced to some extent in the future with social investing which offers real financial return to individuals, companies, foundations and other institutions that invest in non-profit organizations.

- Capital will flow into non-profits by people, foundations, companies and other institutions purchasing "bonds" issued by the non-profit organizations. These bonds will be interest-bearing bonds with varying interest rates and maturity dates, and for organizations with a 501 c) 3) status they will be exempt from the federal and most states securities laws registration and reporting requirements. These bonds will be subject to the anti-fraud laws and contract laws enforced at state and federal levels. These bonds must be issued under strict conditions to promote accountability and will pay taxable interest on either a regular schedule or when the bond matures.

- These bonds will be transferable and the money raised by the bonds will go either directly to the non-profit or to a third party, an escrow agency or some other type of organization, created specifically to manage the huge inflow and outflow of funds that could be invested in non-profits using this mechanism. When a bond matures, the owner can redeem the bond for cash (investment plus interest) or donate all or part of the bond to the non-profit and then take a tax deduction. The purchase of the bond will not result in a tax deduction since at that time it is an investment and not a contribution. Interest can be paid annually or paid after a set period like five years, or when the bond matures.

A fourth aspect of the basic model of bond funding for non-profit organizations is that for-profit companies may guarantee the payment of these bonds as part of their "contribution" strategy and buy reinsurance to protect themselves against the risk of the non-profit organization defaulting on the bond. Finally, these bonds will be issued by the non-profit without any prior legislative enactment as is now necessary for tax-exempt bonds.

In order for non-profits to issue bonds, and in order for investors to be willing to loan the non-profit organization the money, the non-profit will have to have a solid business and repayment plan, allow bondholders to see their open financial books through web access or regular reports and may have to offer a competitive interest rate. In fact, a non-profit could offer bonds at various interest rates over time as some appeals may be of such a compelling nature that low or even negative interest rates could be established for the bonds. The non-profit would be accountable to the escrow agency and the bondholders. It must be able to show that it will spend (and has spent) the money in accordance with the business plan (by showing contracts to be signed for the expenditures, for example, and also show that the business assumptions in the payback plan are reasonable.

Does this sound far-fetched? Do we really expect that non-profits will want to have debt on their books when now they have people willing to just give them money? One official at a large international non-profit told one of the authors, "Why would we borrow money, when people, companies and foundations just give it to us?" Do we really expect non-profits to develop business plans? Do we really expect that for-profit companies might guarantee payment of these bonds? Yes, we do. We expect debt financing to increase significantly for non-profits in the future and this alternative type of financing is already in place under the term "HERO Bonds" (health, education and religious organization bonds).

The problem with non-profit organizations taking advantage of tax-exempt bonds is that the organization must want to borrow at least $1 million dollars to qualify for many government programs. While these amounts are attractive to hospitals and non-profit AAA baseball teams (such as the Memphis Red Birds that is raising $70 million as this book goes to press to bring "AAA" (minor league) baseball to Memphis) it is outside the scope of many smaller non-profits. Although the Memphis Red Birds used a traditional tax-exempt bond route, this non-profit organization is certainly entrepreneurial. Through the foundation, a baseball stadium is being built in downtown Memphis and AutoZone, the huge car dealership, has agreed to pay $4 million for the naming rights to the stadium. The foundation will earn income from the sale of "Red Birds" goods and paraphernalia, and food served at the stadium, and will itself fund an aggressive charitable program to fund baseball activities in the Memphis inner city area.

Non-profit organizations that want to sell bonds directly might be able to sell them in denominations of as little as $35 and still clear a tidy sum after the transaction costs are paid. The authors predict that bond (debt) financing will take hold in the non-profit sector around the turn of the century the way it took hold in the for-profit sector in the 1980s. Strategic planners must be aware of creative ways for non-profits and for-profits to generate capital to run their operations.

While bonds may be new to most non-profits, borrowing is not new to non-profits. They have mortgages on their buildings, finance equipment and have other credit needs. One of the authors was involved in a project where a newly constructed public high school borrowed $49,000 to purchase televisions for every classroom. The high school developed innovative fund-raising systems to repay the creditor (the local school board).

The authors acknowledge that this "bond approach" may "cannibalize" some charitable giving as it may encourage some people, corporations and financial institutions to shift from charitable giving to charitable or social investing, expecting the non-profits to generate financial returns for the investors. The increased use of bonds for non-profits could actually lead to an increase in charitable giving because when the bonds are sold primarily to individuals, there is a reasonable likelihood that when the bond matures, the bondholder will donate the bond to the charitable organization and then take a tax deduction. In addition, this new reliance on bonds and possibly other debt instruments for non-profits will meet the dual goals of transferring billions of dollars of capital to the non-profit sector and simultaneously make non-profits act more like businesses regarding their financial health.

This financing approach is certainly not for every non-profit. Non-profits which are not able to generate revenues to pay back the bondholders will not be able to avail themselves of this system of finance. They will have to rely on the traditional systems of seeking grants, contributions and producing charitable events that produce income.

Other high-growth strategies for non-profits will include generating advertising fees, selling products and services related to their core mission and improving their business practices to cut waste and inefficiency.

Compensation of employees and equity participation

New compensation systems that treat all employees as owners are the wave of the future. Stock options and incentive bonus systems in the for-profit and non-profit worlds, coupled with organizations opening their financial books and records to their employees, represent high-growth strategies that also promote loyalty, social contracts between the employees and the organization and enhance an organization's ability to create work as a meaningful experience for their employees and managers.

In the educational field, compensation systems that reward merit in performance will increasingly take hold as tenure systems (guaranteed employment) shrink. Although there may be labor difficulties in achieving these types of compensation systems in the short run, their dominance in the educational field is likely to be achieved early in the next century.

Strategic planners need to include the compensation and benefit systems and the overall system of rewards as key elements in their strategic plans. Strategic planners can no longer say that is for "accounting" to figure out. Often the compensation and reward system is the key reason why an employee joins your organization or leaves to go to another. And compensation and reward systems can serve as a prime stimulant to improved employee productivity and team productivity, especially when incentive compensation systems are based at the team level.

Strategic partnering and the coming avalanche of mergers in the non-profit and educational worlds

We have already identified the potential for non-profit organizations to become strategic partners with for-profit companies. For executives, employees and strategic planners, there are certain rules that should guide non-profit/for-profit alliances. The goal of a non-profit/for-profit strategic alliance should be a long-term relationship. Often this must start with a short-term renewable contract to allow the parties to test the waters. The non-profit and for-profit must identify the value "propositions" for themselves and the other party, and discuss them freely. Alliance should be based on both parties sharing some of the assets of each organization with the other, including networks, databases, strategic plans and propose that each side in a strategic partnering situation should assign someone from their organization to the other organization's strategic planning effort. A strong strategic alliance should be grounded in the use of virtual teams with members from each organization used to "staff" the relationship. A relationship manager from each organization should be designated to cultivate and measure the benefits and costs of the alliance to each organization. Promoters of strategic partnering between for-profits and non-profits should think big and look to the strategic partnering to fuel significant expansion both financially, geographically and to enhance all of the value propositions of both organizations.

Strategic partnering need not be monogamous. Forming a strategic partnering relationship with numerous organizations at the same time may yield greater results than one-on-one partnering. The concept behind the United Way was to organize charities so that businesses and individuals could target their contributions more easily. The United Way certification, revenue collection and revenue disbursement processes are valuable to people.

We see a coming avalanche of mergers in the non-profit world for several reasons. Most non-profits operate on a scale far below levels of "economic efficiency" that are obtainable through larger scales of operation. Therefore, often larger non-profits will be able to show greater output per dollar than smaller organizations. As federal and state funding sources for non-profits begin to focus on assessing organizational capacity, more and more small non-profits will find their funding drying up. Branding benefits of larger scale organizations will give them a great competitive advantage over smaller non-profits. With the drying up of direct mail and telephone solicitation success for small non-profits, many small non-profits will see their income streams dramatically reduced. Strategic planners need to plan for the end game. In the non-profit world we expect there to be a movement to "roll up" small non-profits who seek to be a part of a larger organization capable of high-growth strategies.

We understand that volunteerism fuels non-profits and will continue to do so. In some cases people will want to volunteer for small non-profits. However, since volunteerism may well be on the decline in the US, we also predict that relying on volunteers alone by small non-profits cannot be a driver of a high-growth strategy. In fact, volunteering for a larger non-profit may put the volunteer into a much larger network of relationships. In addition, it may allow the volunteer to access his or her abilities to use technology for social good. Since larger non-profits can have a greater impact than smaller non-profits, this may result in the volunteer for the large non-profit feeling that he or she is part of some much "larger" good. For these reasons, larger non-profits have a competitive advantage over smaller non-profits in the recruitment, management and support of volunteers. Large organizations such as ASTD and AARP have developed very large-scale volunteer programs that provide socially, and, especially in the case of ASTD, professionally enriching experiences to volunteers.

Mergers, acquisitions, strategic alliances, joint ventures (MASA-JVs)

Strategic planners in the future will become important players in planning, evaluating and implementing merger, acquisition, strategic alliance and joint venture opportunities both in the for-profit and in the non-profit world. Once the domain of lawyers, the large number of failures of MASA-JVs shows clearly that well-drafted legal documents and great visions of uniting two or more organizations to "conquer the business world" are not enough to guarantee success of a MASA-JV. In the late 1990s CISCO bought over 25 other companies. Fueled not only by cash, but by company stock whose value is enormous on the open markets, companies like CISCO, ATT, WorldCom and others are gobbling up other companies to capture their supply chain, secure new services and products for sale and expand to be a global players in a market where market leadership pays great dividends.

Smaller companies and non-profits will also jump on the MASA-JV bandwagon. The economies of scale, the greater research potential, the low cost of joining forces (at least initially) all play a large part in the "if you can't beat 'em, join 'em" mentality that will govern the economic landscape for the forseeable future. However, success is not a slam dunk. In fact, 78 percent of the alliances tracked by one study recently did not cover their costs.

Given the high rate of failure, any entrepreneurial organization is well advised, before even considering any type of MASA-JV, that some breakthrough contribution or value must be identified as the likely result of the alliance. In order to justify the large costs in terms of personnel involvement often associated with an alliance, the potential rewards must be great. Other basic rules are becoming clearer for success in these alliances.

Alliances can be offensive – attempts to gain a major stake in a market – or defensive – attempts to stop market decline. Alliances can:

- combine superior technology
- secure raw material sources
- capture patents and product protection
- create efficient distribution systems
- link strong managerial talent and workforce capability
- capture a capital rich partner
- enroll a local partner where geographic, political and cultural forces are important
- leverage superior reputation, image and public exposure
- aggregate complementary networks of people and institutions
- serve markets which can jointly be served in a manner that benefits from economies of scale.

First, an organization interested in entering into strategic alliances must develop a strategy. The strategy behind the deal is far more important than the deal itself. The strategy must have:

- a dynamic view of how to get into the alliance
- a clear strategy regarding how to create and sustain its infrastructure
- a plan regarding the management and governance
- a resource allocation plan sufficient to feed the alliance
- a plan to integrate the alliance with the other operations of the organization
- a clear set of targets and objectives
- an alliance improvement plan must be agreed to by all parties
- there must be an initial allocation of responsibilities
- a plan to evolve the allocation of responsibilities as the alliance grows
- development of processes, templates and decision-making structures
- a plan for the independent monitoring of the alliance
- a system for making mid-course corrections
- a clear definition of the criteria to use to determine to end the alliance
- an exit strategy.

In short, all alliances must be plan driven but should be flexible enough to benefit from learning, shifting duties, responsibilities and leadership between the strategic partners.

Second, organizations should enter into a "portfolio" of strategic alliances and develop a strategy that each additional alliance adds to the total business value of the alliance effort. In this portfolio the strategic alliances should be "tiered." Groupings of alliances such as "value added reseller," "fully certified partner," "research affiliate," "product development partner," and other categories appropriate for your organization are necessary for three reasons. This grouping often gives your strategic alliance partners a "ladder" to climb, thus promoting future behavior that is in your interest as well as theirs. This "tiering" or grouping system also allows your organization to differentiate in a meaningful way between your partners, create differing levels or expectations and rewards and allows you to educate and train your employees how to interact differently with the different levels of partners. This form of "social ordering" assists in defining differentiated roles and responsibilities for each partner group and making their roles clear from the very beginning.

Third, for strategic alliances to work, there must be trust between partners. At a minimum, the "right partner" must have compatible goals, complementary capabilities and similar values. While the cultures of two organizations seeking to form a strategic alliance will likely be different, these differences should be identified in the planning stage for the alliance and dealt with from the beginning of the relationship. It is incumbent on the strategic planner to identify when cultures of two organizations are so different that a strategic alliance is doomed from the beginning. The onus is on both partners to conduct extensive research on the other and to develop a "profile" of the other organization before entering into a strategic alliance of any significance. The profile should include information on employee, supplier, and vendor morale and satisfaction as well as customer satisfaction. The profile should also include an analysis of the successes and failures of previous alliances entered into by the proposed partnering organization. The research must successfully identify the market opportunity, the resources needed for success, the timetable to meet market demand, the strengths and weakness of the proposed alliance, and of each partner, and the leadership styles of the partners.

Alliances are as important for the self-employed entrepreneur or nonprofit organization as they are for large-scale organizations. There is the impression that the smaller the organizations forming the alliance, the less planning and measurement rigor is necessary. We are not so sure. For small organizations, an alliance can bring it down completely or it can serve as the basis for a high-growth strategy. With so much on the line, small organizations cannot feel that the rules cited above do not apply to them. Certainly a handshake can form the basis for a successful alliance, but alone it rarely serves as the fuel necessary to support making the alliance a key component of a high-growth strategy.

Strategic cost management

As we stated earlier in the book, the worlds of business, non-profit organizations and educational institutions are merging. Nowhere are they merging as quickly as in the area of cost management. When critics say that non-profits must be run more like businesses, they most often mean that non-profits must integrate service strategies with cost management strategies and figure out how to provide more service for less money. In business, strategic cost management makes companies focus on where to make the next investment and how to measure profits/returns from that investment.

Cost management in most organizations is done in an ad hoc, tactical manner. The question, "How can we save money here or there?" is no longer adequate for running even the smallest non-profit, much less the largest conglomerate.

Today, organizations can operate at many different scales. They can sell "x" number of widgets or "10x." Non-profits can do the same with serving "x" number of meals to the elderly or "10x." The cost per unit sold (delivered) may go down significantly as as the number of units involved goes up. Strategic planning must take this type of cost factor into account when arriving at an estimate of the optimal size of an operation. The plotting of this analysis is called the "experience curve" and the generic term for this is "economies of scale."

Similarly, we know that cost per unit levels may go up when a business or non-profit of a given size offers more services or different products. Strategic planning must take into account the impact on the overall cost structure of the enterprise resulting from adding or keeping diverse products and services in its range.

Cost leadership is defined as the ability to produce or distribute a certain product or service at the lowest cost in either an industry or among a certain group of competitors. Low cost per unit is a strong form of competitive advantage. It is the key supporting link in the consolidation wave moving across America. It is certainly the driving force in the boom of "e-commerce" where costs of service can be a fraction of the costs of doing business in the normal bricks and mortar way.

The alternative to cost leadership is a strategy of *differentiation*. By making your products different, by finding your niche, your organization can charge a premium or can seek contributions successfully at very high levels without much direct competition. The strategy

> **By making your products different, by finding your niche, your organization can charge a premium or can seek contributions successfully at very high levels without much direct competition.**

of differentiation involves costs – the costs to make your product or service better or different, the cost to serve one geographical area over another and the cost of educating consumers of your differentiated product. Stategic planning must focus on the costs of differentiation as compared to the returns in order to make economically rational decisions regarding when to pursue cost leadership and when to pursue value-added differentiation.

A critical role for strategic planning under the label of strategic cost management is to identify all of the costs associated with each part of the organization. When a non-profit organization like EMMAUS of Washington, D.C. buys a building, it is in the real estate business even though it may think it is only in the business of serving the elderly population with a range of

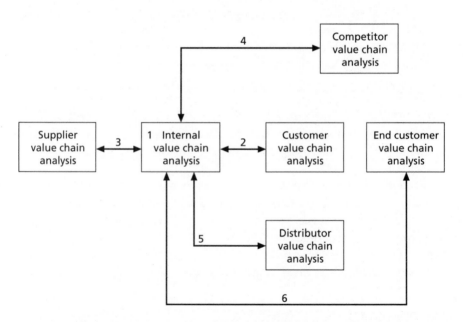

Note: each arrow shows a possible value chain analysis. Number one is in fact internal value chain analysis. In total, six possible comparisons exist. Depending on the situation, different value chain comparisons are more appropriate.

Fig. 13 Six possible value chain analyses

needed services. By identifying each of the costs associated with a business or non-profit, you can identify the "businesses" that your organization is actually in. Once you have identified and isolated each of the "businesses" your organization is in, you can then manage each section by evaluating the costs and the returns of that section. This is often called "activity-based accounting."

This way of looking deeply inside your organization is critical for strategic planning in several respects. Your organization may not need to be in each of the businesses it is in. If you determine that you are losing money from one element of your organization, you can spin off or outsource that activity. The key distinction in deriving value from outsourcing is the notion that "leasing" is sometimes cheaper than owning.

Economic Value Added (EVA)

A central argument concerning strategic cost management is a definition of the term "cost." This simple word turns out not to be so simple, and economists, accountants and even philosophers have struggled with the meaning of this term.

Every organization must understand that *cost* is more than the dollars that we pay for something. The term cost must include an estimate of what the return would have been if we had spent the money on something else. This is called the *opportunity cost* and is a critical concept for the strategic planner. In deciding whether to do "x" or "y," the strategic planner must not only figure out the hard dollar cost of each activity, but must also estimate the return for the activity and the alternatives that could have been pursued with those same dollars. This is true in the non-profit and educational world just as it is in the business world.

When ASTD decides to send a Vice President to Tokyo and Seoul to give speeches, it must weigh the cost of this "international" seeding effort against the cost of developing another publication that might produce sales or sending this same Vice President to Austin, Texas to address the local chapter of ASTD. While the organization has been built on the strong local chapters, it is now seeking to keep these local chapters strong while increasing its presence overseas. To further complicate the matter, the actual cost of sending the Vice President overseas may be close to zero if her hosts pay for the airfare and hotels, but there is still a significant cost in her time and attention being directed thousands of miles away from ASTD's core constituencies. In order to justify the trip to Tokyo and Seoul some notion of economic value added or EVA must be applied.

One important high-growth strategy is to have everyone in your organization begin to focus on how they are spending time and money, and what economic value is being added to the organization with that effort and cost. When no economic value is being added, by the activity in either the short run or the long run there must be some strong reason to continue the activity. A key to this type of thinking is the distinction between investment and cost, long run and short run. ASTD is pursuing a long-run internationalization strategy, trying to grow organically and through strategic alliances, but without mergers or acquisitions in lands where it has never operated. While there is little chance for any significant short-term economic return to the organization from pursuing this strategy, the chance of long-term economic returns (growth) is good. In fact, ASTD is experiencing significant growth of persons from outside the US attending their US conferences and does receive some economic return from these paid conferees. More importantly, in the long run, ASTD could reap huge benefits if it is considered someday as the world's leading association in the field of training and development. By being able to pull together all of the world's thought leaders and leading knowledge development programs in the field of training and development under one umbrella organization, ASTD could function as the synthesizer and distributor of the leading knowledge thought worldwide in the training field. This could be a tremendous contribution to the world's economic and social systems as well as a tremendous growth driver for ASTD.

There would formerly have been little role for strategic planning to make some clear assessment of the costs and probabilities of such large-scale success on the part of ASTD. Today, the role of strategic planning must encompass strategic cost management in order help guide an organization to achieve the maximum benefit to the organization through implementing its strategic plans.

Cost must be looked at not only in terms of what an organization could have done with the money, but also as a function of the expected return that an organization should be deriving from all sources of capital employed in a particular endeavor. Even if an organization's building is paid for in cash (and even with donations) the building is capital. Using the building or part of the building for a certain activity has cost – certainly opportunity cost – associated with it.

Part of the new EVA system of management "incentivizes" employees and gives them uncapped bonuses based on the measurable economic value the employees or their group or division add to the company. The EVA system suggests that the current way employees are paid involves too high a base or fixed level of payment (salary) and too low a variable rate of pay or bonus level. The system also recommends deferring the pay of some of the bonus amount to assure that one period's EVA is not overstated and corrected by a following period's adjustment where the EVA is much smaller or negative.

Every organization must separate out "investments" from "current costs," and distinguish long-run behavior from short-run behavior. However, whenever your organization makes any investment, it must strategically plan the investment so that its true long-term associated costs are identified and its expected returns are documented and analyzed. Organizations have now learned that less than 10 percent of the cost of computer-related technology is the cost of the "hardware," yet organizations' technology plans rarely allocate sufficient budget for the training, software, downtime and other real costs of change that result from changing computer technology. It is the role of strategic planning to assess the relative difficulty of implementing a particular strategy or decision in advance so that organizations are not blindsided by costs, delays and failures of implentation that were really not so "hidden" after all.

Two forms of analysis, return on investment (ROI) and net present value (NPV) are often used to identify the returns of a particular investment. Both systems are based on an effort to isolate the costs and expected returns of an investment and factor in the length of time it takes for the returns to come in. Future returns are to be discounted by some inflation factor, since a dollar in five years is not worth as much to an organization as earning the dollar in three years. The organization could have invested the dollar in year three and received some positive return from that dollar in year three and year four that is not available to it if the return is realised in year five.

Strategic planning must be closely tied to cost management so that the decision to stop or curtail an investment can be made as soon as it is determined that this investment, if continued, will not make the organization more economically fit or will not assist the organization in fulfilling its mission. Daryl Conner, in his books on *change,* clearly points out the need for organizations to be nimble to succeed in these changing times. Being able to stop investment decisions as soon as it becomes clear that they will not pay off is critical to allow organizations to redirect their investment decisions quickly and wisely.

Some investments – especially in the non-profit and educational world – will yield returns that are not quantifiable in monetary terms or will yield returns to other parts of society and not the organization making the return. Strategic cost management still has a central role to play in making these kinds of decisions. For example, it has been the strategy of Washington and Lee University to have a geographically diverse student body. This strategy has significant recruiting costs, and prevents Washington and Lee from accepting additional students from one geographical area which could yield additional excellent students at relatively low cost. Strategic cost management and strategic planning working together with this strategy helps the University to identify the benefits of this approach and to support the realization of these benefits, including having a more diverse student body from different cultures, having a national reputation, having alumni from each of the 50 states and having access to some of the best students from each state in the US. Similarly, The Joy of Sports Foundation founder, Andrew Oser, like many non-profit leaders, spends a substantial amount of time training volunteers for free so that they can provide better service to the youth served by his organization. Although the returns from this effort are hard to measure and usually go to the benefit of those volunteers who receive the training and the children who receive the services of the Foundation, there are benefits to the Joy of Sports Foundation that can be ennumerated, although not precisely measured.

When costs or returns cannot be precisely measured, the effort can still be a high-growth strategy. What is critical for an organization that pursues significant non-measurable activities, is to think strategically about the costs in terms of opportunity costs and think about the returns in terms of the categories of benefits that the organization and others will derive from the activity.

Categorization of costs and benefits represents the best approach in strategic thinking, strategic planning and strategic cost management when hard and fast numbers cannot be generated. Organizations should not steer away from investments and activities that cannot produce a hard "ROI" or "NPV" or "EVA" when the up side can be clearly described in terms of categories of positive results and some order of magnitude of results that can reasonably be expected from the endeavor. A great example of this type of effort is the role the Chamber of Commerce of Austin, Texas plays in bringing businesses and schools together to foster investment by businesses in the Austin Independent School District schools. The "Partners in Education Program" is staffed by the Chamber of Commerce and costs the Austin Chamber of Commerce a significant amount of money. The returns from the program can be put into categories including:

- increasing business involvement and investment in our public educational system
- increasing exposure of school age children to volunteers and resources from businesses
- increase in membership in and revenues to the Austin Chamber
- increase in the reputation of the Austin Chamber
- increase in the leadership role nationwide in this endeavor of the Austin Chamber
- increased employee satisfaction and pride at the Austin Chamber
- improved academic performance and levels of satisfaction in students in Austin
- improved "workforce-ready" students graduating from high schools in Austin.

Strategic planning can go far to driving investment and supporting cost decisions in areas where the benefits cannot be easily quantified, and where many of the benefits will go to someone other than the organization making the investment. Most importantly, strategic planning can help an organization make better decisions regarding these types of investments by identifying the categories of returns and the realistic, potential magnitude of returns that will result overall from implementing one type of program over another.

CHECKLIST OF STRATEGIC COST QUESTIONS

1 What are all of the costs that your organization incurs broken down into normal accounting terms and broken down again programatically (if your organization has more than one program, service or business)?

2 Which costs are discretionary?

3 Which costs can be incurred in another manner – such as leasing rather than buying, outsourcing instead of hiring inhouse, distributing electronically, not manually, moving locations or staying where you are geographically, sharing costs and revenues of an endeavor with another organization or incurring all of the costs and returns within your own organization, foregoing the expense rather than continuing it?

4 Which costs does your organization attribute to overhead that have little economic value added in the short run? In the long run?

5 What economic value added can you attribute to each employee, each division, each activity within your organization?

6 What economic value added can you attribute to each product or service that your organization provides?

7 What are your organization's financing costs and how can they be minimized?

8 What are your organization's cash, receivables and other asset management policies, and how can maximum benefit be obtained from securing the highest possible return from your organization's assets within your organization's willingness to tolerate risk?

9 Is your organization's prevailing culture a "cost aware culture?"

10 Are your organization's cost information systems operable daily, weekly, monthly and are they well monitored?

11 What "sacred cows" are there in your organization that cost money, such as real estate, employee policies, pricing policies, etc?

12 At what price does your organization achieve quality internally in the administration of the organization and externally in services and products for customers and how can the quality/price ratio be improved dramatically?

13 Which 20 percent of your organization's costs offers 80 percent of the potential for improvement?

14 Does your organization set target cost levels systematically?

15 Does your organization benchmark costs and outputs on a regular basis?

16 Does your non-profit or educational institution regularly compare the costs (including time spent by volunteers) of fundraising activities to their returns?

17 Is there significant underutilization of resources in your organization?

18 Are non-quantitative beneficial results targeted rigorously and monitored over time?

19 Are there areas of new investment that could greatly improve economic performance?

20 Are there areas of old investment that are not producing reasonable returns?

21 Are you in the right area of the market or should you migrate to another area of the market where your organization would have a competitive/financial advantage?

22 Is your organization's strategic planning system running in accordance with a schedule?

23 Is implementation of strategies monitored for financial costs and economic or other returns both in the short run and in the long run?

24 Have the actual returns of your organization's business strategies equalled, fallen below or surpassed the expectations expressed in the strategic plan?

25 Is your strategic planning process cost-effective, lean and dynamic?

Conclusion

Strategic planners must focus more on money and resources in their efforts to promote the development and implementation of high-growth strategies. New tools, new definitions and a new emphasis on bringing the financial team (budget personnel, accounting, bookkeepers, etc.), the operational team and the strategic planning team together to form a cohesive working group will be a source of great competitive advantage in the future. Web-based information systems, intranets and other information sharing systems may lead the way. Even if an organization is not adept at using these new tools, a simple handwritten strategic planning system that encompasses a strategic cost management system can change the way your organization works – beginning today.

There is no silver bullet that will marry the strategic planners and strategic thinkers with the front-line workers and the back room green shades (the financial types) in your organization. However, if an organization properly involves each of its component parts in developing a high-growth strategic plan, the organization's component groups will work together in alignment toward that common goal. High-growth strategies can contribute significantly to "high group effort."

The opposite is also true. If an organization simply wants to go along, be mediocre, not grow, ignore opportunities, avoid risk and not use strategic planning for the organization's benefit or for the benefit of its employees or customers, at best it will struggle to survive, have unsatisfied employees, unenthusiastic customers, and at worst it will fail and disappear – as thousands of businesses, non-profits and educational institutions do each year in the US. As Arie de Geus states in *The Living Company*, organizational failure comes at a high price to society as well as to the individuals inside of the organization that disappears from the landscape.

5

Toward the high-growth future of your organization

- Introduction
- Recruit
- Organize
- Manage
- Deploy
- Conclusion

We have to move from the incremental to the radical, toward a fundamental revolution in our approach to productivity and to work itself – a revolution that must touch every single person in the organization every business day.

John F. Welch, Jr.
Chairman and CEO, General Electric

Introduction

The term "stretch goals" best describes what we mean as the goals an organization should seek when it develops and deploys high-growth strategies. Stretch goals, by defintion, are goals *that your organization does not know how it is going to achieve when it sets them*. They are goals that your organization cannot be completely certain of attaining in the time frame that your strategic plan sets out. They are goals that are set rigorously using a gap analysis to let your organization know exactly where it is today and how far it needs to go to reach your stretch goal. Stretch goals and the high-growth strategies used to achieve them take into account your organization's strengths, weaknesses, opportunities and threats. They are based on a clear view of who your organization's main competitors are, and the assumption that your competition will improve significantly over time. They are based on an analysis of the "rugged and changing landscape" that your organization will need to traverse in order to achieve these goals. High-growth strategies are based on a clear understanding of why your organization *needs* to strive for this goal. High-growth strategies require clarity about the highest priority *values* that your organiztion is going to employ in its effort to reach your stretch goal. High-growth strategies require identifying the behaviors that your organization is not going to tolerate in pursuit of the goal and the strategies that your organization is going to reject and since these strategies and behaviors violate the *values* of your organization.

Stretch goals and high-growth strategies incorporate the roles and responsibilities of each participant and the overall capacity of your organization to achieve the goals. They take into account the need for necessary financial, human, intellectual, organizational and physical resources to achieve the goals and the requirement to deploy your organization's resources in a manner to prevent waste and inefficiency. They take into account strategic options that your organization can develop to guide it in reaching the goal of high-growth. And they take into account the overall context, be it individual, local, industry wide, nationwide or global, that makes the stretch goal worthy of the effort. Stretch goals are reached through good strategy, not just good tactics.

Stretch goals and high-growth strategies take into account the dynamic aspects of commerce. To the careful eye, the platform and target are always moving. The laws of commerce, like the laws of physics, apply to high-growth strategies. These laws applied to the young marine biologist from Cambodia who was studying at the University of Bristol, England in 1975 to learn the field of "acquaculture" (the farming of fish) so his village could feed itself and not give in to the communists, just as much as they applied to the Monsanto Company that undertook strategic studies in aquaculture in 1997 and 1998 studying the economic feasibility of becoming the preeminent supplier of genetically improved stock to shrimp farmers in Southeast Asia. Today, they apply to Microsoft whose antitrust suit shows it may be a leader in product design and distribution, but may not be a leader in business ethics. They apply to a cabaret singer, Sally Martin, who in 1997 wanted to start her professional career in cabaret while she was in her 40s, raising two young children as a single parent and living in Washington, D.C. where the cabaret industry was basically dead. She knew that to be successful she had to build up the cabaret industry in the Washington area in addition to raising the capital for her first CD and her website. She knew she had to develop a strong board of directors and a Council of Masters/advisers so that she could be guided through the business world. And she learned that she had to become a CEO, which is not a job title, but a way of life.

The entire system of businesses, non-profits and educational institutions is dynamic. The dynamic system not only allows for increases in organizational capacity, it *demands* it. The system not only creates the opportunity for personal growth and learning, it now *demands* it. High growth is only one approach to business. Some organizations will continue to serve the same customers, from the same location, selling the same goods, services or products, and employing the same infrastructure to meet their business needs. They may even produce the same economic returns year after year. Some owners, boards, employees and customers may find this state of affairs appealing, even inviting.

> **High growth is only one approach to business. Some organizations will continue to serve the same customers, from the same location, selling the same goods, services or products, and employing the same infrastructure to meet their business needs.**

While many of these businesses and non-profits sustain our economy to a great extent, what is clear is that *high-growth strategies create the key opportunities for the future*. High-growth strategies require a certain kind of organizational confidence. As Dave Sherwood, Vice President of marketing for MicroStrategy Inc. puts it, "In software, we live in an artificial world. Whatever we can envision software doing someday, can be done."

High-growth strategies require a certain kind of responsibility. In order to achieve sustainable high growth, an organization needs to be an open book, an open system. As we turn the century, the Asians and Europeans are just starting to learn that part of the American success story in business in the 1990s is a function of the high quality of information that anyone can get on any publicly traded company and any non-profit institution. In fact, there is also excellent information available on privately held companies. Accurate, reliable information is not quite power, but such information can lead to insight, to better judgment, to better strategy and can serve as a fundamental platform or knowledge base upon which to create a high-growth strategy. Closed organizations, be they in the business and non-profit world or in the governmental sector, represent a cultural phenomenon that is not likely to produce high-growth strategies in the coming century. Their time is past.

In this chapter, we outline some of the steps that your organization can begin pursuing now to move quickly in the direction of developing and deploying successful high-growth strategies. To the extent your organization is small or short on capital or other resources, consider yourself lucky. Your organization is capable of growing in percentage terms faster than any really large organization could ever dream of. This chapter comprises four basic sections:

- recruit
- organize
- manage
- deploy.

Recruit

A high economic growth strategy requires resources, a team. There has been a great emphasis on hiring the "right" people, the "talented" people, people with high intellectual and emotional intelligence. There is a $100 billion worldwide training industry attempting to make workers more productive, executives smarter and leaders just plain better. There is the new data warehousing industry collecting and analyzing terrabytes of data and information to help organizations make better and more timely decisions that may well put many organizations on "auto-pilot." There is the knowledge management industry turning white collar workers into "gold collar" workers as "knowledge managers." There are new materials, health care and food products, new financial systems that measure wealth and a growing venture capital world that will someday be so efficient that money will flow to a great business idea and management team without the current set of hurdles now in place.

There is a growing acceptance of *capitalism with a human face* which combines the responsibility to produce goods and services efficiently and also to create opportunities for more and more people around the world to have access to these goods and services. IC^2 at the University of Texas calls it "constructive capitalism." There is a growing sense of connectedness created not only by the Internet, but also by the desire to work with others rather than gaining pleasure from defeating others. Jim Moore's 1996 book, *The Death of Competition*, leads the way. This book follows closely behind.

There is a new emphasis on economically viable strategies to create a better world, on openness, on creating meaning in the workplace and on leading by sharing what you have and what you know with others. There is a new opportunity to extend one's vision beyond the normal 40–80 year maximum life span that people live in various places around the world. When people begin to address the question of how they will want to live their lives from the age of 80–100 or beyond, they will begin to ask the question how can they spend their years between 20–65 as workers to help create the kind of world they will want to live in for their last 30–40 years of life between 65–105 which includes years of life or longevity basically unknown to humankind until the 21st century.

Within your organization, the most important first step in the process of creating and implementing successful high-growth strategies is recruiting. Webster's third definition of "recruit" is "a fresh supply of something." In fact the word *recruit* comes from adding "re" to the French word "croite" which is related to the word "crescere" which means "to grow," and "recrue" which means "new growth." Recruiting, broadly defined, means that someone or more likely some a group in your organization will need to bring to the table a "fresh supply of somethings" to be used in creating, documenting, weeding out, testing, implementing, evaluating and revising high-growth strategies.

We start with *recruit* because every organization, regardless of its size and resources, *can recruit successfully*. Recruiting is a fundamental part of the human spirit that children less than one minute old accomplish so well and most often continue to do well throughout their lifetime. Recruiting is a fundamental talent that does not dissipate with age, as older persons are more than adequate in the skill of recruiting people to aid in their cause. (Witness the phenomenal success of the 32 million-member organization, American Association of Retired Persons, AARP or the efforts of Ben Margolin, a 90-year old man affiliated with Growth Strategies, Inc. who can still recruit an effective team to work on business and social projects).

Recruit for what? Recruit into what? Who do you recruit? How do you pay for those you recruit? These are some of the key questions that your organization must answer on the road to high-growth strategies.

Defining your organization

In order to recruit successfully, you need to *define* your organization. Again we turn to Webster. Webster's dictionary says the word *define* means:

"to state or set forth the meaning of _____" and "to explain or identify the nature or essential qualities of _____."

Your organization must answer the following questions.

- What is the nature of your organization?
- What are the essential qualities of your organization?
- What is the meaning of your organization?

Successful recruitment starts with powerful answers to these three key questions. It is currently fashionable to ask and re-ask the question, "What business are we really in?" And this question applies equally to non-profit and for-profit organizations.

High-growth strategies start with every member of the organization answering these questions and carefully analyzing and reporting the answers. *Alignment* means that everyone in the organization answers these questions in a consistent way. Our work and the work of many others has proven that alignment is critical to the high performance, high satisfaction environment that produces sustainable high-growth and winning results. As we describe in the section on the role of the CEO and the board of directors (see page 152), the CEO's first job is to ask and listen to the answers to these three key questions. Strategic alignment must be achieved and maintained throughout the entire organization in order for there to be longstanding success in any organization.

Once your organization is well defined and aligned, it will become clear who to recruit and who to separate from the organization. The model of lifetime employment ran into the reality of the laws of commerce in the 1980s in the US and in the 1990s in Japan. The static idea of "hired now, hired forever" could not compete with the dynamic evolution of businesses where the skills, attitudes and talents needed for a particular job or position one year may not be the skills, attitudes and talents needed the next year. More importantly, the model of lifetime employment ran into the fact that there may come a point in someone's career when the goals of the organization and of the individual employee diverge to such a great extent that separation is the only sensible approach.

At some times in an organization's life, it may be appropriate for person "X" to hold a certain position, but just a year or two later, due to no fault of anyone, it is now appropriate for person "Y" to hold that position. For example, at MicroStrategy, in its early years, the head of customer technical support needed to be one of the most technologically wise people in the company since he was called on to answer detailed questions about the company's decision support software. However, after MicroStrategy grew into an organization with hundreds of customers and a well-established technical support department, the head of the department needed to have great organizational skills and human resources knowledge. Technical acumen was no longer a requirement for the job since other people in the department then handled the customer technical support calls. Moving a person from a job to another job within the organization or moving a person out of an organization altogether must be done based on objective criteria. However, if the organization is to be successfully aligned with achieving high-growth strategies, it must give the right people the right areas of responsibilty. In addition, it must separate those from the organization who do not contribute to high-growth and are not willing to be trained or otherwise change their behavior and attitude as necesssary for them to be able to contribute significantly to the high-growth future of the organization.

Therefore, recruiting has two sides to its "coin." As an organization aligns toward the goal of a high-growth future, new people and ideas will be added. And those in positions of substantial responsibility who do not perform in concert with the high-growth goals of the organization must be let go. The good news is that the person leaving the organization may well find a better fit in another organization, but this cannot be guaranteed.

Clarity and emergence

Defining your organization must be done in three historical contexts – the past (if any), the present and the future. Stock markets, foundation funding managers and potential employees all base their evaluations and their decisions on their assessment of an organization's future, not its past or its present. One of the authors likes to say "No one ever gets on a train because of where it is."

History is important for the lessons learned and the resources that the past success of the organization gives to the present. However, when history is used to put chains on creativity ("we don't do things like that around here") or when it is used to negate the unique possibility or opportunity that the present or future can yield ("we've never done that before" or "we tried that before and it didn't work") then history, and those that cling to it, can be a significant drag on your organization.

Most organizations do not record their defining moments. They do not document the lessons they have learned. They do not train their employees, CEOs or board members to be "conscious" or aware of why they have been able to achieve success or incur a failure. Simply put, history is valuable when an organization learns from it in a cumulative way. This is all knowledge management is about anyway. Knowledge management will become a $10 billion industry by 2005 because there is a lot of catching up to do and new knowledge is being created at the speed of light.

An organization's history is also the history of its employees, its customers, its products, services and leaders. This history can be tapped for the "relationship capital" that is created whenever one person treats another person right. Therefore, as part of any recruiting or growing process, organizations must have a person or group charged with the responsibility of reviewing the history of the organization to find the pearls of wisdom, the defining moments, the distinctive features of the organization that can only be gleaned from looking systematically at the history of the organization.

Looking at an organization from the perspective of the present allows it to achieve great clarity regarding its current goals, its current practices and operations, as well as its strengths, weaknesses, opportunities and threats. A critical element in understanding the present is having a financial accounting system that is accurate, updated daily on a broad number of financial elements and communicated widely throughout the organization. Focusing on the present is a means of allowing everyone in the organization to be heard as to what is going on in the organization from their perspective. A trend in modern management is called 360 degree feedback. Simply put, this is a system where a person evaluates the person above and below them (and on the side of them) as well as themselves so that one can learn how people at different vantage points judge other workers on criteria relevant to their jobs.

One company we interviewed, NetCapitol, Inc., shows how easy it is for all companies with simple e-mail to find out what the employees are thinking on a daily basis. NetCapitol sets up systems with employers and unions that inform each employee regarding a political issue of concern to the organization and gives each employee a chance to register his or her feelings on the subject (usually through picking one of several preset, widely varying choices). The employee checks the box most closely aligned with his or her views and automatically an e-mail is created and sent to a Congressman or Senator or The White House. In fact, the e-mail could be sent to every member of Congress. Companies can employ this type of system to canvass every employee, every vendor, every stakeholder, every customer and many others about every significant topic of interest on a daily basis. The system will tabulate the responses and present the results in easily readable charts. Therefore, focusing on the present allows organizations to know where they stand, to listen to all parties and to gain the collective insight and wisdom from many people. Simple software programs can assemble and analyze the data and generate reports on a daily basis that all managers can understand.

However, the *most important time dimension* in defining your organization when it comes to high-growth strategies is the *future*. The concept of *emergence* best describes the approach we recommend your organization to undertake as it creates a vision of its future. Implementation forces change, personnel change, opportunities change and what looked like a high-growth strategy last month may look so conservative today that a serious rethinking must be undertaken. The question of how your organization will emerge over time focuses the organization on two key areas – its *organizational capacity* and the *rugged and changing external landscape* in which it must succeed in order to emerge.

Michael Saylor, President and CEO of MicroStrategy, has developed a unique approach to training and nurturing the company's employees with rigorous training and educational programs. When asked why he spent so much of the company's time and resources on training employees and building a strongly bonded community at MicroStrategy, he said "We are building an institution here, not just a company." Institutions like the US, the Roman Catholic Church and others invest in their people. Given how much these great organizations have done for their constituents, it is clear that even with all that MicroStrategy does for its employees, there is always more that can be done. Michael Saylor keeps his company focused on the future, while it consistently learns from its short past.

ASTD defines itself as a world leader, yet there are no world standards for assessing the need for training, measuring the impact of training and sharing best training practices across cultures. ASTD is currently undertaking global projects that are designed to create a world market and a set of world standards in the training field. And to show you how ambitious that goal is, ASTD only has 120 employees and not one of them today is located outside of the US.

Clarity and emergence are important keys to defining your organization. This process will make clear who your organization should recruit as employees, as strategic partners, as vendors, as members for your board of directors and as members of your Council of Masters/advisers. In addition, this process will clarify the roles that need to be carried out within your organization to create and implement high-growth strategies.

Focus and breadth

What business are you in? This question applies equally to businesses and non-profits alike. You will find that regardless of how small your organization is, your organization is actually in numerous businesses at once. It has been reported that 95 percent of the businesses and non-profits in the US have five or fewer employees. Most of them, in all likelihood, do not have an active, worthwhile board of directors or an organized Council of

Masters/advisers. In addition, fewer than 1 percent have a history that has been written, nor any way to capture in a conscious manner what it could have learned from its past. Most of these small businesses and non-profits do not have an annual budget, written human resource policies, nor have they ever written down a high-growth strategy. Many are not incorporated. And many, in all likelihood, put high-growth in the "dream" category, rather than "likely to occur." This does not have to be the case.

How does a business or non-profit organization gain focus, while not losing sight of its full opportunities? Again the answer comes back to our broad definition of *recruit*. Once your organization has become clear on its vision, once it has set its core values and surveyed the rugged landscape, the market and need for its products and services and evaluated the possibility of success, how does your organization begin to draft the high-growth strategies that are most appropriate for your organization? The current standard tool used to identify, focus and encompass breadth is called the "business plan." For many non-profits it is the "annual plan" or the budget. Some business or annual plans are full of statistics, market analyses, biographies of the senior management team, organizational charts, cost estimations, pricing structures, organizational financial histories and projections, and often describe the potential for the organization and its products and services in glowing terms. We propose that your organization replace or supplement its the standard business plan with a simplified "Economic Growth Plan" (EGP) as described below.

Takeover mentality: growth = inclusion

High-growth strategies rely on including either people or economic activity that previously was not included in your scope of operations. High-growth strategies also include having the people in your organization do things that they previously have not done. Daryl Conner's recent work focuses on *creating and maintaining the nimble organization*. An entire consulting industry is built around "change management." Often when new systems are put into place organizations fail to take into account the "trauma" (and we do not use the word lightly) that employees experience when faced with change.

High-growth strategies rely on an organization's ability to innovate, be flexible and create sufficient security and involvement among its employees that they are willing to undertake new activities, learn new things and experiment. High-growth strategies are a function of planned activities, experimental activities, feedback and pure "improvisation" that we often refer to as "flying by the seat of your pants." Strategy, strategic thinking and strategic planning form the *glue* that guides each of these activities. Strategy can lead you and your organization toward making the right decision,

149

Contents of an Economic Growth Plan (EGP)

1. Description of the organization – three paragraphs:
   (a) financial, organizational and product/service history
   (b) description of current management and operations of the organization
   (c) description of the future of the organization and its capacity.

2. Description of the market/product/service opportunity – four paragraphs:
   (a) product/service need/utility
   (b) competition
   (c) description of the customers and why they choose (will choose) the organization
   (d) marketing strategy.

3. The economics of the organization – seven paragraphs:
   (a) current economic picture
   (b) start up/expansion/initial high-growth costs
   (c) ongoing operating costs in high-growth state
   (d) prices for various products/services
   (e) numbers of product or service units to be sold/distributed in a timeframe
   (f) financing needs
   (g) future economic picture.

4. General description of high-growth strategies – one paragraph for each growth strategy (select fewer than 10).

5. Ownership and compensation – six paragraphs:
   (a) ownership allocation plan – present and future
   (b) compensation, benefits and bonus plan – present and future.

Assuming a large number of high-growth strategies, 10, for example, this plan is only 33 paragraphs long and would include fewer than 5 charts. That means in 10 pages your organization can have an economic growth plan (EGP) to guide it into the future. The plan will assist your organization in capturing both its focus and its breadth of opportunities and may help you raise money from investors.

---

undertaking the right experiment, generating the correct feedback and analyzing it correctly, and most important, assist your organization in eliminating tempting, but wrong decisions.

There is a strong movement toward diversity in the workplace. George Bush, Jr., Governor of Texas, recently said, "Diversity creates new life, new energy and new blood." Today, with globalization and increasing migration of cultures, for the reasons Governor Bush has noted, it is the goal of many organizations to excel in "multi-cultural competencies." This movement makes sound business sense – there is great wisdom in including diversity as a key element of your organization's high-growth strategy. Globalization in business and commerce has shed light not only on the cultural differences that exist in various parts of the world, it has also shown global leaders that members of the human race from different cultures are not so fundamentally different from each other after all. The 21st century will teach us what Teilhard de Chardin and others have known for years. This is one world. We are creating a global market. The goal of the economy is to include all people as customers, clients, employees, strategic partners. *Inclusion* is the new rule, the new *organizing element* for growth.

The question that *inclusion* brings to the for-profit sector, the non-profit sector and our educational institutions is simply this – How do we include more people and "peoples" in our organizations? How do we cross national, cultural, racial, religious, and other barriers? How do we promote the active participation and involvement of those in our organizations in creating future high-growth for the organization. The answer is *leadership*.

High-growth strategies require *leadership*. Promoting involvement of all employees and members of a business or organization requires leadership. Whenever one recruits, one leads. Whenever one says this is how the future will be as a *prescription*, not as a prediction, one leads. Whenever one innovates, charts a different course, or says that a product or service will make money or serve a need, leadership is being exercised.

An "era" used to last a long time. The "industrial era" lasted for over a century, the "information era" lasted decades and some predict the "knowledge era" will also last a few decades. We doubt it. For those who begin to craft high-growth strategies for their organizations and for those organizations that begin to implement high-growth strategies, the *leadership era* will begin. Leadership is no longer just the job of the CEO or the board of directors. While shared leadership is now in vogue with the increased use of virtual teams, even shared leadership misses the essential building block of high-growth strategies. High-growth strategies depend on *evolving leadership* where employees, CEOs and every member of the organization is always ready to step up to the plate and provide the suggestion, the extra effort that he or she believes would best address the issue at hand and the issues that will come up in the future. High-growth strategies require a leadership culture and eventually leadership will be taught to all in our schools, not just those lucky enough to be selected by teachers or others as "leaders." High-growth strategies require that leaders of organizations create an environment where everyone is willing and eager to lead. As Oakley and Krug discuss in their 1991 book, *Enlightened Leadership,* a key role of a leader is to get everyone in the organization focused on the goals of the organization and involved in every stage of planning, decision making and implementation of changes designed to create the future of the organization. In our words, the leader of an organization is the chief recruiter.

Organize

The role of the CEO, COO, the president and the executive director

The terms CEO (Chief Executive Officer), COO (Chief Operating Officer), president and executive director often mean very different things in organizations. For our purposes, we lump all of these titles together and refer to the position as "the CEO." Broadly defined, the title "CEO" could be applied to a president of a nation, a president, principal or headmaster of a school or the head of a non-profit organization. Thousands of books have been written on the role of the CEO. Our work with hundreds of organizations suggests a role that is different from those commonly described in these books under the title "CEO."

Throughout our consulting practices, we have had the privilege and duty on occasion of telling CEOs that they should step down for the good of the organization. We have also seen people who rise to the occasion and perform excellently. We have seen some leaders such as Michael Saylor of MicroStrategy define their jobs as being the master of all aspects of their business including finance, technology, marketing, scholarship, service and product quality, recruiting, location and real estate, compensation and benefits, the culture of the organization – and so the list goes on. We have seen other leaders say "I don't understand this Internet stuff, so we hired Tom." They think they manage by hiring others to do the job, but it does not work that way.

We agree with Prabhu Guptara who has argued for over 20 years that no CEO can be a leader of a high-growth organization without having a clear understanding of the opportunities that technology offers today. We also believe that a CEO cannot delegate any important area of their organization completely to someone else. Michael Gerber's phrase in his book, *The E-Myth Revisited, management by abdication* is ripe with meaning as he demonstrates how some "leaders" give away the responsibility for some part of their company or organization and therefore abdicate their responsibility in that area, often with disastrous results.

The role of the CEO, as we define it, is broader than anything we have seen in print. We believe the role of the CEO is to *create, support, manage and sustain the right kind of conversation taking place within and about the organization.* Two leaders, Bill Clinton and Bill Gates, in late 1998 and early 1999, clearly did not achieve this. The conversations they created by their actions and their words were destructive to themselves and the organizations that they led. Managing the conversation means managing every aspect of the organization so that the conversation that goes on is fully aligned with your organization's high-growth strategies.

There are many definitions of an organization. The lawyer says that an organization is a *series of contracts*. The sociologist says that an organization is *a system of behavior governed by a distinct culture*. The organizational development specialist says that an organization is a *system of defined relationships with the participants working toward a common goal or set of goals*. The psychologist says that an organization is *a number of persons or groups with specific responsibilities and united for some purpose or work*. The military commander says that an organization is *an ordered, fixed set of relationships with specified roles, authorities and objectives*. The linguist says that an organization is a *set of purposeful conversations*.

For our purposes, the linguist wins. The linguist's definition of an organization gives us the most to work with in the context of high-growth strategies. *High-growth strategies start with a conversation.* They are fueled and guided by conversations. They gather momentum by becoming a conversation that more and more people join in at an accelerating rate. High-growth strategies achieve success by the willingness of people to act consistently with the conversations that are created, supported, managed and sustained first by the CEO and then by everyone else acting like the CEO – owning the project, taking responsibility for the results produced and improving the strategy and implementation on a constant basis.

Conversation is the most powerful peacetime business and organizational tool ever devised. It is the ultimate tool in creating and sustaining high-growth strategies. It is measurable, through active listening. It is changeable, through taking a stand. It is robust, through the use of accountability and credibility. It is contagious, ever-spreading and can be directed and guided over time. While others stress the word communication, to us the word *conversation* is the better approach for two reasons. First, communication, as the word is normally used in everyday life, is usually one-sided. Second, conversation implies an exchange of views, or as Julio Olalla says, "a changing together." Third, communication focuses on the act of getting an already designed and known message out, while conversation implies two or more people jointly seeking some knowledge, truth or strategy that they individually have not yet figured out entirely. It is therefore through *conversation* that high-growth strategies are born, mature, are revised and ultimately succeed. It is the role of the CEO, regardless of his or her exact title, to insure that the people in the organization, as well as those outside of the organization, are generating and participating in conversations that promote high-growth. The new word in the business literature that almost captures this idea is "buzz." "Buzz" is the talk around town, in the media and in the hallways where people talk about how your organization is going places fast, growing and becoming a significant part of the economic and social landscape.

There is no more important job of a CEO than to create and support the right kind of conversation within an organization and the right kind of "buzz" outside of the organization. In order to accomplish this job the CEO will have to be the master of many, if not all aspects of the enterprise. But mastery of the enterprise, as Bill Gates and Bill Clinton have learned, is a necessary, but not sufficient condition to promote the right kind of conversation about your enterprise or sustain high-growth strategies. It takes more.

The role of the board of directors and Councils of Masters/advisers

Treatises have been written on board selection and performances, and the new trend, how to evaluate your board of directors. In the context of supporting high-growth strategies, we know the following: *Every organization needs a board of directors that is willing to conduct some work and meet regularly on behalf of the organization.* People need to be selected carefully and monitored even more carefully. Boards of directors in the non-profit world must be called upon to be more than money-collecting agents for the organization. Board members must make continuous, significant contributions to the organization, be it a business or non-profit, or they should resign or be removed without delay. Places around the board table are too scarce to allow anyone to occupy such a place without making regular contributions to the organization. Simply put, there is no room for driftwood, spent wood or dead wood at the board level.

Boards of advisers, what we at Growth Strategies, Inc. call *Councils of Masters*, are one of the best, low-cost approaches any business or non-profit organization can employ to add interested and dedicated people to its organizational structure. Councils of Masters are groups of people asked to serve as advisers to organizations in their areas of expertise. They can be paid or be volunteers. These Councils of Masters can meet as seldom as twice a year, although we recommend a minimum of quarterly meetings of your organization's Council of Masters. The Council of Masters can be an essential element of a high-growth strategy through Council-generated insights, linking up with the networks that Council members posess, the development of mentoring relationships between Council members and management and employees in the organization, and through the specific expertise which the Council members share with the organization. In our experience, Council members often willing to serve voluntarily, but Councils can also be created by paying the Council members for their time. In fact, like trading website links, someone in your organization can offer to serve as a member of another organization's Council of Masters in exchange for someone in that organization serving on your organization's Council of Masters.

The creation and maintance of an advisory group to your organization can be an important element of your high-growth strategy. While recruitment is the critical first step to having people join your Council of Masters, the key to the effectiveness of such a council is making sure that it is well organized, has a well-developed *performance strategy*, and is integrated with the operations and strategic planning of your organization.

The role of employees

High-growth strategies require the best of everyone in your organization. Employees are not simply the means to achieve strategic objectives. Employee "well-being" must be one of the key strategic objectives of the organization if it is to achieve success in its high-growth strategies. Organizing a workforce today requires that careful attention be paid to what workers think and feel about the organization. Our consulting practices have shown a strong relationship between employee participation in planning and decision making, employee morale and employee productivity and longevity. Employee surveys that are biased with words and structure that suggest to the employee that he or she say nice things about the company or organization are worse than worthless. Survey methodology through use of e-mail has become a snap. Even if your organization is not e-mail-ready, surveying employees about a broad range of topics is both easy and probably long overdue.

Incentive systems, accountability and acknowledgment must be built into your organization's compensation and benefits packages. In for-profit companies, stock options and employee ownership packages make an important difference not only for the employees but also for the organization's bottom line profit. In non-profit organizations measuring the productivity of workers is only now coming into the limelight. In the educational world, measuring the productivity or quality of teaching is not even on the radar screen as yet in most institutions. Without incentives, accountability and acknowledgement based on an agreed upon set of performance objectives, employees are lost and management is in the dark when it comes to promotion and getting the "best of everyone all of the time." These incentive systems, accountability standards and acknowledgement programs must become part of the culture and the calendar of your organization. The good news is that in these areas, *experimentation and asking employees* how to incentivize their compensation, pursue accountability and provide acknowledgement is usually the best way to start your organization toward designing these systems and becoming a better place to work.

Training and learning

For organizations that want to pursue high-growth strategies, the goal of every employee should be *to be able to do something by the end of every day that he or she could not have done at the beginning of the day. And this should be the goal of the organization itself.*

> **For organizations that want to pursue high-growth strategies, the goal of every employee should be *to be able to do something by the end of every day that he or she could not have done at the beginning of the day. And this should be the goal of the organization itself.***

In order to secure the right kind of training, organizations must assess their training and knowledge gaps. Prior to giving someone on-the-job training, course work, or another form of training, some rudimentary assessment should be made regarding how that individual or group learns best. This will allow the training to be tailored to the individual or group's learning style.

After the training is provided there must be a clear application for the trained employee to use the training on the job on a consistent, regular basis. There should also be the opportunity for the trained employee to share (teach) the training to others in the organization in order to sharpen even further what the person learned in the training.

Then, the impact of the training must be assessed. Several key questions will guide the evaluation effort and these questions must be formulated prior to the undertaking of the training. Some examples of these questions are listed below.

- What are the goals of the training program from the organization's point of view?
- What are the goals of the training program from the trainee's point of view?
- Did the training make any difference to the behavior (or attitude) of the individual or group that received the training?
- What did the trainee or trainees think they learned from the training?
- What results in terms of productivity, profit, or other set measures have occured as a result of the training?
- Did the results of the training diminish, stay the same or grow cumulatively over time?

- If the training did not have any measureable or observable effect, why not?

In order to answer some of the questions, the organization must have data from before the training period to compare to data on the same metrics from a period of time after the training. In order to answer the last question, employee interviews will be essential.

Much has been written about *learning organizations*. Peter Senge's ground-breaking work in this field states that in order for an organization's participants (employees, managers, suppliers, vendors, board members, etc.) to embrace learning opportunities and use what they learn daily, the organization must establish a *culture that demands learning, and rewards learning at the same time*. Since high-growth strategies imply accomplishing tomorrow what the organization at present does not know how to do, *learning and training* become essential tools in designing and implementing high-growth policies.

Membership, values and performance

Earlier we referred to Charles Handy's concept of "membership" replacing the old concept of employees. The relationship of membership and values to performance is well known in the non-profit sector, where money and other financial resources are often scarce and most of the people involved are volunteers in the traditional sense of the word. From a businessperson's perspective, what non-profits accomplish on small budgets is often amazing, and certainly worthy of further study.

At the core of every organization are values. Values are the ideas, beliefs and ways of doing things that are universally considered important by the people involved with the organization. They can be operational in nature such *as efficiency, speed, quality*. They can be moralistic in nature such as *fair, honest, trustworthy*. They can be forward looking such as *futuristic* or historically based such as *traditional*. They can be practical such as *reliable* and *dependable*. It is interesting to note that two organizations, Coca-Cola® and Wal-Mart use the term "Always" in their advertising. KPMG, the consulting firm uses the word "Clarity."

The key question for you to ask, in conjunction with others in your organization is what are your organization's core values? The operational question to ask then is, "How does your organization manifest these values?" And "How can it perform more consistently with these values in *everything it does, all of the time?*"

Values drive behavior and performance. As Michael Saylor says, "It is not enough any longer just to try to make money. Your company must try to do something that people really need to improve their lives." In the non-profit world, the alignment of values of thousands of volunteers each day makes this sector productive, often on low budgets and limited organizational capacity. However, just as businesses can no longer operate effectively without a clear and consistently stated set of values, non-profits are realizing they cannot operate without stronger organizational capacity, cash flow analysis and strategic planning.

In today's world where products can be customized to any customer's wishes by enlightened organizations, and where zero defect rates can be expected and demanded even in million unit production runs, an organization's values can be the differentiating element between it and a competitor and between the success or failure of a high-growth strategy.

Every organization can develop its own version of a "values-driven growth process" where it identifies its current, predominant values, and then actively identifies the *new values* that it will need to adopt in order to achieve its high-growth strategies. Through strategic planning and through conversation an organization can proactively set forth what its key values will be, create alignment around those values and create high-growth strategies that embody these values.

These elements are driving a new approach to organizing that will stimulate the development and success of high-growth strategies. This new "values-oriented approach," in combination with key elements of the old approach including organizational charts, and the responsible allocation of duties and authority among those employed by your organization, combine to create an approach to management of high-growth strategies.

Manage

Knowing which rules/molds to break – the art of strategy

Business strategy is, by definition, creative. Continuing to do what you have done in the past, or merely improving on what you have done in the past can be suicidal for businesses as well as non-profits and educational institutions. *Knowing which rules or molds to break and reshape is the essence of the art of strategy.* We cannot provide a complete list of the rules or molds to break in your industry, company or organization. However, we can assure you that gone are the days when the phrase, "We have never done that," or "We have never done it that way," have any validity by themselves in stopping an organization from undertaking some activity. In addition, the phrase, "We tried that before and it did not work," must no longer by itself serve as a show stopper.

For example, when an after-school science program that teaches hands-on science programs stated that it wanted to expand overseas, one of the authors recommended that the organization market its program to the military schools serving US children around the world. One official in the organization stated that they had tried that before and it had failed. When asked how it was tried, the consultant was told, "We called the Pentagon and they never returned the call." When the consultant suggested that the organization recruit an active or retired high-level military official in charge of educating the youth of the military for a place on the organization's board, a leader of the organization informed the consultant that "We already have 15 members on our board and that is all our bylaws allow for so we cannot do that."

The first rule your organization might consider breaking or changing comes under the title *Bylaws*. Leaders and employees of organizations rarely even know what their bylaws say. Bylaws should be reviewed every year and should be amended (another word for "broken") in order to promote the growth of the organization in the face of a changing economic environment and changing opportunities. The organization we just described could have benefited from additional board members, but was not aware that the number of board members it had was a rule that could be changed and changed easily.

It was also clear that the organization never really had a strategy to penetrate the military education market. Failure in an approach is often not the result of the inadequacy of the idea which serves as the kernel of the approach, it is the result of the failure to *create a robust strategy that will recruit, organize, manage and deploy the appropriate resources to accomplish the goal.* Saying "we tried that before" or "we thought of that before" is no longer an excuse for an organization to refuse to revisit a potentially successful idea. Of course, we never recommend putting the person who offers the statement, "We tried that before," in charge of the reinitiated effort.

A third area where rules/modes must be broken is in the area of job descriptions and the current allocation of roles and responsibilities in an organization. Today, shared leadership means that for one period of time or in one area someone named "Kathleen" will lead the effort and for the next period of time or for another area someone named "Jason" will lead it. Our consulting practices have shown that often putting someone permanently in charge of an effort or worse, not undertaking an effort because the person in charge of that area will either not want to do it or cannot do it well, is a stranglehold that organizations cannot afford. One major consulting firm operates all of its activities on the basis of "projects." One great advantage of organizing high-growth strategies around the term "projects" is to remove aspects of the project from the normal hierarchy of a particular division or section of the company or organization. The mold called "this is my area of responsibility" is one of the first molds to break in your organization.

Organizations seeking high-growth strategies should allocate responsibility to the person or group that can best accomplish the mission regardless of where they fit on the organizational chart.

Risk tolerance

High-growth strategies require that organizations bring to the surface rules that exist within the organization that are not openly discussed—*the implicit rules*. Assessing your organization's *real willingness to take risks* is a critical function of those responsible for strategic planning. At present we are not aware of reliable, quantitative measurement devices publicly available to measure an organization's willingness to take risks, but we suspect they exist. Earlier, we outlined the flexibility/innovation analysis tool (see Chapter 2) that we add to the current market place of MBA-type analytical devices that can be useful in developing the best high-growth strategy for your organization. Since this tool is in its early stages of development, each organization must improvise on its use to discover what is permissible risk taking and what is not. It is easy for consultants and advisers to recommend taking large-scale risks, since they are not risking their livelihood or their assets when the organization takes the risk. However, in the current, ever-changing economic environment, there is no high-growth strategy that is totally risk free.

Risk tolerance is a muscle that must be developed over time. The US military in the late 1990s developed the concept of the "soft failure" in order to cut costs. This concept may allow your organization to adopt a more aggressive risk tolerance stance without losing sleep. "Soft failure" is an approach that allows systems to have parts that do not work correctly all of the time but which do not cause the system to crash. For example, in the past military planners might purchase the most expensive computing or navigational device, since if it failed, the equipment would crash. Today, many military-funded operations are allowed to use cheaper materials and components with inexpensive *back-up systems* in the equipment so that when (not if) the primary component fails, the back up unit or units will be able to allow the equipment to either continue its mission or abort the mission, and return back to a safe location for repairs. The use of fault-tolerant systems is instructive to businesses and non-profits in the area of strategic planning, since they allow for the creation and use of inexpensive supportive elements of a system or plan rather than the reliance of one, make or break, element that became expensive due to its critical nature in the operation.

Robust plans – how "soft failure" systems work

Strategic plans are comprised of many components and we now have the ability to plan that when one of the components of the plan fails, we can substitute a secondary component or secondary strategic path to replace the failed component or path. The ability to identify a failed or failing aspect of your strategic plan early in its implementation is now critical to business or non-profit organization success. For example, currently in the US we may be experiencing a decline of the "direct mail" industry used by companies for sales and marketing and by non-profits and educational institutions for fund-raising and membership/student enrollment.

Today, an organization must design a marketing campaign by employing numerous activities such as direct e-mail, regular direct mail, other web or telephone-based systems, specific location (store) based sales, traditional sales personnel, multilevel marketing, print, television or other advertising and affinity relationships to name just a few. The key to knowing almost instantly the day-to-day success of each of the strategies that your organization employs is available through the use of "data warehousing" or smart data collection. Organizations that collect and analyze their data daily will have a huge advantage over the organizations that wait months, or which never analyze carefully the results of their specific operations. This aspect of evaluation and feedback and this level of investment of economic, technological and personnel-related resources in determining the measurable success or lack of success of discrete aspects of your growth strategy will likely break the mold of how your organization has done business in the past. Failure to become sophisticated about measuring which strategy is most successful and understanding why your growth strategies yield varying outcomes, may retard your organization's growth potential and become a strong competitive disadvantage.

Having this information on a daily basis and creating "soft failure" systems significantly lowers the risk your organization takes in adopting new high-growth strategies. While standard terms such as "return on investment," "return on innovation," "economic value added," and "return on change," and "return on capital or equity" give us some guidance, when used properly, on the success of a given strategy, each measure severely underestimates the real contribution breaking the rules and breaking the molds of the organization have on the real growth potential of the organization.

The learning organization

It is not only important for organizations to be successful in their high-growth strategies, it is also important for them to know why the strategy was successful. Daryl Conner uses the term "consciously competent" to describe the situation when a person or organization is both successful and has learned from its success (or its failures) the key ingredients and processes that will assist it in achieving future success.

Organizational capacity for growth is enhanced by the creation of conscious learning resulting from experimentation, from implementing new strategies and from undertaking new activities. In many businesses and non-profits the approach is to try "x" or "y" approach and see over time if it works. Most often, people inside of the organizations can rarely tell you why an activity "worked' or "did not work." While we acknowledge that serendipity may play some role in organizational success, more often than not serendipity is a word used for success where there is no clear, agreed upon, understanding of the key factors that led to that success. However, understanding why an organization's actions produced the exact results that were produced is critical to that organization being able not only to replicate that success, but also to build on that success and promote breakthrough growth in the future. An organization is *consciously competent* when it understands why its actions produce, both internally and externally, the results produced, and it can teach its entire organization (and others) why the result occurred. An organization is not consciously competent when it cannot determine quickly why something is working or not working. For example, two chefs may each produce a great dish. Ask one how he or she did it and the chef may not be able to describe the recipe at all. The chef may be able to produce the great dish over and over, (and other great dishes as well) but cannot teach others how he or she does it because the chef is not *conscious* about all of the ingredients, their amounts, the order, the cooking process for each ingredient or why the exact combination of the ingredients and the cooking process worked so well for the dish. Ask another chef who has studied cooking from a different, more *conscious*, vantage point and he or she can show you exactly the recipe followed, the technique employed, and can describe the role of each ingredient in the making of the final result. The first chef over time will not have the ability to teach others or transfer his or her knowledge, skill or ability to others in his or her organization and will not be able to create a legacy of improved culinary skills in succeeding generations. Most importantly, the chef who is not consciously competent will not be able to generate breakthrough economic growth through creating a cooking school and opening up four star restaurants at many locations around the globe.

While the chef example may seem somewhat far-fetched in a book about high-growth strategies for entrepreneurial organizations, a close look at the restaurant industry reveals there is *no successful large scale "four star" restaurant chain in the world*. The restaurant chains that thrive are generally "no star" operations, yet they are very consciously competent in their ability to make bad food that sells well. The high end restaurant market is dominated by chefs that are fabulously competent, but not consciously competent and therefore cannot expand their economic base.

Becoming *consciously competent* is one of the silver bullets to high-growth strategies as shown by the fast food and other franchising type of operations. In the software development world, accurate, clearly worded documentation represents the consciously competent part of this highly creative industry. Yet, software developers often require six months to a year after the development of their custom-made software to document each step in the process. Outsourcing companies like Information Experts, Inc. are now growing rapidly to meet the demand to write documentation and on-line help systems for the software industry.

A critical test for high-growth, entrepreneurial organizations is to devote sufficient resources to becoming consciously competent while at the same time not getting so bogged down in the process that the creative and entrepreneurial elements start to lag. Today with the use of video and other forms of technology, organizations will be able to document more carefully how they undertake activities and document them so that the knowledge obtainable from a careful study of "best practices" can be "bottled" and disseminated throughout the organization almost instantly and at low cost. And with the communication technology available that gives each organization the ability to test the knowledge of each employee (and customer) periodically, if not daily, we can begin to measure quickly just how much of the newly created knowledge and conscious competence is spreading throughout your organization.

Rules that cannot be broken

There are numerous rules and molds that cannot be broken in your effort to achieve breakthrough growth. The first rule that cannot be broken deals with employees. The rule is that "front-line employees count." From Three Mile Island, we learned that staffing aspects, the human factors, the front-line employees will determine more about the ultimate success of a high-growth strategy than the elegant, precise design of a system on paper.

> **Many organizations create, adopt and attempt to implement strategy without giving employees and customers the opportunity to participate in the development of the strategy.**

Today, just as the nuclear power industry was stopped in its tracks by failing to take human performance matters sufficiently into account, many organizations create, adopt and attempt to implement strategy without giving employees and customers the opportunity to participate in the development of the strategy. Even more egregious is that many organizations do not give employees sufficient training, forewarning, explanation or sufficient power and authority on the front lines to modify the strategy to the better. The company that can combine high technology with high touch will be in a better position to develop and implement successful high-growth strategies.

Another example of the failure of an entire industry to take its employees well-being into account is the securities industry. Many believe as this book goes to press that the reasons e-commerce brokerage houses such as "e-trade" and "e-schwab" are being so successful are their low price, their active engagement of the consumer and the fact that so much investment-oriented information is now publicly, instantly and cheaply available to traders. These factors are of great importance. They are certainly "growth drivers" in the industry. However, there is another reason why the traditional brokerage houses are slipping – *employee/broker turnover*. The failure of the traditional brokerage houses to provide adequate training, adequate incentive systems that promote longevity and their failure to provide other non-monetary support systems to their brokers cause many traditional brokerage houses to have huge turnover rates. Not only is this inefficient, it destroys customer loyalty and hurts the branding potential of traditional securities firms. In addition, these high turnover rates may also be playing a significant role in the traditional brokerage houses' huge failure to recruit and keep large numbers of minority and female brokers. Behind the scenes, the failure of an entire industry – the traditional securities industry – to be successful at creating loyalty among its employees, to create a unique culture from company to company, and to attract minorities and females may actually be a stronger contributor to its weaker and weaker showing against the new e-commerce invaders than the standard "on-line is better" thinking that most people believe is driving the on-line success in the brokerage industry.

The second rule that cannot be broken by an organization seeking high-growth is have a clear and expansive definition of the term *customer*. The customer is not only the person who buys your organization's products and services. The customer is also the person *who would buy* your products and services if they were better, easier to purchase, cheaper, more customized (with skim or low fat milk as Starbucks found out) or packaged more consistently with their needs. This broader definition of "customer" is essential to support high-growth marketing and sales strategies.

Our educational system is becoming fragmented in the US, with more and more charter schools, home schooling, vouchers for parochial schools, magnet schools, and public schools varying in quality from great to harmful to our youth's intelligence. Marketing books, products and services to this industry has been a huge challenge. Innovation has been rare in this industry for the reasons specified earlier in this book. Improvement is not measured except in terms of a few test scores. The idea of having the *customers* (student, their parents, the businesses that will hire these students, colleges and universities and the military) *systematically evaluate* the performance of the educational institutions and educators is considered too far out and revolutionary to be given even a reasonable discussion in today's environment. So, the education industry below college level in the US stagnates and educational services delivered to minorities and children of low income parents in public schools are often abysmal by any reasonable, objective standard.

How to become "customer-centric"

High-growth strategies in the educational field could focus on delivering a better educational product to the primary customer, the student. High-growth strategies in the educational field could focus on understanding what the customer (more broadly defined as parents, businesses, universities and colleges and the military) wants, and working with all of these customers to reinvent the educational experience for greater success. The idea of "partnering" with one's customers, broadly defined, is as old as commerce itself, but it has not been generally employed by the educational industry so that the customers rule and not the teachers' unions, not the administrators, not the courts and not the school boards. High-growth strategies must focus on knowing your customers and your potential customers. Michael Gerber's "psychographic" profile of an organization's customer base is one approach that suggests how a company or non-profit organization can achieve high-growth by learning who its customers and potential customers are, why its customers buy (and why potential customers would buy) its product or service and how its product or service fits its customers' needs better than the alternative products and services available. Every pricing decision, every decision regarding how to market your goods or services, and every high-growth strategy should be designed to promote either the addition of satisfied customers or satisfying fewer customers with higher priced, more value added, more profitable services and products.

The approach used by many companies, including Mattel with its "Barbie®" line of products, giving customers a product choice at almost every conceivable price range is called *"pyramiding."* This is also called "versioning" and is an excellent approach to high-growth. Such a sales or marketing high-growth strategy not only produces a broad market response to your products and services, it also provides your organization with valuable information about which feature or product is considered worth the extra cost by the buying public. In today's market, the non-profit membership organizations that have only one class of membership ignore a hundred years of knowledge created by the for-profit sector that people want choices in membership category selection options just as they want choices in product selection or service options.

Profit is often generated by adding additional value to a product or service and marketing it for a significantly increased higher price, while keeping its additional cost (variable cost) far lower than the additional per unit (marginal) revenue. One of the authors was flying from Washington to Paris at a cost of $199 each way. When asked how much it cost to fly in the first class section of the same plane, he was told that it would be $4,000 each way! Obviously the airline is doing something in first class to add significant value for its passengers!

If a non-profit organization cannot develop a strategy that will give potential and current members a broad range of membership options at a broad range of varying prices, the organization may want to consider outsourcing the entire membership operation to a company or other non-profit organization that understands the economics and practicalities of this mildly innovative high-growth strategy.

Entrepreneurial organizations must be "open systems"

A third rule that your organization cannot break in developing high-growth strategies is the need to include new people, new organizations and new strategic partners as active participants and decision makers regarding your high-growth strategies. Entrepreneurial organizations must be open, inviting, expanding systems. The pace that ASTD, MicroStrategy and other companies and non-profits are creating new strategic alliances is dizzying. The geographic reach of these new strategic alliances is staggering. Today, a company can literally operate around the world in only a short period of time.

The ability of an organization to link up on a daily basis with another organization is giving new meaning to the phrase "life is a team sport." Today's team must be bigger and better than last week's team. And tomorrow's team will likely include some members that your organization had not even considered as team members just one short month ago. Therefore, a critical element of an organization's high-growth strategy must be the successful building of an ever growing set of alliances, partnerships (broadly defined) and other types of relationships that promote the growth of the organization. In the 1990s the new linkages between businesses and universities, between non-profits and for-profits, between business competitors and between governments and businesses will pave the way to the future when an organization's network of alliances will cut across industries, continents, languages, cultures and economic systems. These linkages must be created based on a clear, agreed strategy and in their early stages can be fragile. These linkages can promote both successful activities or, if not properly created and supported, can create discord, friction and lost opportunities.

On the positive side for example the Organization of American States' current effort to teach entrepreneurialism throughout the western hemisphere is a project that could have potentially 1 million individuals, businesses, governments, educational institutions, industry leaders, politicians and non-profit organizations all participating and will be organized and managed by a core staff of fewer than ten people. And, this OAS-generated entrepreneurial activity may, itself, generate more income than its cost of operations and have funds to invest in assisting start up companies and non-profit organizations as well as accomplish all of its educational goals. For this ambitious project to succeed, it must add "partners" at a lightening speed and at a very low cost per new participant. In fact, it must add to its own economic resource base when it adds partners and participants because each new partner and participant will represent a "cost" to the organization in the time and effort necessary to manage them and maintain their alignment. To remain viable as a project, the entrepreneurialism project, called the Young Americas Business Forum of the OAS, must figure out a way to grow exponentially and to pay for this growth as it goes along without sales revenues and without a large amount of start up, financial capital. While this project may sound somewhat out of the ordinary, the business model is exactly the same as the business model that many other non-profits and some for-profit organizations face as they attempt to achieve rapid growth quickly, through virtual organizations, with limited economic resources.

Successful, high-growth strategies create a "growth trajectory" that builds on itself and uses its own previous success as both the benchmark to compare future results and the fuel to achieve them. High-growth strategies are fluid because the competition is fluid, the rugged landscape or economic terrain is fluid, the business rules are fluid and the resources that an organization has to work with are fluid. *Strategy is the art of accomplishing more than has ever been achieved before with fewer resources than one would like to have at one's disposal.* This is accomplished in the final stage of the business model, a stage often called implementation, but that we call "deploy."

Deploy

Growth and leadership with every step

High-growth strategies are not just for Tuesdays or for the first of the month, or when a new CEO arrives or when the new consultant arrives or when your organization is in need of a "turnaround." Leadership by everyone in the organization is not just for the day after the company pep rally or after you have spent a tidy sum for Tom Peters or Tony Robbins to give an address to your organization. The new model of high-growth strategies for entrepreneurial organizations is that growth and leadership occur *at every step* of every activity on every day when your organization is operating. Does this mean that no one ever has a vacation? The answer is both "yes" and "no."

Today, high-growth strategies require the discipline of the marines, the creativity of the novelist and the quality demanded by a great orchestra leader. They require not only empowered employees, they require empowered customers who are given the means and incentives to notify companies when they have ideas for new or improved products and for better customer service. With today's sophisticated communication systems, all companies and non-profits have the ability to create and maintain high quality relationships with employees, customers, vendors.

High-growth strategies rely not only on the successful deployment of the 12 tools provided in Chapter 2, they require two other aspects: *evangelism*, and *devotion* or *loyalty* by a large and growing following. Many writers have begun to focus on the need to execute growth strategies with greater precision, greater sensitivity to the human element, greater awareness of likely customer and employee responses to the changes proposed, and the need for an organization to stay focused by not undertaking too many growth or change projects at the same time. The stakeholder analysis shows how critical it is for strategic planners to understand that every growth strategy needs not one champion or sponsor in the organization, it needs a "majority." And over time, it needs a larger and larger number of followers and leaders to sustain the momentum or acceleration necessary for high-growth strategies to be successful.

Certainly high quality products to some extent create their own following. However, to an even greater extent, whether it is in the rarefied venture capital worlds or in the department stores that cater to teenage, impulse shopping, all organizations that seek to create and sustain high-growth strategies must create a following. No other word captures the process of creating a following as the word "evangelism." While this word has been tarnished by a few "TV preachers," the word *evangelism* has great utility for companies, non-profit organizations and educational institutions attempting to create the necessary foundation and sufficient strategies to promote high-growth strategies. Stripped of its religious overtones, "evangelism" refers to the art of converting non-believers to one's way of thinking, acting or living. High-growth strategies require that organizations modify the human behavior of employees, investors (contributors) and customers to act in concert with their high-growth strategies. While we might want to believe that rational based systems of incentives, employee stock options, better advertising, product quality improvements and improved productivity will provide all that an organization needs to create and sustain high-growth strategies, they are not enough. High-growth strategies must capture a following and address the emotional needs of customers as well as employees to be fully successful over long periods of time.

Growth and leadership *at every step* requires that an entire organization adopt a culture, a way of doing things, that is fully supportive of the high-growth objectives that are written into the organization's plans for the coming week, quarter, year or decade. In the organization, whether it is a company, a non-profit or an educational institution of any size, there must be "unity." Unity or strategic alignment does not mean that everyone becomes a "yes person" to the leader. *Quite the contrary.* What it does mean is that there is a period of strategy formulation and a period of strategy execution. During the period of strategy formulation there must be a careful listening to different viewpoints since people will view a proposed goal from different perspectives and diverse paradigms. During the period of strategy execution there must be decisive action consistent with the strategic plan, followed by monitoring, honest feedback and the free expression of opinions that may lead to modifying the strategy to take into account new information or expose poor choices made at the outset of the strategy. Unity does require everyone in the organization who seeks to achieve a high-growth strategy to become "invested" in the execution of the tactics that are employed by the organization to achieve its growth targets. Unity also demands that the leadership of the organization separate those individuals in responsible positions from the organization who show either an inability, a lack of will or a lack of interest in being a part of the successful implementation of high-growth strategies.

High-growth organizations are not for everyone and high-growth strategies are not for every organization. Employees and leaders who fail to contribute to the organization's alignment around growth, will not fit in. Today, there are diagnostic tools that can assist organizations in weeding out (by not hiring them or by separating them from the organization) those who will "back stab" an organization when they do not share in the alignment of the organization to achieve high-growth. Some organizations, as they are presently configured or staffed may not be able to align behind high-growth. Maybe they can be transformed by leadership or maybe that same "pro-growth" leadership would be better off going to another organization where alignment can be created behind high-growth strategies.

Employees today need be *leaders* for high-growth strategies to achieve their maximum potential. Employees must be engaged *at every step* to bring to the table all of the energy, brains, creativity, intelligence and knowledge they can muster to help organizations create and implement high-growth strategies.

Our work over the past 25 years has demonstrated that attitudes and behaviors, (just like laughter and some illnesses), are contagious. Leaders must promote, through evangelical statements, programs and role model behavior, certain behaviors that promote high-growth strategies so that these attitudes and behaviors expand in their organization. Employees' attitudes, their own individual goals, their adaptive (change) capacity, their true feelings about their supervisors, their co-workers and their organization must be clearly understood both before high-growth strategies are implemented, and through the implementation and strategy modification process. Gone are the days when employees hate or do not respect their new CEO and the CEO survives for long. Gone are the days when employees do not respect the CEO and the organization can achieve consistent high-growth. Gone are the days, when CEO's and their organizations can achieve high-growth through the use of fear and applying sanctions on a regular basis to employees.

Growth and leadership *at every step* requires that employees grow in their cognitive, technical and productive skills *"at every step."* Organizations may think they are doing good and doing well when they provide training to employees. Yet, the results or benefit from training does not occur at the point of giving an employee training. It occurs when management insures that the employee is given an opportunity to use the training on the job and when management rigorously studies whether the employee given the training opportunity actually learned anything, actually changed his or her behavior on the job positively as a result of the training, and whether the employee has taken the opportunity to teach and train others in the organization what he or she learned in the training. It is now conventional wisdom that only through the regular application on the job of the skill or knowledge obtained in the training program, will the employee be able to maintain the skill or knowledge obtained. And

An organization promotes growth by giving its employees training. However, an organization's failure to measure, monitor and promote the application of knowledge and skills gained through training on the job is an example of an organization that is not "growing with every step".

only then will the organization benefit in the long run. An organization promotes growth by giving its employees training. However, an organization's failure to measure, monitor and promote the application of knowledge and skills gained through training on the job is an indication of an organization that is not "growing with every step".

Growth *at every step* requires that the knowledge, skills, mission and learning of an organization grow cumulatively. Just as muscles require rest to grow in the most arduous physical training program, organizations must balance "doing" growth with reflection and learning. Organizations and employees must be able to change gears at the right time to absorb the lessons they and their employees may be able to glean from their growth "activities." Growth *at every step* requires not only that someone be responsible for getting that new customer or closing that sale, but also that someone in the organization be responsible for writing down the lessons learned from development and pursuit of high-growth strategies. Some organizations call this person the "V.P. for Knowledge." In fact, growth *at every step* requires that no one person be expected to get each new customer, close every sale or write down all of the lessons learned. Growth *at every step* requires that each employee contribute significantly to both getting the new (or keeping the current) customer and documenting and sharing the lessons learned along the way.

Leadership at every step is clearer in concept, but, in our experience, rarely practiced. Leadership *at every step* is most ably demonstrated by Sir John Templeton who many regard as one of the world's most successful investors. He lived his life spending only one-half of his after-tax income (even when he was just starting out) and expected companies in which he invested or recommended investing in to be conservative with their assets and aggressive with their growth goals. After retirement, he assisted non-profit organizations and brought exactly the same level of economic rigor to those organizations that he demanded of for-profit companies throughout his life.

Leadership *at every step* does not mean that the leadership of an organization cannot be allowed to make a mistake. Coke's "new Coke" was a huge financial mistake. But it was not a mistake of leadership. It was the result of a flawed strategy that failed to take into account customer preference, customer reluctance to change and failed to win over much of the rank and file of the downline distributors who sold Coke (but were independent companies from Coca-Cola, Inc.) before it launched ahead with its disastrous new product. Leadership *at every step* requires that organizations seek to identify and promote the leadership qualities of their employees, board members, management and customers and to create a synergistic (successful working) relationship in support of high-growth strategies.

The good news is that when the communication channels are open within your organization, it will become clear quite quickly whether your organization is actually up to the challenge and risk of developing and embarking on high-growth strategies. Some organizations are not and never will be. Would the CEO risk his or her house or job, would employees risk their bonus, expected raises and "guaranteed" benefits, would the organization risk its very existence on the effort necessary to promote and sustain high-growth? These are the important questions that each organization needs to address for itself in the beginning stages of developing high-growth strategies.

Growth and leadership *at every step*, begins at the first step – knowing your organization today and its true willingness to become a high-growth organization. The opportunities for high-growth have never been greater. Through globalization, there is an entire world that can benefit from your organization's goods and services. Your organization can now reach them if you want to. Through technology we can learn customer preferences and customize goods and services to such an extent that the product or service that reaches the customer may not even look like the original product that was designed on the drawing board. Through the willingness of humans to work across racial, educational, wealth, class, ethnic, cultural, national, language, religious, philosophical and geographical differences, the potential of an organization to create teams to deliver its goods and services has never been greater. Through shared leadership and participatory systems, where employees and even customers can find a means to contribute to the improvement of the product or service produced by an organization, a collective intelligence is now available to every business or organization leader who is willing to expend the resources and has the mind-set capable of effectively listening. Through the availability and use of volunteers, creative incentive systems and the creation of meaning at work in businesses as well as non-profit organizations, we are now at the threshold of a time when our economic system is creating clearer sets of rules, our governments are becoming more supportive of letting the market rule within reason and our workers are willing to be full participants in the high-growth opportunities that every organization can now legitimately seek to attain.

High-growth is not a part-time job for an organization. An organization must allocate its scarce resources across many areas when it seeks high-growth. We have touched before on the need for learning and training, the need for strategic alignment and unity, the need for developing clear and innovative growth strategies using the best business tools available and the need for a clear understanding of your own organization, its adaptive resources, its ability to change and grow, the need to know what unmet needs there are and will be for goods and services and how to fill those needs economically. Entrepreneurism requires not only all of these aspects of commerce to be addressed, it requires one often neglected aspect to be addressed – *measurement and precision.*

Measurement and precision

In the approach "recruit, organize, manage and deploy" one aspect of running or working at a business, non-profit organization or educational institution transcends time and strategic categories. This is the aspect of measurement. Much has been written about the work of Robert S Kaplan and David P Norton, whose book *The Balanced Scorecard: Translating Strategy Into Action* and consulting services have made the term "balanced scorecard," synonymous with an organization creating and implementing a system of measuring carefully numerous aspects of your operations and using this information to help guide your organization. We endorse wholeheartedly the concept that organizations seeking to develop and implement high-growth strategies should:

- identify carefully what it is they intend to measure ("the metrics")
- identify benchmarks or levels that are considered "success"
- determine how to measure key aspects of the organization and its results
- allocate resources for measurement and analytical efforts to insure that adequate resources are deployed in this effort
- develop a plan to integrate the results of their measurement and analytical efforts so they are properly used by the organization in strategic planning and implementation efforts.

Earlier in the book we touched on the use of the term "economic value added" (EVA) (see page 131). This approach by the consulting firm Stern Stewart and others emphasizes that the measurement of "profits" or "earnings" using generally accepted accounting principles for some companies may be seriously flawed and must be modified if we are going to use valid economic measures to drive bonus systems, resource allocation and investment decisions, and measure economic success accurately of a for-profit enterprise. Both the "balanced scorecard" and "EVA" represent advancements to the state of the art in measuring important elements of organizational behavior and their results.

Often large and small companies, non-profits and educational institutions fail at measuring key elements of their economic activities, employee behavior, customer attitudes or true growth potential in terms of either revenues or profits. No company can or should measure everything that some analyst can imagine. However, it is critical for non-profits as well as for-profit organizations to expand the number of items about their existence and operations that they do measure and to measure them over time to discern trends and patterns. For example, one non-profit, Child Trends, Inc., is in the business of measurement. The 30 researchers at Child Trends, Inc. measure poverty levels among children, teenage pregnancy rates, the impacts of new federal programs on child well being and are considering creating a "youth well-being index" that will track over time changes in youth well-being. The organization has an annual budget of $3 million. One of the authors asked the organization's leaders if they realized that the organization was spending only a nickel per year per youth of this country (there are approximately 60 million people under the age of 18 in the US). Not only did the organization's leaders admit that they had never made this calculation, they were quite surprised when asked if their research, their publications and their findings were worth $1 per youth per year. The CEO's unequivocal answer of "Yes" to this question did reveal that in their eyes their agency should be a $60 million per year organization and not the $3 million per year organization trying to eke out a few percentage points of growth each year.

High-growth strategies must be based on some rational belief or aspiration regarding just how big a company or non-profit organization can become within a given period of time. Measuring with precision key elements of the economic and demographic landscape in which a businesses or a non-profit operates provides critical insights regarding how much growth potential it really has. Measurement of the outside economic environment, competitors, the total market size and market share within your particular markets is critical to becoming intelligent about your organization's high-growth potential. This high-growth potential will change over time and only through measurement will an organization know whether it has vast room for growth in its market segment or needs to begin to explore other markets for high-growth opportunities. Non-profits may have a tougher research task than for-profit companies in measuring the appropriate indicators of their external economic marketplace, but the job is no less important in the non-profit sector than it is in the for-profit sector.

Precision is required when measurement takes place, especially if wages, jobs, investments, resource allocation and other important business decisions depend on the measurement results. The segmentation and fragmentation of the training industry today may serve as a "growth brake" limiting either service providers (trainers or their companies) or service receivers (trainees or their companies) from ever doing rigorous research on the actual impacts of the training in such areas as changing workplace behavior, contributing to increased productivity or profits or enhancing employee well-being.

Companies and non-profits cannot wait until the perfect measurement devices are created to begin to evaluate the effectiveness of the training programs in which they invest billions of dollars each year. Organizations, before they send someone to training, must have a clear set of expectations of the results they expect from the training and measure employee behavior against those sets of expectations both before and after the training. Econometricians are not needed, though they may be helpful at a steep price, to help organizations figure out whether a training program has increased productivity, has increased profitability, has reduced costs or has been a waste of money.

Measurement of human capital is in its infancy though it has been discussed for a 100 years. Human capital, as we described earlier, is a measure of the relevant skills, knowledge and ability of the individuals that comprise an organization. While it may be arbitrary to say "John's Ph.D. is worth 'x' dollars," we can assign a value to it because organizations are willing to pay Ph.D.s, on average, more than they are willing to pay for those with master's degrees if the knowledge gained or human capital gained through the Ph.D. program is expected to be useful to the organization. And even more important than measuring the static value of the human capital on a particular day in an organization, if the organization wants to grow in its skills, knowledge(s) and abilities, it is important to measure the change over time of an organization's employees' skills, knowledge(s) and abilities. While precision is always preferred, crude measures of human capital and the changes of human capital in an organization may be useful to an organization that seeks high growth. They are certainly better than no measures at all.

Measurement is a way that an organization says to everyone that what is being measured is important. Measuring the number of suggestions that employees make for improving an organization and measuring the number of suggestions that management has adopted from the total number of employee suggestions sends a strong signal to employees that their suggestions "count." Measurement programs can create opportunities for the rational allocation of rewards and friendly competition within different sectors of an organization.

Measurement has never been cheaper. With new technology, a simple measurement system could be designed that would ask every employee every week to measure such factors as:

- employee attitudes
- employee self-assessments of how well they performed that week
- assessments of how well their co-workers performed that week
- assessments of how well their managers performed that week
- how much they learned on the job that week compared to previous weeks
- how willing or able they think they are to implement new procedures
- how willing or able they think others in the company are to implement new procedures
- how good their products or services were that week compared to previous weeks

- how satisfied or not satisfied their customers were that week compared to previous weeks
- how wasteful or efficient they believe their organization was that week
- other questions relevant to your organization.

Having employees, suppliers and customers (and students of educational institutions) pencil in answers in a multiple choice format on a precoded answer sheet or respond by e-mail to questions posed by the organization can reveal, for pennies per answer, tremendously valuable information that the organization can use to assess where it is, how to improve and give it direction in developing and implementing high-growth strategies.

The implementation and improvement of measurement activities do not require a bevy of consultants, although many consultants will sell you fancy measurement tools that may be a step up from your home brewed version. But some of us from the old school still appreciate "home brew" for what it was, "the best we could afford under the circumstances and a lot better than nothing." One of the silver bullets to high-growth strategies is that your organization, regardless of its size, can improve its measurement of key factors immediately and can learn and grow from the process.

Precision is important regardless of the size of the organization. Certainly, precision in space engineering is important because a small mathematical error can send a spacecraft thousands of miles off target due to weightlessness in outer space. In outer space, imprecise approaches and calculations can costs millions of dollars in a split second. The importance of your organization, your business, your applications of your talents, energies and dedication is no less valuable in a very real sense than the millions that we shoot into outer space. Precision is the goal, but the inability to reach it with your organization's first efforts at measurement must not get in the way of starting in earnest to begin to measure what previously has been unmeasured.

Non-profit organizations would be well served to calculate the costs as precisely as possible of each service they provide (using some form of "activity-based accounting"). In addition they should also enter into that equation a "cost" for capital that is donated to the organization and is employed in providing the service. Measures of efficiency can be created for non-profits and educational institutions, just as an efficiency measure can be created for for-profit companies and NFL quarterbacks. The goal of a measure of efficiency is not to figure out to the last hundred of a cent how efficient your organization is at the present time. The goal is to track over time how efficient your organization is in delivering its goods and services in order to be able to think rationally about how to become more efficient over time.

High-growth strategists often suggest that "reinvention" will yield greater results than "improvement." From our consulting experience, we are clear that there is generally room for both improvement (which must always be based on some formal or informal measure system) and reinvention which is the use of a new approach to success. Measurement does not always require the use of an outside party to do the measuring or the analysis of the information or data generated by the measurement system. Self measurement, by employees and managers, may well produce valuable information at low cost. In all measurement systems, the quality of the information generated will be the result of the quality of the questions asked and the integrity of the answers and analysis generated through the effort.

Measuring employee output and performance, measuring the amount and types of leadership exhibited by a senior manager, measuring the contribution of a member of the board of directors, measuring the efficiency of your direct marketing program, your sales and training efforts, measuring the value of the office location your organization has compared to other alternatives are just the tip of the iceberg of measurement activities that can be performed today in your organization. Measurement systems will evolve, and some will be abandoned along the way. Organizational growth does not occur just because someone wants a bigger bottom line or higher revenues. Organizational growth is not just the result of trying to create a better product or advertising campaign. Organizational growth is promoted by knowing the current level of success or failure that each part of your organization is currently experiencing and this requires measurement.

Organizational growth requires two types of measurement. First, it requires measurement of what is going on today. Second, it requires the setting of a standard that each part of your organization is to achieve as part of your high-growth strategy. The term used today to discuss these types of measurement is called "metrics." Every organization seeking high sustainable growth must firmly answer the question of "What metrics are important to the organization?" Identifying the metrics that best describe your organization's current level of performance, current level of ability, its willingness to adapt and grow and its ultimate growth potential are as critical to creating high-growth strategies for entrepreneurial organizations as road maps are to the family going on a vacation for the first time to a new area.

The good news is that there are many places companies, non-profit organizations and educational institutions can turn to for help in getting new measurement systems put into place in addition to high-priced consultants. Often professors and students from MBA programs, organizational development programs and other programs at the community college, college and university level can assist your organization in developing measurement systems. Other companies and non-profits are often willing to share or give away the descriptions of their measurement efforts. Joining into a strategic alliance with another company or non-profit organization can also speed up implementation and reduce the cost since some of the measurement issues will overlap between your organization or company and the organization or company down the hall or across the street. Early implementation efforts of measurement systems will be experimental in nature and patience is required in implementing full scale, intensive measurement systems. The rewards from these systems can be bountiful and can contribute handsomely to your high-growth strategies. In fact, the existence of such measurement systems can be a significant asset in promoting your organization to foundations for contributions, to venture capitalists for funding and to other companies as they seek merger or acquisition candidates.

The costs of failure

We often hear about costs in terms of dollars. The six recent space satellite failures in the US cost billions of dollars. The Three Gorges Dam project (which may yet succeed) cost $25 billion. Dollars are measures of costs, but dollars are not the only real costs of failure that we want to discuss. Important scientific data and knowledge will be permanently lost due to the satellite failures. Hundreds of thousands of lives in China will be uprooted and harmed if this massive project fails to meet its objectives.

Today, our economic system has figured out – with substantial governmental help – how to land people on the moon, how to blow up entire cities, how to link computer users worldwide through the use of the Internet and, possibly, how to clone human beings. We now know how to live longer, look younger, run faster, consume more, have our companies stock prices trade at over 100 times earnings and reduce pollution all at the same time. And certainly many economic advances have occurred without any governmental assistance. With all of these successes, why do we need to talk about the costs of failure that we as humans will experience if we are not able to improve our ability to create and sustain high-growth strategies in our entrepreneurial organizations. The reason that we need to discuss the real costs of failure is that, despite all of the late 20th century economic successes, much of the world and much of the US, itself, is not participating in or getting much benefit from the entrepreneurial accomplishments of the past half century. More importantly, at present there is no guarantee that the first half of the 21st century will be blessed with similar economic growth or that economic growth will become more widespread throughout the world.

The role and influence of entrepreneurial organizations is expanding rapidly throughout the world. Recent US government publications such as *Businesslike Government* by Al Gore and Scott Adams (yes, Dilbert®) suggest that government is starting to get the message that the "business as usual" paradigm of government will no longer work in a fast-paced, customer-centric society created during the last quarter of the 20th Century. Areas that were exclusively the province of government, such as collecting child support and issuing drivers' licenses and automobile, boat and truck tags will soon be the province of the private sector since government has proven that it cannot perform these functions with the efficiency, the effectiveness or with the proper care and concern for the customers of these services that the private sector can provide.

One of the authors recently had the opportunity to ask presidential candidate, Bill Bradley, if under his administration we would have less of a bureaucratic government and more of an entrepreneurial government. Bradley replied that there cannot be an entrepreneurial government, but there can be an innovative government. Under our broad definition of entrepreneur with which we started this book, there is ample opportunity for government to be entrepreneurial. Privatization is an entrepreneurial response to an non-entrepreneurial government. Privatization means that the performance of an organization and the salaries it pays, the number of jobs that it supports and the incentive rewards given to its leaders are all intertwined, a feat that government has never seemed to accomplish. The culture of government with its emphasis on process rather than results, job security, political favoritism, unwillingness and inability of employees and agencies to take risks, its inability to create policies and innovations on the spot, its lack of demonstrated due care and concern for its customers and its cumbersome, hierarchical systems have rendered many of the activities that government has performed in the past unpopular and the butt of many jokes. What is not a joke is that the justice system in the US often takes several years to adjudicate even simple disputes among citizens and businesses. The failure of the justice system to produce speedy trials in civil cases is tolerated by a citizenry that is slowly beginning to seek alternatives to government monopolies such as our court system, our police departments and our utilities which have been run by governments since the beginning of the country. While the Governor of Maryland in 1999 is trying to make the case that the State should take over the county judicial systems, others may look to the private sector serving as the manager of the county judicial systems in the future.

Government's inability to provide effective child support collection, effective traffic administration, effective housing for the poor, effective and timely court systems points the way to the huge costs of failure that we deal with on a daily basis. The hope is that entrepreneurial systems that reward improvement and reward the creation of new business and economic models to solve the delivery and implementation problems that so often plague government run programs will lead to no lines at the department of motor vehicles, no waiting ten years to collect child support, no waiting three years for a trial of a civil matter, no abuse by IRS officials and fewer government programs that fail to address people's real needs in a timely and cost-effective manner.

Government is not the only source of failure that we need to address. Today more businesses fail than succeed. The cost of these failures is enormous. The percentage of non-profit organizations that waste their resources without ever making a significant contribution to the economic and social landscape may be higher than the percentage of businesses that fail. Each new organization that is created, be it a business, non-profit organization or educational institution, represents not only an investment of financial capital, but also the investment of real people, their dreams and their forever lost opportunities to devote their lives and financial resources to other activities that could actually have been successful and improved the world. Failed businesses and non-profit organizations impoverish the world. They do not enrich it. Their costs are huge.

On occasion a failed business or non-profit organization may lead to unexpected growth and success of another business or non-profit organization. In most instances, however, huge amounts of waste, inefficiency, conflict and demoralization occur when a business or non-profit organization fails. The tools provided in this book and its insights on entrepreneurism are designed to assist your organization in avoiding such failure. These tools have been provided to promote high-growth strategies and are also designed to promote your business or non-profit organization operating more effectively and efficiently at whatever level of growth it seeks.

Real wages in the US have not significantly increased for a majority of workers since the early 1960s. Today entire subpopulations of the country located in specific geographic pockets believe they have no opportunity to become entrepreneurs and know they have no opportunity to advance economically by working at poverty level wages. The failure of our economic system to engage the minds, creative talents, intrinsic motivation and leadership potential of the *entrepreneurially disenfranchised* represents one of the greatest wastes of human talent known today. Through the use of microcredit, some would-be entrepreneurs can get a little financial head start toward the road toward entrepreneurism. Unfortunately, a little credit, by itself, is often like one little swimming lesson. It may be marginally useful, but not when someone has to swim across a large lake to survive.

Entrepreneurism, and especially high-growth strategies for entrepreneurial organizations, can be an important remedy to assisting people out of poverty, out of low wage, dead end jobs and out of a cycle that people experience when they are associated with business failure after business failure, on top of educational failure after educational failure. The fact that most of our public high schools do not teach business or entrepreneurism is merely a symptom of how our government-sponsored educational system is failing those who need it most. In one high school in Maryland, in the second wealthiest county in the nation, in a new school built at a cost of nearly $46 million, 49 percent of the general student population in the ninth grade had below a "C" average in 1998. These students not only fail at the general curriculum they are not taught the basic skills of entrepreneurism nor taught some of the essential lessons of developing high-growth personal or business strategies. Our work over the past three decades shows that some of these key lessons that youths need to be taught today include teaching people to master the following:

- creating and communicating a clear vision for yourself and your organization
- enrolling others and working successfully with an ever growing team to achieve your goals and market success
- participating in an ongoing activity while adhering to core values agreed upon by all major participants in your endeavor
- measuring and monitoring your implementation results in order to check them before they stray too far or become too expensive to correct quickly
- adhering to the discipline necessary to meet, if not beat, your competition
- constantly emphasizing and learning how to serve your customers better, more efficiently and more creatively.

These are the lessons of high-growth strategies for entrepreneurial organizations. Today, many *entrepreneurially disenfranchised* people do not have a clue regarding how to start and run a business, how to start and run a non-profit organization or how to start and run an educational institution. When we look at the distribution of income and resources in the US and throughout the world and how it has changed over the past three decades with wealth and income becoming more, not less concentrated in the few, it is clear that those who do understand and can apply these entrepreneurial lessons are the ones who have been able to increase their wealth the most.

High-growth strategies for entrepreneurial organizations are based on the fundamental belief that a person or group can form together to improve not only their lot, but also the lot of their customers, their vendors, their investors and the overall economic and social landscape as a whole. The key driving force behind high-growth strategies for entrepreneurial organizations is the spirit, the hope, the planning and the becoming prepared to address the changing needs of our business, social and physical environment for goods and services. There are no guarantees of financial success in the entrepreneurial economy, no perfect job security (as Japan is learning), no instant reward for a good idea especially if that idea is pursued without sufficient skills, resources, commitment and discipline. However, there are guarantees that those who are allowed to participate in the creation and management of a high-growth-oriented entrepreneurial organization will have the opportunity to learn the skills of customer service (respect), the skills of looking at the world with the intention of improving it (service, hope and dedication), the skills of working with others (cooperation) and most importantly, the skill of pushing one's self to the fullest extent of one's intellectual and physical potential (fulfillment).

The costs of the failure of our society to teach and embrace high-growth strategies for entrepreneurial organizations is the cost of short-changing millions of people of the chance to learn these skills and to have a chance of working together with others to improve their lot and the lot of others simultaneously. The cost of failure is very high.

This lesson applies even more forcefully to countries that are less developed economically and have less of a history of entrepreneurism. Just as companies can often leapfrog technological steps that other companies have spent millions of dollars in perfecting, less developed countries and impoverished pockets of more developed countries can use the tools provided in this book to teach entrepreneurism and make great strides in both human development and economic development at a quicker pace than was previously possible in the countries that spent decades developing these tools and strategies.

The costs of the failure of certain geographical areas and peoples to learn and adopt the values and high-growth strategies of entrepreneurial organizations is shown in the starvation of people worldwide and the starvation of the human spirit in many countries. The role of values can never be underestimated, and the roles of the unbreakable rules that serve as the foundation of entrepreneurial organizations form the only basis of agreement on how competitors compete, how employers treat employees and how all groups in society should be encouraged to participate in the entrepreneurial economy.

Several examples from our consulting experience show how the clash of values (or lack of values) can severely limit the role of entrepreneurism in a society. Entrepreneurism requires the accurate keeping of financial books and records, honesty in dealing with co-workers, managers and subordinates, the creation of non-physically threatening, safe work places, the creation of value and perceived value for customers and employees alike and the inclusion of all races, cultures and ethnic groups as customers, employees, investors and vendors. With the new *open books movement* gone may be the days when financial books and records can be regularly cooked for long without someone finding out about it and taking appropriate action against the organization. With the rising cost of government and private litigation against organizations that allow or promote racial discrimination or physically or sexually threatening work environments, it is becoming a significant competitive advantage to operate a humane workplace. With the trend to larger and larger, even global entrepreneurial organizations, *multicultural competencies* within an entrepreneurial organization are becoming the minimum standard required to achieve high-growth strategies with different populations of customers and employees and over different geographical regions.

Entrepreneurial organizations will fail to meet the test of sustainable high-growth strategies if they do not:

- pay their workers the applicable minimum wage
- treat women and minorities equally as other workers
- provide training and safe work environments for workers
- seek ways to produce their goods and services with a minimum of consumer health and safety risk and environmental pollution
- contribute financially to needed projects in their communities
- promote the empowerment of employees and customers
- keep accurate financial books and records.

Michael Saylor's emphasis on building an "institution, not a company" is a shorthand way of saying how true entrepreneurs have a social responsibility that goes far beyond meeting payroll and turning out products and services that are of value to customers.

The costs of failure are not only high, they are growing. As governments pull safety nets, as non-profit organizations are called upon to fill a growing gap between the entrepreneurially successful and the entrepreneurially disenfranchised and as educational institutions fail to provide even the basics to students to teach them how to live in the 21st century, the solutions to many of the worlds problems of poverty, lack of education, pollution, peace and safety, and failures in communication are beginning to fall more and more into that sector of the economy we call the entrepreneurial sector. Leaders of multi-national companies such as Canon have found this to be true as they begin to spread across vast territories and begin to experience first hand the limits of governments to deal effectively with these issues.

In the future, whether two or more countries go to war in the 21st century against each other, or whether a country is on one side or the other in a war may well depend more on the relationships between the entrepreneurs of those countries than the relationships of the political establishments or political viewpoints of the countries. Whether pollution will be allowed to grow in a country or part of a country may depend more on the stance that leading businesses take to tackling the pollution problem than on some government edict against pollution. Whether the educational system will successfully do its job in creating the workers and entrepreneurs we need in the 21st century may depend more on the role that the entrepreneurial sector plays in demanding and providing schools directly for educational success than federal or state funding or local school board edicts. Whether low income people will have adequate housing may depend more on entrepreneurs who develop new ideas for making housing cheap and reliable (through the use of cardboard compounds and other new materials and production methods) rather than on government funding for regular housing stock that is expensive to build and more expensive to maintain. Whether crime and drug abuse will be curbed may depend more on the ability of the entrepreneurial sector to enroll people into the system of rewards available from and the personal demands required by the entrepreneurial sector more than it will depend on governments hiring of police to threaten drug users and criminals with the sanction of jail or criminal records.

High-growth strategies for entrepreneurial organizations entail addressing social problems created, fostered, tolerated or just not resolved by early capitalism, middle age socialism, late communism, dictatorship and non-democratic monarchial forms of government. The restrictions placed by *entrepreneurial disenfranchisement* on the human spirit, human potential and human capabilities of billions of human beings throughout the world is the true cost of failure of high-growth strategies of entrepreneurial organizations. As shown in the last section of this book, starting with your entrepreneurial organization, the one you are currently associated with in some way or the one that you will form as a result of reading this book and catching the spirit, your organization can be part of the significant transformation of the world's economic and social landscape that will take place in the early part of the 21st century.

The hope that high-growth strategies represent for the world's future

This is a business book. A book about the laws of commerce and a toolkit for businesses, non-profit organizations and educational institutions interested in high-growth strategies. This book is premised on the idea that the laws of commerce apply to for-profit businesses, non-profit organizations and educational institutions alike. This book is also premised on the idea that the laws of commerce know no geographical boundry, favor no race or ethnic group and render useless those institutions, governments and organizations that ignore these laws.

Lester Thurow predicts, in *The Future of Capitalism*, that over time, the wages of all countries' workers will even out. Capitalism's ugly side, as Marx suggested, was the exploitation of workers. Today, in advanced capitalistic countries where workers are in short supply, wages have started to rise above their 1960s level and many workers who seek temporary or part-time positions are able to accommodate that wish. However, while wage parity between countries may exist someday in the future, huge wage differentials between the US and Mexico, its neighbor and Germany and its neighbor, Poland, continue to exist – without much showing of equalization in the near future.

Modern economic theory has surpassed the ghosts of its past, the class struggles of Marx, the gloom and doom of Malthus who feared that the growth of food and goods could only be arithmetic (incremental) while the population grew geometrically (explosively), the industrial era when pollution controls were non-existent and worker safety not considered important by the governing elite and the factory owners. Modern economic theory is also currently leaving behind the imperialistic era when a nation's entrepreneurs, with the help of their own governments and the governments who sought their investment, barged into underdeveloped countries, built factories, paid dirt wages to the workers, developed and managed plants that would occasionally blow up killing hundreds and injuring thousands of local citizens all the while shipping goods back to the entrepreneur's country for sale at high profits. Maybe Thurow will be correct that wage rates will become similar across nations and that living standards will similarly even out, since the great wealth being created through high-growth strategies in entrepreneurial organizations could be the rising tide that raises all boats.

One of the key lessons that entrepreneurial organizations learn early in their development is the lesson of "focus." Since an entrepreneurial organization must produce some fairly high quality good or service at a reasonable and competitive price to enter a market and sustain high-growth, most entrepreneurial organizations early in their development cannot at the same time pursue the creation of hundreds of products or the supply of many different types of services, and be successful with each product or service. But entrepreneurial organizations can learn quickly. Amazon.com's entry into the music and grocery marketplaces, Starbucks' entry into the ice cream business, AAA's entry into the driver's education business and MicroStrategy's transformation from a decision support system company to a communication company all show how quickly an entrepreneurial organization can take a successful business model from one area of the economy and apply the lessons learned to become successful in another area.

There is much talk about "learning organizations" and one of the hopes for high-growth strategies is that a high-growth strategy will always be a high-learning strategy as well. High-growth strategies, by definition, require humans to accomplish tomorrow what they could only dream of today. No one has the skills or knows how to feed the world's population even though we have been producing enough food to do so for over a decade. No one knows how to house the world's population, even though there is no shortage of physical and mental capability to accomplish this objective. No one knew how to link up millions of people and knowledge data bases until the government started the Internet and turned it loose to the private sector. No one knows how to build crops that are not destroyed by floods and weather, although we are making great strides through government and private sector funded research on creating crops that are heartier, more bountiful, more insect resistant and less reliant on deadly, polluting chemicals. No one knows how to guarantee freedom of expression in every country, but it is clear that if governments seek to stop all such expression now that the Internet exists, they will waste huge resources without accomplishing their mission.

The basic concept of entrepreneurism *is that an entrepreneurial activity done today will produce a return tomorrow that is greater than the investment and effort that went into the original activity.* All entrepreneurial activity and all high-growth strategies seek to secure significantly greater returns from an activity or effort than the cost of the activity or effort that was invested in the first place. Entrepreneurial activities have a benchmark, a starting point where we must carefully invest resources with a clear vision and a good plan that our endeavor will be greeted successfully by the marketplace by our customers.

Twenty short years ago in the US government policies drove markets. Now, economic markets drive government policy. There is still an essential role for government, so long as it too begins to live by the laws of commerce, spending as little as possible to achieve a clearly thought out, desired result. Passing laws such as the Clean Air Act does little good on those occasions when government agencies like the EPA and their state counterparts do not catch or prosecute the violators. Privatization of the enforcement of many of the laws on the government's books and creating stronger bridges between government funded research and development and entrepreneurial companies who will commercialize the successful R&D activities can create a win-win situation for the government, the entrepreneurial sector and the taxpaying citizenry.

> The basic concept of entrepreneurism *is that an entrepreneurial activity done today will produce a return tomorrow that is greater than the investment and effort that went into the original activity.*

High-growth strategies for entrepreneurial organizations mean squeezing greater and greater output from fewer and fewer resources. The spread between the cost of the "inputs" and the "outputs" can be shared between higher profits to the owners, higher wages to the employees and lower costs to the consumer of the goods and services. Efficiency can produce many winners. Investments in training, research and development and other forms of improving skills and learning represents one of the greatest strengths of entrepreneurism today since these activities will have the ability to improve not only our workers and our inventions, but also improve the species we refer to as "human beings."

Conclusion

Tomorrow your business, your non-profit organization and your educational institution can embark on a high-growth strategy. Today, you and your organization can begin the process of determining whether you and your organization are committed, are willing to invest, have the discipline, the focus and are willing to be flexible and innovative enough to undertake a program that will lead to high-growth. High-growth strategies require a substantial amount of personal development and organizational development, require a careful study of your economic, social, technological and political (internal and external) environments and require the willingness to empower everyone in your organization to participate in a meaningful way in the strategic planning and implementation/ execution of the strategies required for successful growth. High-growth strategies require the willingness to trek into the unknown and remake it in the image you have set forth for your organization.

This book has presented some of the tools taught in programs called Masters in Business Administration (MBA) at the graduate level of many colleges and universities throughout the world. We have presented these tools not only so that you cannot only use them in your organization, but also so you can understand the basis for these tools and analytical devices and build your own tools and your own systems for assisting your organization to become a high-growth organization. Today, the economic and social landscape is littered with companies, non-profits and educational institutions producing mediocre goods and services with marginal or negative profits, and whose goal is merely to survive rather than thrive.

Tomorrow we predict that many of these organizations will be part of the economic wasteland, overtaken by entrepreneurial organizations with higher standards, better treatment of workers, higher quality goods and services, empowered customers who participate in product improvement and new product development and who are committed to using every new technology and every new management approach available to improve sustainable profitability and improve the human condition on the planet.

Our work is committed to ensuring that every organization recognizes its responsibility to produce the most by using the least amount of resources, and to improve the quality of its workforce alongside improvements in the production of goods and delivery of services. Our commitment has been fueled by the many people who for hundreds of years have not only held this ideal, but have risked all of their capital and all of their days to delivering high-growth strategies through entrepreneurial organizations. As we move toward the 21st century, we see the trend toward entrepreneurism growing so that millions of additional people annually across the globe can attain the high status, awesome responsibility and opportunity that wearing the mantle "entrepreneur" entails. We see successful entrepreneurism being synonymous with growth of individuals, growth of economic statistics and improved measures as they apply to the social and physical landscapes that we inhabit.

We know that your role in this movement toward improved entrepreneurism and high-growth strategies begins with the organizations where you work, the organizations you lead and the organizations where you will assist in creating in the future. Welcome to the future. Welcome aboard.

Appendix: mission and vision statements

Growth Strategies, Inc. (GSI) Mission Statement

GSI is a group of leaders drawn from many fields of study and experience who work together to promote the growth of small, medium and large companies and non-profit organizations. GSI assists your organization in understanding its full potential and in determining the demand for your products and services in the US and abroad.

GSI assists your company or non-profit organization in creating a strong and effective board of directors and an effective network of employees, management, suppliers, vendors and customers who are proud to be affiliated with your organization.

GSI develops strategic alliances for its clients that are productive and enduring and is creative in fashioning custom-tailored business growth strategies.

GSI conducts research based on the highest standards of technical proficiency and provides honest, rigorous feedback designed to improve the growth and innovation trajectory of its clients.

GSI uses the latest technological developments in communications to be in touch with its clients. It utilizes strategic plans, systems and operations to develop:

- the **human capital** of your employees and management
- the **technical capital** necessary to create the finest possible product or service at a reasonable cost
- the **finance capital** to remain strong and competitive
- the **organizational capital** necessary to leverage the knowledge of your employees.

Growth Strategies, Inc. (GSI) Vision Statement

GSI is a leader in the field of business, organization and personal development. The senior consultants of GSI have been developing successful growth strategies for profit-making organizations, non-profit organizations and individuals for over forty years. GSI's board members and consultants have served with distinction as high-level corporate executives, lawyers, doctors, scientists, university professors, union leaders, finance experts, educators, commercial real estate professionals, government officials, directors of non-profit organizations, members of respected think tanks and laborers.

GSI has the integrity, the vision, the technology and the resources needed for success in the 21st Century.

GSI is guided by the goal of creating assets, value, and growth.

GSI establishes and maintains long-term, mutually rewarding business relationships.

GSI has developed carefully-tailored growth strategies that foster an environment where each significant group related to the business or non-profit organization including employees and management, customers, investors and suppliers participate in the growth of the organization.

GSI works with companies and non-profits in order to identify and exploit unknown organizational assets.

GSI's Values-Driven Growth Model empowers companies and non-profit organizations to grow rapidly in a manner consistent with each organization's values.

Bibliography

A Struggle to Survive: Funding Higher Education in the Next Century, edited by David S. Honeyman, Corwin Press/Sage Publications, 1996.

Schools must create new forms of value. Corporations are new competitors, K-12 schools are partnering with businesses. Private tutoring companies are on the rise. New competitors are customer oriented, are willing to be innovative and provide new services and to focus on excellence.

Anderson, James C. and Narus, James A. *Business Marketing: Understand What Customers Value,* Harvard Business Review, Nov.-Dec. 1998, 53–65.

Answering the question "Why do customers buy from us (or the competition)?" is critical to business success. Focus groups, surveys and other field approaches (including observation) will allow your company to build a "customer value model." The model is a summation of each element in your product or service that a customer holds in high value. Since all customers are not alike, data should be collected on specific characteristics of the consumers and cross-tabulated with the values they hold highest. This information will allow sales tools and varied product offerings to be developed that take into account how customers value your products.

Arnenault, Jane *Forging Non-Profit Alliances: A Comprehensive Guide to Enhancing Your Mission Through Joint Ventures and Partnerships, Management Service Organizations, Parent Corporations and Mergers.* Jossey-Bass, San Francisco 1998.

Suggests that non-profits consider linking up with other non-profits over the next ten years in either joint ventures, sharing administrative functions through management service organizations or mergers. The book outlines the key procedures a non-profit organization should undertake in its investigation and implementation of a merger, acquisition or other type of strategic alliance.

Andrews, Kenneth, *Directors Responsibility for Corporate Strategy,* in "Strategy: Seeking and Securing Competitive Advantage," edited by Cynthia A. Montgomery and Michael E. Porter, Harvard Business Review Books, 1991.

The role of the board of directors in corporate strategy is usually minimal. However, through the use of a Corporate Strategy Committee and broad involvement of board members in developing strategy, an organization can develop a better strategy and a better strategic planning process.

ASTD's Guide to Learning Organization Assessment Instruments, compiled by Mark E. Van Buren, American Society for Training and Development, 1997.

This compilation of articles takes best practices that measure key elements of an organization's learning efforts. Three elements of a learning strategy are to promote knowledge acquisition, knowledge sharing and knowledge utilization. The goal of the assessment tools is to develop and refine a learning organization strategy. The strategy is a game plan for building learning organization capabilities. Learning is viewed as operating at numerous levels of the organization: 1) individual; 2) team; 3) organizational. Learning is facilitated in organizations when they: 1) assess the need for learning looking both internally and externally at competitors and other industries; 2) measure learning activities and results; 3) have a willingness to experiment: 4) are open minded; 5) promote continuous education for all employees; 6) have the full leadership committed to supporting learning throughout the organization.

Ault, Richard, Walton, Richard, and Childers, Mark, *What Works. A Decade of Change at Champion International,* Jossey-Bass Publishers, San Francisco, 1998.

Two key elements of success in high-growth strategies is the demand within an organization to become the best in the world and promoting extreme openness in expressing disagreements at all levels and across all levels of an organization.

Baker, Wayne E., *Networking Smart: How to Build Relationships for Personal and Organizational Success,* McGraw-Hill, 1994.

This book describes the need for improved and strategically planned networking in the new age of networked organizations. It also gives a detailed "how to" primer on what individuals should do and what organizations should do to improve their chances of success. The "how to" sections suggest communication strategies, relationship audits and forward thinking about what type of relationships you and your organization would find most useful in accomplishing your goals. An appendix of networking organizations and a section on networking with your competitors provide guidance and structure to this area of business and organizational development that is often pursued haphazardly.

Band, William A. *Touchstones: Ten New Ideas Revolutionizing Business,* John Wiley & Sons, Inc., 1994.

Organizations must focus on four areas: quality, service, cost and time. Authority in organizations should be shared broadly with employees participating in all key aspects of strategic planning and decision making. Partnering is necessary for strategic advantage. Organizations must articulate their values and have a value strategy. Promoting the learning of all in the organization and the sharing of new knowledge throughout the organization produces excellent results. Change management strength is a key source of competitive advantage. Leadership must focus on facilitating and empowering others, promoting vision, successfully anticipating the future.

Barker, Joel A., *Future Edge: Discovering the New Paradigms of Success,* William Morrow & Company, 1992.

Anticipation, Innovation and Excellence are the key strategies to success in the future. The author suggests that returning the spirit to the workplace will be a crucial element in an organization's capability for success in the future. Asking all organization leaders to focus on the question, "What is impossible to do in your industry, but if it were possible would fundamentally change the industry?" the author seeks to have organizations and their members think outside of the box and to seek innovation. Defining a leader as "someone you would follow to a place where you would not go by yourself," the author seeks to instill a sense of mission among people to be leaders and to care deeply about the quality of their work and their ability to produce intellectual property, the key to future wealth.

Baskin, Ken *Corporate DNA: Learning from Life,* Butterworth-Heinemann, Boston, 1998.

The control, top down, do-it-by-the-system approach is waning and being replaced by organizations that encourage corporate evolution rather than reengineering and increased involvement of employees in all of the decisions that affect the workplace and the company's success.

Bauman, Robert P., Jackson, Peter, Lawerence, Joanne T. *From Promise to Performance: A Journey of Transformation at SmithKline Beecham,* Harvard Business School Press, 1997.

Employing "strategic communication" where everyone in the organization becomes aware of the strategic direction of the company was critical in developing and managing the culture necessary to achieve everyone working together toward common goals.

Beatty, Jack *The World According to Peter Drucker,* The Free Press, New York, 1998.

This book reviews the life, thought and contribution of Peter Drucker and the Peter Drucker Foundation.

Becker, Franklin and Steele, Fritz *Workplace by Design: Mapping the High-Performance Workscape,* Jossey-Bass, San Francisco, 1995.

The physical dimensions of the workplace often interfere with optimal performance of workers. The physical design of the workspace should promote change, define the corporate image, and promote teamwork and healthy interaction among workers. The workplace should be "vision-driven" and create a healthy work environment.

Benjamin, Gerald and Margulis, Joel *Finding Your Wings: How to Locate Private Investors to Fund Your Venture,* John Wiley & Sons, Inc., 1996.

This book explores the world of "angel" investors and the structure and operations of the private venture capital system in the US. Acknowledging that this system is secretive, inefficient and laborious for individuals and small companies to go through, the authors suggest that finding "angel" investment is always possible given the right business plan, the right management and the right strategy for finding the investor. The book presents a list of funding sources, discusses approaches to valuing your company, product or idea, explains due diligence and presents common questions and their answers.

Bennis, Warren, *Managing People Is Like Herding Cats,* Executive Excellence Publishing, Provo, UT 1997.

Great leaders manage the attention of others through a compelling vision, manage meaning by creating organizations that have a strong chance of achieving their vision, manage trust through displaying, delivering and demanding integrity, and manage themselves and their reputation to communicate and represent leadership at all times. Leaders are pioneers, not managers and seek to involve those affected by a decision in the planning efforts associated with the change. Leaders know their audiences,express their unspoken dreams and provide a road map and enroll the resources necessary to begin the realization of those dreams. The five basic ingredients of leadership are: vision, passion, integrity, trust and curiosity.

Bennis, Warren, *Organizing Genius,* Addison-Wesley, 1997.

Putting together teams of talented people with a strong mission and vision is essential for producing great works. Teams must have a strong leader who acts as a conductor and facilitator.

Berendt, Robert J. and Taft, J. Richard, *How to Rate Your Development Office: A Fund-Raising Primer for the Chief Executive,* Taft Corporation, 1983.

A "how to" book dealing with all aspects of traditional fundraising for non-profits including the type of person to hire for the development job, how to structure a development office, the role of the board of directors, and evaluating your development office (including return on investment analysis). The book has a list of common questions and answers at the end.

Binney, George and Williams, Colin, *Leaning into the Future: Changing the Way People Change Organizations,* Nichols Bealey Publishing, 1997.

Leaders in the current environment need superior listening skills as well as the ability to speak frankly and openly with all levels of the organization. Leaders lead change by demonstrating to their organizations that they also can and will change and making clear to everyone in the organization the nature and extent of the needed change. Changing organizations requires encouraging people at all levels to take the initiative in the change process and supporting them in taking that initiative.

Blackwell, Roger D., *From Mind to Market: Reinventing the Retail Supply Chain,* HarperBusiness, New York, 1997.

With most companies being able to produce goods of high quality at a reasonable price, excellence will become standard in terms of customer service and quality of goods and services. Competitive advantage will come from superior knowledge of customer wants, desires and future needs. While management of supply chains is essential to produce and distribute goods and services effectively and efficiently, the management of the demand chain will become a central practice of tomorrow. Organizations will be better able to mass customize products and services tailoring them to specific target groups in the population with differing demand characteristics. In addition, businesses will seek, have access to and analyze larger and larger amounts of data regarding consumers, their spending patterns, their decision-making patterns and their preferences.

Blanchard, Kenneth and Johnson, Spencer, *The One Minute Manager: The Quickest Way to Increase Your Own Prosperity*, Berkley Books, New York, 1982.
There are important management tasks that can be done in one minute including giving praise, setting goals and reprimands. It is important to be in regular communication with those you manage and to take the time to show that you care deeply about those you manage.

Boyett, Joseph and Boyett, Jimmie, *The Guru Guide: The Best Ideas of the Top Management Thinkers*, John Wiley & Sons, Inc., New York, 1998.
The ideas of 79 "gurus" are described in this book that focuses on leadership, learning organizations, managing change, pursuit of market leadership, managing and motivating people, teamwork and "business, work and society."

Bradford, David L, *Power Up: Transforming Organizations Through Shared Leadership*, John Wiley & Sons, Inc., 1998.
High-growth strategies in organizations require the competencies of many people and sharing leadership broadly brings these competencies to the top and builds sustainable growth strategies.

Lawlor, Edward E. III, Mohrman, Susan A. Legdford, Gerald E., Jr. *Strategies for High Performance Organizations – The CEO Report: Employee Involvement, TQM and Reengineering Programs in Fortune 1000 Corporations*, Jossey-Bass, San Francisco, 1998.
Employee involvement in all aspects of the process is identified as a part of a well developed high performance strategy. However, many organizations do not have a high degree of employee involvement in key decisions affecting the organization and the work of the employees. Most companies rate their TQM and reengineering efforts as being successful.

Brandenburger, Adam M. and Malebuff, Barry J., *Co-Opetition: A Revolutionary Mindset that Combines Competition and Cooperation – The Game Theory Strategy That's Changing the Game of Business*, Doubleday, 1996.
The authors from the Harvard School of Business and the Yale School of Management describe the conceptual framework and practical side of how competitors are now working together and can work together in the future to be more successful in business. This book which applies equally to the non-profit world and the world of educational institutions shows how to cooperate with suppliers, customers, competitors, complementors (forming buying coalitions) and forming long term relationships that bring value to both partners. The book has many examples from high tech organizations and others of working together in ways that add to the "value net" of both organizations. Individuals and organizations seeking to cooperate should be very clear from the beginning about the expected benefits of the arrangement and the value added that each partner brings to the business proposition.

Breakout Creativity: Bringing Creativity to the Workplace, edited by Rick Crandall, Association for Innovation in Management, 1998.

A compilation of short essays on intellectual capital, whole brain approaches to organizational development, brainstorming, using visual imagery, humor, putting creativity in sales and the use of mental models to unleash creativity. The book emphasizes planning, participation by a wide range of members of an organization and the devotion of significant time at work in collective pursuit of creative solutions to business problems.

Byham, William C. and Cox, Jeff, *Zapp!: The Lightning of Empowerment – How to Improve Quality, Productivity and Employee Satisfaction,* Ballantine Books, 1988.

A story book which presents the concept of "zapping" employees by creating at the workplace an attitude among employees that they "own their jobs," they are responsible decision makers, their work is important both to the company and to themselves and that they are cared about deeply by management and other employees. The book gives examples of how productivity and employee satisfaction rises greatly in organizations that place great emphasis on these principles.

Carver, John and Carver, Miriam M., *Reinventing Your Board: A Step by Step Guide to Implementing Policy Governance.* Jossey-Bass, San Francisco, 1997.

A detailed presentation of the role of a board of directors and specific measures an organization can use to improve or reinvent a board of directors. boards of directors serve as representatives the members and the public at large being served by the non-profit. Boards must hold officers of the organization accountable for the organization achieving success in pursuit of its vision.

Carver, John. *Boards That Make a Difference: A New Design for Leadership in Non-Profit and Public Organizations,* Jossey-Bass, San Francisco, 1990.

This book defines the job of the board of directors and the documents that a board should generate. The book presents a theoretical and practical view of a board member's duties for both the governance of an organization and the results the organization produces.

Carver, John, *Strategies for Board Leadership,* Jossey-Bass, San Francisco, 1997.

Board talent and energy is usually wasted. Boards need to be forward thinking, value generating and leadership organizations. Boards should be focused on increasing the human capital of an organization, take a lead role in developing and monitoring strategic plans, look out for the interests of the customer, be innovative and seek constant improvement in organizational governance and performance.

Celebrate Customer Service: Insider Secrets, edited by Rick Cranfield, Select Press, Corte Madera, CA., 1999.

This series of articles by Dr. Joan E. Cassidy, Ed.D. and others focuses on such topics as cross-cultural customer service, customer service training, analyzing the value of customer service, internal customer service, creating a customer service culture, on line customer service and implementing a quality service model inside organizations.

Chapman, Gary and Rhodes, Lodis, *Nurturing Neighborhood Nets,* Technology Review, Volume 100, Number 7, Oct. 1997, pp. 48–54.

Free terminals have been placed in low income areas in Austin and training is supplied in order to promote access by low income people to computers, create and promote networks among low income people, other individuals, organizations and institutions and to enhance neighborhood effectiveness in policing and other community services. This effort is designed also to increase public participation in civic activities and policy making. Austin, Texas is a high-growth area, especially in the high tech area and this effort is designed to address the technology gap developing between high income and low income people in the Austin area.

Charan, Ram, *Boards at Work: How Corporate Boards Create Competitive Advantage,* Jossey-Bass, San Francisco, 1998.

Corporate boards in the past have been an untapped source of competitive advantage for organizations. Boards now assist organizations by identifying opportunities, scanning the external environment, establishing goals and evaluating CEO's. Boards in some innovative companies perform rigorous self-evaluations, are change agents for the organization and constantly seek to improve themselves by adding talented, interested, hard working new board members.

Clutterbuck, David and Dearlove, Des, *The Interim Manager: A New Career Model for the Experienced Manager,* Financial Times, Pitman Publishing, 1998.

This book describes the roles, experience and career path of the interim manager who is hired for a specified period of time to assist a company. It identifies the salaries and personal characteristics of leading interim managers, and is designed to assist persons in joining the increasing ranks of people working in this manner.

Messick, David M. and Tenbrunse, Ann E. *Codes of Conduct: Behavioral Research Into Business Ethics.* Russell Sage Foundation, New York, 1996.

Ethics is a good business practice. Long-term financial gains and stability far outweigh any short-term gains that can be realized by unethical behavior. Other gains in employee morale, customer loyalty, strategic alliance opportunities and improved organizational coherence make ethics a high-growth strategy.

Cohan, Peter S. *The Technology Leaders: How America's Most Profitable High-Tech Companies Innovate Their Ways to Success,* Jossey-Bass, San Francisco, 1997.

These companies use entrepreneurial leadership attracting smart, energetic people, infusing the environment with a clear sense of the company's mission and values, promote communications, reward exemplary performance and have a humanistic approach to employees. In addition, these companies seek to be industry leaders in high-growth industries, keep abreast of customer needs and new technologies on the horizon. These companies include broad segments of people and technology to create products that produce superior value for customers. High-tech companies select out key customers who are early adopters of technology and learn from them about customer needs. High-tech companies innovate in a disciplined manner. They invest in enhancing organizational learning, estimate the success of each innovation prior to significant expenditures of capital, uses a portfolio (asset allocation) approach to allocate risk of wasted innovation dollars and focus the entire organization in the direction of learning how to learn more quickly and efficiently than its competition.

Collins, James C. and Porras, Jerry I., *Built to Last: Successful Habits of Visionary Companies,* HarperBusiness, 1994.

Many visionary companies make their best decisions using experimentation rather than complex planning. Visionary companies see themselves as their major competition and benchmark their success against their past success and their expected future success. Core values of visionary companies are never compromised.

Conner, Daryl, *Managing at the Speed of Change,* Villard, 1993 and Conner, Daryl, *Leading at the Edge of Chaos: How to Create the Nimble Organization,* John Wiley & Sons, Inc., 1998.

The pace of change is so fast now that organizations must be flexible and nimble to respond to market opportunities. Organizations must be adaptive and managers must introduce enough change to keep up with and lead the competition, but not too much change to overwhelm the organization and throw it into chaos. In order to be adaptive and nimble, organizations need to be consciously competent, they need to know that what they are doing is right and reflect this action in writing, in processes and in the ability to teach others in the organization. Organizations must document their insights on a daily basis and communicate it throughout the organization so that everyone will benefit daily from knowledge gained and insight derived from someone in the organization.

Contingent Work: American Employment Relations in Transition, edited by Kathleen Barker and Kathleen Christensen, ILR Press/Cornell U. Press, Ithaca, New York, 1998.

Contingent workers are workers actually on a temporary assignment or that are "hired" by a third party organization and leased to the organization where they work. Estimates of the number of contingent workers is between 5% and 29% of the workforce depending on the estimation methodology. The book makes the argument that many contingent workers are not as well off, economically and psychologically as they would be if they had full time traditionally structured jobs.

Costa, John Della, *The Ethical Imperative: Why Moral Leadership is Good Business,* Addison-Wesley, Reading, MA, 1998.

As reputation grows in importance for entrepreneurial success to be sustainable, new business models are being developed to guide businesses. John Della Costa's model includes 1) promoting strategic clarity; 2) integrity; 3) respecting dignity; 4) honoring the environment; 5) being fair; and 6) no discrimination. Since trust is becoming so important in virtual teams and in the networking world, it is essential to understand that trusting companies attract trusting people and partners. Further, Costa asserts that a trusting work environment fuels creativity and is more responsive to change.

Crainer, Stuart, *The Ultimate Book of Business Gurus: 110 Thinkers Who Really Made A Difference,* American Management Association, New York, 1998.

Short discussions of leading business thinkers in the 20th century.

Crandall, N. Frederick and Wallace, Marc J. Jr., *Work & Rewards in the Virtual Workplace: A "New Deal" for Organizations and Employees*, American Management Association, New York, 1998.

The new deal suggests that employers focus on the processes that are central to the organization's mission and structure job roles around these processes instead of thinking of fitting job descriptions in an organizational chart. The new deal also suggests a new sense of mutual accountability of employers and employees. Improvements in training, increases in human capital of the work force, compensation systems built on some measure of the economic value added to the enterprise by each employee and the expansion of the use of teams are all suggested by the authors.

Cranfield, Jack and Miller, Jacqueline, *Heart at Work: Stories and Strategies for Building Self-Esteem and Reawakening the Soul at Work*, McGraw-Hill, 1996.

A large selection of stories that focus on the key role that promotion and development of self-esteem plays in the improvement and building of successful organizations. A key focus of the book is that self-esteem of each member of the organization is, in part, the organization's responsibility and suggests nurturing self-esteem is a key element in not only humanizing management practices, but improving their contribution to the bottom line success of an organization.

Creech, Bill, *The Five Pillars of TQM: How to Make Total Quality Management Work For You*, TrumanTalley Books/Dutton, 1994.

This book calls for dramatic improvement in management of American businesses using the TQM approach. This approach is an organizational-wide quality assessment strategy focusing on the product/service, the organization, the processes used by the organization, the commitment to quality and the quality of leadership in an organization. The book provides many examples of businesses deploying TQM and achieving substantial improvements throughout their organizations. TQM is based on an organization undertaking several fundamental actions as part of the early stage TQM process. First, the character and culture of the organization must be firmly established and communicated throughout the organization. Second, employees must be involved through a decentralized approach that seeks a clear understanding of the marketplace environment as well as knowing what motivates employees to build commitment to the highest quality and productivity possible. Third, employees should be given ownership status and decision-making authority. Fourth, small teams will be the organizing principles of the future. Fifth, focus should be on product quality not on the internal aspects/inputs or minutia to produce the item or service. Sixth, results should be measured including the quality and productivity of your organization. Seventh, the marketplace and the customer should be known and strong customer alliances and linkages should be created. Eighth, promote pride in your organization. Ninth, provide focused, appropriate and ample training to employees at all levels. Tenth, promote strong communication flow in your organization. Eleventh, create a holistic team with all involved sharing a common purpose and vision of the organization.

Cruikshank, Jeffrey L. and Sicilia, David B., *The Engine that Could: 75 Years of Values-Driven Change at Cummins Engine Company*, Harvard Business School Press, Boston, 1997.

Organizational competence is defined as "know-how" at all levels of the organization. Embracing change is one of the keys to success for Cummins. Cummins broadly defines the word stakeholders to include the community, labor, government, vendors, distributors and customers and emphasizes building relationships with all stakeholders. Cummins emphasizes the importance of having clear value systems to guide stakeholders in making key decisions. He also emphasizes long-term relationships with employees and planning carefully for succession of leadership.

Daft, Richard L. and Lengel, Robert H., *Fusion Leadership. Unlocking the Subtle Forces That Change People and Organizations*, Berrett-Koehler, San Francisco 1998.

Change occurs most successfully in an organization when all levels in the heirarchy work together and "fuse" and every department and level in the organization changes simultaneously. This fusion can only result from creating connections within the organization, sharing information, open and honest communication and joint agreement by individuals at all levels to be responsible for organization wide change.

Davenport, Thomas H. and Prusak, Laurence, *Working Knowledge: How Organizations Manage What They Know*, Harvard Business School Press, Boston, 1998.

Sustainable competitive advantage comes from what an organization knows collectively. Smart organizations manage knowledge so that each person in need of information can access it quickly and each person can add to the store of knowledge on a daily basis. Knowledge is becoming the new inventory of many businesses. Companies have chief knowledge officers and focus on both sides of the coin – having a knowledge-based culture and profiting from the sale of the knowledge of the organization and its members. Knowledge management, to be successful in an organization, should start with collecting, organizing and disseminating high value knowledge in a focused pilot project using technology to make the process work smoothly for as many people as possible.

Davis, Bob and Wessel, David, *Prosperity: The Coming 20-Year Boom and What it Means for You*, Times Books, New York, 1998.

High-growth strategies will benefit from the increasing reliance on community colleges to educate and train our workforce. Globalization will produce cheaper and better goods and contribute to an increase in worldwide productivity.

Davis, Stan and Botkin, Jim, *The Monster Under the Bed: How Business is Mastering the Opportunity of Knowledge for Profit*, Simon & Schuster, 1994.

Electronic education is revolutionizing the education industry. Industry need for constantly retrained workers and new learning annually has extended the education marketplace to lifetime learning. Schools must become more businesslike to improve and there is a significant problem in these efforts promoting inequality in learning and opportunity.

Davis, Stan and Meyer, Christopher, *Blur, The Speed of Change in the Connected Economy*, Addison-Wesley, Reading, MA, 1998.

The distinction between products and services is being erased. Economic webs are blurring the lines between organizations and what used to be considered valuable. Capital assets, are now often viewed in the new economy as liabilities. The book suggests that companies focus on intangible asset growth, connect with everything they can, always link products with services and services with products, use the Internet to the fullest with e-commerce, promote branding and stimulate freshness in their organizations and their products and services. In addition, the book calls for careful analysis of one's economic environment and gathering and analyzing information from every sale, every customer contact, every internal problem faced in the organization and every opportunity imaginable. The book recommends partnering, suggests massive deregulation of the economy and to strive to capture the attention of people and markets.

Davis, Stan, *Future Perfect*, Addison-Wesley, 1997.

Organizations must manage in anticipation of the future and not merely be reactive.

de Geus, Arie, *The Living Company*. Harvard Business School Press, Boston, 1997.

There is great waste when companies die prematurely since the life expectancy of a company is only 40–50 years. Successful companies are learning organizations, are conservative with their capital and are living organisms that exist for their own survival and to fulfill their potential.

Dees, J. Gregory, *Enterprising Non-profits*, in Harvard Business Review, Jan-Feb, 1998.

Linking up with for-profit organizations to generate revenue can backfire. Non-profit organizations must craft their entrepreneurial strategies carefully taking into consideration their cultures, their socially oriented mission and organizational capacity. The author recommends a social enterprise spectrum to aid non-profits in commercialization. Accepting grants from the government is one way to commercialize operations as is creating a business owned by the non-profit. Corporations are giving money based not only on the merits of the non-profit's programs, but also based on the value (marketing, reputation, employee involvement, etc.) of the relationship. Market-based funding will rise in the non-profit world. Non-profits can also explore third party payment options, contracting for services, advertising revenues (endorsements) and co-branding. The key question non-profits must ask is "how can they create value" for someone or some company or institution that is willing to pay. All revenue generating activities of non-profits should be mission related.

DiBella, Anthony J. and Nevis, Edwin C. *How Organizations Learn: An Integrated Strategy for Building Learning Capacity*, Jossey-Bass, San Francisco, 1998.

Learning is the result of deliberative, strategically planned effort. Learning organizations must develop competence in enhancing factors in the employee's environment that promote learning, promote the rapid and regular use of what is learned, promote change and development to allow for the learning to have a maximum impact and a clear understanding of how learning takes place. Learning strategies must be developed, implemented, assessed and revised. A certain percentage of gross revenues should be applied to learning programs.

Dible, Donald M., *Up Your Own Organization: A Handbook for the Employed, the Unemployed and the Self-Employed on How to Start and Finance a new Business,* Entrepreneur Press, 1971.

A study of entrepreneurship both within organizations and by individuals. The book guides the reader through the business planning process, recruitment of partners and employees, use of consultants, training and educational programs, paid and unpaid advisers, copyright protection and developing a solid reputation. The book also suggests 40 sources of money for entrepreneurial activities and has checklists for new businesses.

Downes, Larry and Mui, Chunka, *Unleashing the Killer App: Digital Strategies for Market Dominance,* Harvard Business School Press. 1998.

A "killer app" is a new product/service that dominates a market. In fact, it can "create" a new market. Since the digital world is changing so quickly, strategic plans can now only run 12–18 months rather than the traditional 3–5 year time frame. This book recommends that organizations unleash new products that will destroy the markets for their old products.

Doz, Yves L. and Hamel, Gary,. *Alliance Advantage: The Art of Creating Value Through Partnering,* Harvard Business School Press, Boston, 1998.

It is now essential for companies to plan and execute a strategy of partnering with many other companies to take advantage of economic opportunities. Competitors are becoming allies, partners share information, resources, strategic plans and implementation programs on a seamless basis. One of the advantages of partnering is that it allows the partners to create and combine insight and it promotes learning at a faster level and at a broader level than would be possible without the partner. A key to making partnering successful is the management of numerous alliances, the power relationships and the allocation of rewards. The new emphasis on partnering is the logical result of identifying economic value (a value proposition) in each alliance, and in the network of alliances, that organizations cannot create quite quickly and support quite economically on their own.

Drucker, Peter F, *The Discipline of Innovation,* in Harvard Business Review, Nov.-Dec., 1998, pp 149–157.

Most innovations are not the result of pure serendipity. They result from a conscious search for "innovation opportunities." Demographics, rapid changes in industries, changes in perception (which alter meaning) and new knowledge are sources of innovation opportunities in addition to chance occurrences that are deftly exploited by persons in tune with market needs. Often it takes advances in more than one type of knowledge to create innovation since market knowledge and technological knowledge are often both essential elements in innovation. An innovation should be simple, focused, start small and have a clear application. One seeking innovation must seek to become the true standard setter, the industry leader, the new market, the directional beacon or else the innovation is "unlikely to be innovative enough."

Drucker, Peter, *Peter Drucker on the Profession of Management,* Harvard Business School Press, Boston, 1998.

This collection of essays has a section on "What Business Can Learn From Non-Profits." It makes suggestions for board improvement, reduction of layers of management, outsourcing, making information powerful and states that in this post-capitalist era executives are responsible for their own career development. Drucker is concerned with underpopulation of the labor market age group in developing countries and believes that productivity improvements in the future will be the result of improvements in the area of knowledge work and knowledge workers.

Gerber, Michael, *E-Myth Revisited,* HarperCollins, 1995.

Focusing on small businesses this book suggests creating a full organizational chart and outlining all of the tasks required for success in any business. The key to success is developing a systems approach to each task, allocating each task appropriately and setting the goal of having the business operate successfully without the original business owner being involved. The book points out that many entrepreneurs are owned by the business rather than owning the business and they work for the business, but the business does not work for them. Numerous strategies are determined to be essential for the business including: people strategy, operations strategy, learning strategy, management strategy, expansion strategy and others.

Earning Curve, in Entreprenuer Magazine, December, 1998, pp 63–65.

Entrepreneurship programs are growing on college campuses. Universities are becoming more successful in helping companies get started, grow, raise capital, improve management, identify market niches and develop strategic planning processes.

Ehrbar, Al, *EVA: The Real Key to Creating Wealth,* John Wiley & Sons, Inc., 1998.

Based on the work of Miller and Modigliani, the book proposes a new measure to replace the "inaccurate" terms "profit" and "earnings." EVA or Economic Value Added is a measure of the returns produced by a business, or division within a business, that takes into account the cost of all sources of capital. EVA=NOPAT-C%(TC) or Economic Value Added equals Net Operating Profits less the percentage cost of capital times the Total Capital used in the activity. This system seeks to capture the concept of "opportunity cost" and seeks to reward those elements that produce economic value added. Part of the EVA system of management provides incentives for employees and gives them uncapped bonuses based on economic value added. The EVA system suggests that the current way employees are paid involves too high a base or fixed level and too low a variable or bonus level. The system also recommends deferring the pay of some of the bonus amount to assure that one period's EVA is not overstated and corrected by a following period's adjustment where the EVA is much smaller or negative.

Enhancing Organizational Performance, edited by Daniel Druckman, Jerome Singer and Harold Van Cott, National Academy Press, Washington, 1997.

Organizations must be consciously aware of their business environment and the context in which they seek to survive and grow. Organizational change is a finely tailored process and, given the fast-paced economy, often research on organizational change cannot keep up with changes in practice. At present, the authors conclude that both the research base and theoretical framework in the field of organizational performance are in their infancy. The Committee could not draw any conclusions [based on scientific evidence] regarding what works and what does not work in enhancing organizational performance.

Evaluating with Power: A New Approach to Organizational Effectiveness, Empowerment and Excellence, edited by Sandra Trice Gray, Jossey-Bass, San Francisco, 1998.

Proper evaluation systems should be ongoing and built into the operations of non-profits. Evaluations should be part of an organizational learning strategy and improvement strategy and can be performed by internal actors to promote self-accountability.

Fine, Charles H., *Clockspeed: Winning Industry Control in the Age of Temporary Advantage.* Perseus Books, Reading, MA 1998.

Time has become an essential element in high-growth strategies. The ability of computer companies to "obsolete" their products in less than one year is funneling growth in this industry. The management and the design of the "supply chain" are the most important competencies of high-growth firms. There must be a fit between the design of the product, the design of the processes to manufacture, market and support the product and the design of the supply chain to insure all elements are in place for high growth.

Finnie, William, *Strategic Partnering: Three Case Studies,* in Strategy and Leadership, Sept.-Oct., 1998.

Organizations must identify the breakthrough opportunity or contribution that a potential strategic partner will make before making the alliance. Since the costs of these alliances is high, the rewards must be very high in order to justify the cost. Alliances can combine superior technology, access to raw materials, intellectual property or business processes, distribution systems, workforce capabilities, managerial talent and many other attributes of two or more organizations (or individuals) to promote increased or improved business or organizational practices. In the research for an alliance partner, a partner profile of a potential partner must be developed in depth in order to assure compatibility. Each alliance needs an improvement plan operating at the individual and organizational level from the very beginning. Every alliance must be based on a clear conception of what the customer is looking for and the alliance must be an effort to serve that customer need with higher quality or at lower cost. All alliances must be based on trust.

Fisher, Kimball and Fisher, Mareen Ducan, *The Distributed Mind: Achieving High Performance Through the Collective Intelligence of Knowledge Work Teams,* American Management Association, New York, 1998.

The effect of an organization that promotes learning and knowledge management is that individuals in the organization are more effective. Knowledge work teams foster the sharing of information and knowledge as tools to construct an environment where creativity is generated and the organization improves its capabilities on a daily basis.

Fitz-enz, Jac, *The 8 Practices of Exceptional Companies: How Great Organizations Make the Most of Their Human Assets,* American Management Association, 1997.

Eight important practices are 1) a constant focus on value and values; 2) commitment to long-term core goals and strategies; 3) design and management of a company's culture; 4) open, honest communication among all stakeholders; 5) partnering with stakeholders and involvement of them early on in the decision-making process; 6) collaborative work places where people from different areas interact and work together; 7) a strong emphasis on innovation and the taking of risks; and 8) a competitive passion where the company views itself as its own competitor and seeks to gather new ideas from every possible source and to make improvements on a regular basis.

Fogg, C. Davis, *Team Based Strategic Planning: A Complete Guide to Structuring, Facilitating and Implementing the Process,* American Management Association, 1994.

Involving all those who will be affected by a change is a key to successful strategic planning. Organizations should set a few high priority strategic objectives and monitor implementation very carefully. Strategic planning must always be focused on the ends/goals and not become a laden process with a goal of merely writing a plan.

Friedman, Lisa and Gyr, Herman, *The Dynamic Enterprise: Tools for Turning Chaos into Strategy and Strategy into Action,* Jossey-Bass, San Francisco, 1998.

Every member of an organization must be included in developing strategy, understanding the changes that are taking place in the market and be able to work together. Employees are empowered when they share the vision of the organization. Strategy must be based on an accurate assessment of where an enterprise is, where the market is and where it is moving to, the structure of the organization and the task at hand to be viable in a market. Strategic planning must take into account the environment and people in the organization to develop the right steps at the right time for the organization.

Future Vision: Ideas, Insights, and Strategies, edited by Howard F. Didsbury, Jr., World Future Society, 1996.

A compilation of articles focusing on the future of work, education, management, ecological sustainability, globalization and medical ethics.

Gans, Rabbi Moshe, *Success: Bringing Out the Best in Yourself and Others,* Mesnorah Publications, Ltd., 1996.

A synthesis of many ancient hebrew teachings that focus on how (and why) individuals and organizations can be more successful. The book presents a combination of positive thinking approaches, problem solving techniques and strategies derived from hebrew texts designed to promote self and organizational esteem, motivation and improved productivity and customer/self-satisfaction.

Gates, Bill, *The Road Ahead,* Penguin, 1996.

Gates maps out ideas for new technology and states that technology will become a very important platform upon which new education, training and learning will occur both inside and outside of the workplace and classroom.

Gates, Jeff, *The Ownership Solution: Toward a Shared Capitalism for the 21st Century,* Addison-Wesley, Reading, MA 1998.

Through employee stock option plans and other means a company can finance its operations internally, can promote improved employee productivity, morale and longevity and encourage employers to view employees as more important stakeholders in the business enterprise. Employee ownership will likely promote employees providing constructive feedback to management and improving customer service.

Golden Arches East: McDonald's in East Asia, edited by James L. Watson, Stanford University Press, 1997.

McDonalds adapts its local stores in other cultures to suit local circumstances. While the basic system and values stay in place, the store will take on new roles suggested by local communities including being youth clubs and leisure centers.

Goldman, Steven L., Nagel, Roger N., and Preiss, Kenneth, *Agile Competitors and Virtual Organizations: Strategies for Enriching the Customer,* Van Nostram Reinholm, 1995.

The book suggests that in 1995 there was a new emerging order to business structure and dynamics. The authors identify the key attributes of virtual organizations as opportunism, excellence, technology, open borders and trust among all participants. The authors provide over 100 examples of organizations, virtual and more traditional, focusing on their ability to change and adapt rapidly to changing market demand. The book presents an "Agility Audit."

Goleman, Daniel, *Emotional Intelligence,* Bantum Books, 1995:

and Goleman, Daniel, *What Makes A Leader,* in Harvard Business Review, Nov.-Dec. 1998, pp 93–102.

The five components of emotional intelligence are: self-awareness, self-regulation, motivation/enthusiasm/passion, empathy and social skills. Emotional intelligence is increased through proper training, practice and feedback. As relationship management increases in value in business, social skills and empathy will increase in value.

Gomes-Casseres, Benjamin, *Do You Really Have An Alliance Strategy?* in Strategy and Leadership Forum, Sept.-Oct., 1998.

Alliances succeed or fail based on the soundness of the strategy upon which they are built. An alliance strategy must be completely integrated with the organization's business strategy. Every alliance should have a clear path to development and exit, with clear goals, responsibilities, management, leadership and support. Groupware and other tools promoting communication are essential for success. All alliances must be calendar and plan driven. Alliances should be created on a portfolio basis with each type of alliance clearly structured, identified in its position relative to other alliances and allocated certain duties and responsibilities consistent with its position within the overall alliance structure created by your organization. Alliance partner selection requires an analysis of each partner's values, capabilities and goals.

Gore, Al and Rubin, Robert, *Reinventing Service at the IRS,* National Performance Review, US Government, 1997.

A description of key roles and attributes designed to change the way the IRS treats people and businesses in the US. Introducing the notion that the taxpayer is the customer, this book focuses on improving services to IRS customers, tracking data on complaints, creating a balanced scorecard and treating employees of the IRS better by providing better training, improving the service culture of the IRS, creating family friendly workplaces and hiring the right people for the right jobs.

Gore, Albert with Adams Scott. *Businesslike Government,* National Performance Review, US Government, 1997.

Using a humorous approach the book urges the federal government of the US to become more customer oriented, technologically fit, change-ready and willing to enter into strategic partnerships with other agencies and with businesses to become more efficient and effective.

Gross, Bill. *The New Math of Ownership.* Harvard Busiess Review, Nov.-Dec. 1998, pp.68–74.

It is in everyone's interest for employees to act like owners, taking responsibility for the ultimate success or failure of an organization. In order to get them to act like owners it is important that employees own a significant portion of the company.

Grove, Andrew, *Only the Paranoid Survive,* Doubleday, 1996.

The Chairman of Intel describes how his corporation analyzes the marketplace and how it develops strategies to be the leader in the chip industry. Presenting the concept of the strategic inflection point, where the rate of change in an industry changes dramatically, Grove says that a "strategic picture" changes at certain times in every industry and to be a leader one must attempt to figure out, before anyone else, when this change will occur and what direction the change will take. Leadership in an industry is acting before you know exactly where the industry is going, because by the time you figure it out exactly, the leadership opportunity will have gone. The title comes from Grove's point of view that every business person must be wary of the business environment, keep the organization's collecitive eyes open to competition, changing business dynamics and move swiftly to counter potentially negative changes in the environment and within your own organization.

Grundy, Tony, *Breakthrough Strategies for Growth: Delivering Sustainable Corporate Expansion*, Financial Times Pitman Publishing, London, 1995.

An MBA textbook that provides an in depth look at key strategic tools for the corporation. The book defines "breakthrough strategies" and discusses the role of strategic management. Chapters focus on defining strategy, explaining strategic tools, acquisitive growth factors, international strategies and through case studies and examples show how strategic planning pays dividends in corporate decision making.

Grundy, Tony, *Exploring Strategic Financial Management*, Prentice Hall, 1998.

A textbook for linking strategic and financial issues, covering organic and acquisitive development, managing for value and strategic cost management.

Grundy, Tony, *Strategic Behavior*, Financial Times Pitman Publishing, London, 1998:

A research based study from British Telecom of how top team behavior influences strategy making and implementation. The book shows how cognitition and human emotions work through personal and political agendas to shape strategy. The book introduces powerful diagnostic techniques for identifying how strategic behavior can be harnessed and channeled.

Hagel, John and Armstrong, Arthur G., *Net Gain: Expanding Markets Through Virtual Communities*, Harvard Business School Press, Boston, 1997.

A new net-based business model is developed, marketing and servicing virtual communities where people perceive themselves to be members, share trust and commitment and form both marketing opportunities and employee/production opportunities. The book discusses ways to create a virtual community using a gardening metaphor where one seeds, feeds and weeds the community. The book also discusses the technology employed and how numerous industries will be reshaped by this new model.

Halal, William E., Jull, Michael D. and Laffman, Ann, *The George Washington University Forecast of Emerging Technologies: A Continuous Assessment of the Technology Revolution*, in Technological Forecasting & Social Change, Vol. 59, No. 1, 1998, pp 89–110.

85 emerging technologies are tracked with the information revolution taking the lead among the technologies over the next several years.

Hamel, Gary and Prahlald, C.K., *Competing for the Future*, Harvard Business School Press, 1994.

Organizations must successfully predict where a market is headed and seek to dominate the competitive space. Employees are encouraged to create stretch goals and to attempt to go beyond what they believe are their capabilities. Resources must be leveraged to secure maximum value and be used in accordance with the vision of how the future of the industry is to unfold. The blueprint for winning the future relies on strategic architecture that promotes intelligence gathering about the future and quick response to that insight. Strategic planning departments that become slow, too ponderous and too detailed in their focus should be disbanded. In order for an organization to see the future clearly, all of its levels must be sources of valuable information that will promote a collective wisdom.

Hammer, Michael, *Beyond Reengineering: How the Process-Centered Organization is Changing Our Work and Our Lives*, HarperBusiness, 1996.
A process is a complete set of activities that creates value. To improve an organization's performance all processes must come under scrutiny. Reinvention of the processes, their management and implementation is necessary to secure the highest improvement in organizational capacity and capability. Managers must be open in their inquiry, look to see how all of the processes connect and form a complex system.

Handy, Charles, *Understanding Organizations,* Oxford University. Press, New York, 1993.
Organizations will have the capability to disperse knowledge among workers and management, pay fees for performance rather than salaries. Quality is the new focus in service and products. Outsourcing will make organizations appear "federal" with a small core and many semi-autonomous groups dispersed geographically and experimentation will be used more and more as change increases in speed.

Hartwick, P.J. and Farren, Caela, *Specialist or Generalist? A False Dichotomy: An Important Distinction in Future Vision: Ideas, Insights and Strategies*, edited by Howard F. Didsbury Jr., World Future Society, 1996 pp115–132.
A task oriented specialist focuses on one area. A generalist links together knowledge and information from many areas. The business generalist has prevailed over the past several decades because when we immerse ourselves in a topic of complexity, (such as strategic planning which combines an assessment of the external and internal environments, assumptions about human behavior and the future) we actually build brain tissue. The brain establishes a "knowledge network" which benefits the generalist in other areas as well. Thus, our movement to "knowledges" (Drucker) and knowledge management (everybody) will have the advantage of improving the ability to learn. Learning will be the key to the creativity necessary to take the static and dynamic tools of strategic planning and combine the tools and results of this discipline with the ability to innovate, improvise and intelligently experiment for entrepreneurial success.

Henton, Douglas, Melville, John and Walesh, Kimberly, *Grassroots Leaders for a new Economy: How Civic Entrepreneurs Are Building Prosperous Communities*, Jossey-Bass, San Francisco, 1997.
Collaborative communities are formed and supported by teams of civic entrepreneurs promoting high-growth strategies through creating strong strategic alliances. Civic entrepreneurs should be recognized, future ones should be trained in civic entrepreneurship, corporations should become a part of civic entrepreneurship and non-profit organizations should focus on starting and supporting

civic entrepreneurship. The model of networking represents a great potential for jump starting a low income area toward economic and social revitalization.

Hiam, Alexander, *Obstacles to Creativity and How You Can Remove Them, in "The Futurist"*, Vol.32, No. 7, Oct. 1998, pp 30–34.

This article lists errors that individuals and organizations make that hinder creativity. One error, failure to record ideas, is a problem that modern day knowledge management systems are designed to address. A second error, failure to ask questions or do adequate research suggests the importance of promoting open communication among all employees, members and stakeholders in organizations.

Hirschhorn, Larry, *Reworking Authority: Leading and Following in the Post-Modern Organization*, MIT Press, Cambridge, MA 1997.

Organizations must build greater openness in communication. Today, this is becoming more practical and employee-centric organizations can be valuable safety nets for employees.

Hope, Jeremy and Hope, Tony, *Competing in the Third Wave: The Ten Key Management Issues of the Information Age*, Harvard Business School Press, Boston, 1997.

Learning how to define and acquire knowledge and how to learn are critical components for companies today. Organize around processes and networks rather than traditional layers of bureaucracy. It is essential to create customer capital-loyalty and profitability through providing superior value for strategic customers. Organizations should measure intellectual assets by changing components of their accounting system since intellectual assets are the true source of wealth. Workers should be empowered, not controlled. Future management of education and training of employees and management should be undertaken after careful questioning of the knowledge needs of the organization and the probability that the considered education or training program will successfully address that knowledge or skill need.

Hopkins, Bruce R, *The Law of Tax Exempt Organizations*, Fifth Edition, John Wiley & Sons, Inc. 1987.

A thorough review of the laws of non-profit organizations. This text book catalogues all of the different types of non-profit organizations and includes a section on tax exempt organizations and for-profit subsidiaries. The book also discusses how charitable organizations are becoming more innovative and entrepreneurial and how combinations of organizations, some non-profit and some for-profit are springing up. The author suggests "it is becoming more commonplace, is not frequently essential, for a tax-exempt organization to utilize a for-profit, taxable subsidiary." The book concludes with a look to the future where the author suggests that Toffler's analysis in *The Third Wave* is accurate in that this sector will have an expanded role in the future.

Howe, Fisher, *The Board Member Guide to Strategic Planning*, Jossey-Bass, San Francisco, 1997.

An indepth look at how members of the board of directors can participate and govern the strategic planning process of organizations.

Igbaria, Madid and Tan, Magaret, *The Virtual Workplace,* Idea Group Publishing, 1998.

Working at home or being located in different places will all contribute via technology to more and more people working in virtual environments. These teams will require advanced work flow management systems and the development of a process for virtual team work products to be produced on time and on budget. The book also analyzes the use of e-mail between workers as a new form of improved communication.

Imai, Masaaki, *Kaizen: The Key to Japan's Competitive Success,* Random House, 1986.

Kaizen means improvement. It is the driving force in the Japanese economy. It has led to the Japanese making the best products and has supported its export driven economy. The key to kaizen as a management approach is that everyone in an organization and every process in the organization adheres to this concept in every action performed on behalf of the organization. Kaizen is an ongoing process of continuous improvement. Improvement is never questioned. Rather, it is a given that everything and every process can always be improved and it is the responsibility of everyone associated with an organization to strive for improvement. A key element of kaizen is that the goal of the organization is to serve the customer and therefore improvement in service to the customer is the essential improvement desired by everyone associated with the organization. Kaizen is a process-oriented thinking approach which holds as its basic principle that if one improves processes, the end product or service will be improved. Kaizen requires substantial attention to and investment in measurement (data collection and analysis) as key elements in the improvement process.

Jaworski, Joseph, *Synchronicity: The Inner Path of Leadership,* Berrett Koehler Publishers, 1996.

Written in a biographical format, this book focuses on the inner drives necessary to create a life of leadership. Leadership must provide a shared meaning, a special environment that promotes high energy and intelligence. A key to success is to come from the point of view of possibility. The book also discusses the use of scenario planning at the Royal Dutch Shell Group.

Jones, Edwin R. and Childers, Richard L., *Contemporary College Physics,* 2nd ed., Addison-Wesley, 1993.

Physics text which is a general survey course using a non-calculus approach covering the natural laws and filled with analytical problem solving exercises. This book ties physics with public policy and shows that the study of physics can lead to generalizable insights into other disciplines and areas of interest.

Kao, John, *Jamming: The Art and Discipline of Business Creativity,* HarperBusiness, 1996.

The management of ideas must be raised to a central place in organizations. Creativity audits should be conducted and creativity must be considered an imperative, a must do, for an organization.

Kaplan, Robert S. and Norton, David P., *The Balanced Scorecard: Translating Strategy Into Action*, Harvard Business School Press, Boston, 1996.

This book makes the argument that businesses need to think strategically about what to measure in their operations. The measurement devices and their results become the "balanced scorecard" which is designed based on the vision and strategy of the organization. Understanding what is important to your organization is the starting point of a detailed process presented by the authors for creating a set of measures to capture how well your organization is actually working. The measures provide feedback for improvement, help organizations with their strategic planning and setting of goals and objectives and promote communication both within the organizaition and between the organization's members and departments and the outside environment that will refine and improve the organization's approaches to accomplishing its goals in many areas of its operations including customer satisfaction. The book provides numerous examples and shows how incentives within an organization can be tied to the measured results produced and captured by the organization.

Kawasaki, Guy and Moreno, Michele, *Rules for Revolutionaries: The Capitalist Manifesto for Creating and Marketing New Products and Services*, HarperBusiness, 1999.

This book provides many suggestions on marketing through virtual organizations, collaboration and gives real life examples of mistakes made in business, called "death magnets," and provides suggestions of how to avoid them. The book has an excellent bibliography and is written in a chatty, conversational style, but provides important business strategy information and tactics.

Kehrer, Daniel, *Doing Business Boldly: Essential Lessons in the Art of Taking Intelligent Risks*, Simon and Schuster, 1989.

Focusing on Coca Cola and other examples the author provides a detailed explanation of how to analyze risk, take risk and recover from risks taken that do not work out. The book suggests that the costs of risk should be viewed as investments to learn from rather than sunk costs to put in the loss column. Risk strategy is best carried out by an organization that has a "risk culture." The organizations that embody a risk culture see intelligent risk taking as essential to creating wealth. And they correctly perceive less risk than others when embarking on a potentially successful endeavor. Cultures that support risk support individuals in the organization in taking risks.

Kelly, Kevin, *New Rules for the New Economy: 10 Radical Strategies for a Connected World*, Viking, New York, 1998.

A key source of competitive advantage is being able to coordinate and manage decentralized points of control. With more connections a company's economic returns increase as the value of the network increases exponentially with growth. A connected world requires a new "relationship technology" to enable companies to create successful relationships quickly. Companies should pursue opportunities before efficiencies or cost reduction programs since the returns of going after significant opportunities (high-growth strategies) can be far greater than any cost saving programs.

Kolbe, Kathy, *The Conative Connection*, Addison-Wesley, 1990.

This book describes "conative ability" as the ability to perform a task or accomplish an objective. The book identifies four key characteristics of individuals that guide their behavioral approaches to work and tasks. The four categories are: 1) quick start; 2) fact finder; 3) implementer; and 4) follow-through. The author suggests that knowing what categories best describe you and people in your organization will help the organization assign tasks and work more effectively together. An assessment tool is included in the book for determining which are your dominant characteristics.

Korey, George, *Technique for Strategic Management in Future Vision: Ideas, Insights and Strategies*, edited by Howard F. Didsbury, Jr., pp 182–201. World Future Society, 1996.

Linear Responsibility Charting. This process using charts identifies each task to be performed and shows who has responsibility for 1) gathering information necessary to accomplish the task; 2) analyzing the information; 3) developing the plan of action; 4) making the decision; 5) implementation; 6) evaluation; and 7) changes in the plan based on the evaluation. This procedure shows graphically who is responsible for each key area to be included in a strategic plan. Strategic management not only guides the planning process it sets the timetable and budget for the strategic planning process. The goal of strategic planning is a strategic fit between the organization and the outside environment.

Kraus, Herbert, *Executive Stock Options and Stock Appreciation Rights*, Law Journal Seminars Press, 1998.

A compilation of the conceptual framework behind stock options, the laws, accounting and tax issues dealing with this subject. Sample plans are included regarding each of the major types of stock option, plans currently in use today. This book is updated yearly.

Learning from the Future: Competitive Foresight Scenarios, edited by Liam Fahey and Robert M. Randall, John Wiley & Sons, Inc., New York 1998.

Scenario planning is not a predictive model. Instead it is a guided research and learning model that, once some assumptions are made about the future, people can use to develop their views of how the future will turn out with greater depth and greater value for strategic planning. Scenarios must include a careful analysis of environmental forces and focus on the gathering of knowledge and information around the key decisions that must be made by the organization.

Lett, Christine W., Ryan, William and Grossman, Allen. *Virtuous Capital: What Foundations Can Learn from Venture Capitalists*, in Harvard Business Review, Mar.-Apr. 1997.

Giving money to non-profits only for programs keeps them from building a proper infrastructure to continue to serve people after a big grant runs out. Foundations should pay for overhead costs and should provide management assistance to non-profits much in the way venture capitalists do.

Lewis, Patrick C., *Building A Shared Vision: A Leader's Guide to Aligning the Organization,* Productivity Press, 1997.

This book describes how vision serves as a pulling force that helps organization create alignment. Implementation of a strategy without a vision is much more likely to fail than one inspired by a strong and compelling vision shared by all members of the organization.

Lewis, T.G., *The Friction Free Economy: Marketing Strategies for a Wired World,* HarperBusiness, New York, 1997.

In the new economy, size matters as the more market share you have, the more you get. It is important for a company to stay in the leadership role to improve or change its products so regularly that it makes its own products obsolete. Business in the new economy must use the Internet to the fullest and focus on learning as quickly as possible at all levels of the organization.

Lipnack, Jessica and Stamps, Jeffrey, *Virtual Teams,* John Wiley & Sons, Inc., 1997.

This book describes the concept and technologies of virtual teams and provides guidance on how to make virtual teams productive. Virtual teams take more time to get started and trust is a key factor to breaking the ice. Defining the purpose of the virtual team is critical to success and great attention must be paid to the quality of the technology that is used and the experience received by the team members. The book argues that virtual teams will be more efficient, more productive and will allow for greater globalization of the marketplace than teams that are co-located. Virtual teams allow a company to be open 24 hours a day with the work being shifted from one time zone to another throughout the day.

Little, Charles H., *Investing in Attitude Capital to Improve Service Quality,* in "Future Vision: Ideas, Insights and Strategies", edited by Howard F. Didsbury, Jr., pp.202–212. World Future Society, 1996.

Front-line workers are not in low-skilled jobs. Interaction with the customer is a highly skilled activity. Success in the area of customer service may start with the goal to delight the customer. Attitude Capital is the phrase coined by Charles Little to emphasize the need to train workers in the often neglected area of "attitude," since service provider attitude is one of the strongest determinants of the quality of service provided to the customer. Teaching service skills and attitudes is a never-ending process that we believe can go far in supporting high-growth strategies.

Luke, Jeffrey S., *Catalytic Leadership; Strategies for an Interconnected World,* Josse- Bass, San Francisco, 1998.

Leaders must present multiple strategies and options to decision makers and stakeholders. Leaders must be able to facilitate group learning and create systems where they get information back quickly in order to create and maintain momentum of their projects and make regular course corrections. Future leaders of organizations will more easily share leadership and seek to establish trust among all stakeholders. through integrity and will create a sense of urgency about their projects through creative use of deadlines (like "a man on the moon in this decade").

Lynch, Daniel C. and Lundquist, Leslie, *Digital Money: The New Era of Internet Commerce,* John Wiley & Sons, Inc., 1996.

This book describes on line businesses that can expand with the use of the Internet and focuses on the interrelationship between the Internet and high-growth strategies available on a global basis.

Maccoby, Michael, *Why Work?: Motivating the New Workforce,* 2nd ed., Miles River Press, 1995.

This book examines theories of motivation and describes the "motivating organization" and "motivating leadership." Based on hundreds of interviews, the authors divide managers into five generic types: 1) experts who excel in specialized fields; 2) defenders who operate in large part to keep the rules in place and the status quo from changing too quickly; 3) self-developers who are most concerned with individual growth; 4) helpers who strive to assist others; and 4) innovators who are generalists who promote multidisciplinary approaches to solving problems and implementing solutions. The author suggests that power in society in the late 1900s has shifted from experts to innovators and the key to motivating employees is to make their jobs challenging and to give them the learning opportunities to accomplish success in their jobs.

Mackay, Harve, *Dig Your Well Before You're Thirsty,* Doubleday, 1999.

A series of anecdotal stories that provide the reader with a hands on approach to running a business. The book is based on the strategy of networking as a means of growing your company, your reputation and your ability to create and to respond to opportunities in the marketplace.

Maira, Arun and Scott-Moran, Peter, *The Accelerating Organization: Embracing the Human Face of Change,* McGraw Hill, 1997.

The ability to change quickly, more quickly than competitors, is becoming a source of competitive advantage. In order to change quickly, organizations need 1) strategic flexibility and willingness to change direction in order to achieve organizational goals; 2) readiness to adopt change by all employees, management and the Board; 3) alignment of systems within an organization so that change can be harmonized throughout the organization; 4) involvement of all key employees in the change process; 5) continuous learning and strong infrastructure to support learning.

Manassee, Lori A., *From Organizations to Relationships: New Ways of Working and their Implications for Learning,* in "Futures Research Quarterly", Vol. 13, No. 3, 1997, World Future Society, pp 21–30.

The new paradigm for working includes telecommuting, employee ownership, self-directed work teams, coaching rather than supervising and a renewed emphasis on hiring the right people. Workers will emphasize learning types of jobs and the employee's ties to a company will be lessened as workers work for multiple employers either simultaneously or sequentially over short periods of time.

Marks, Mitchell Lee and Mirvis, Philip H., *Joining Forces: Making One Plus One Equal Three in Mergers, Acquisitions and Alliances,* Jossey-Bass, 1998.

World wide mergers and acquisitions totalled $1 trillion in 1996 and an estimate of the number of alliances world wide was 25,000. In the 1990s in the US there have been 30,000 mergers. 75 percent of these mergers, acquisitions and alliances fail. Strategic planning is required to make a deal a success over the long run. Often M&A's fail due to poor management of the joined enterprise.

Maslach, Christina and Leiter, Michael P., *The Truth About Burnout: How Organizations Cause Personal Stress and What To Do About It*, Jossey-Bass, San Francisco, 1997.

Burnout is caused by the social environment where people have high stress jobs, are accountable for specific results, but are not given discretionary authority to perform their jobs in the manner they deem most appropriate. Burnout affects the bottom line and it is economically more efficient to prevent burn out rather than deal with it at a crisis time. The authors believe that burnout is reaching epidemic proportions and many workers are suffering from high blood pressure due to the work strains and stresses they face.

Matheson, David and Matheson, Jim, *The Smart Organization: Creating Value through Strategic R&D*, Harvard Business School Press, Boston, 1998.

R&D can be haphazard in organizations. It is estimated that through strategic decision making the value creation of R&D can be improved by 20–200 percent. Every R&D program should have a technology strategy, a portfolio strategy (similar to the concept of asset allocation) and a project strategy. Each of these strategies become part of a strategically managed R&D process that can yield both breakthrough results and excellent expected results in a timely and cost-effective manner. R&D decisions must be the result of weighing strategic choices for value and coordination of everyone in the R&D group and management to dialogue to create alignment between R&D and the rest of the organization and to empower the R&D teams to produce world class results.

McCall, Morgan W. Jr., *High Flyers: Developing the Next Generation of Leaders*, Harvard Business School Press, Boston, 1998.

It is the responsibility of management and those in control of the organization's assets to create an environment that strongly supports talent development. Business strategy must be linked with experiences people need in order to learn to lead the company. Leaders are developed, not born. Leadership development must be a strategic priority and careful assessment of competencies and flaws must be made through rigorous research. Organizations should have a formal succession process with internal reports that identify the top and second tier candidates for every key position in the organization.

McCormack, Mark H., *What They Still Don't Teach You at Harvard Business School*, Bantam, 1989.

Advice is given on many areas of business including sales, negotiation, time management, entrepreneurship, acquisitions, management philosophy and working on the road. Practical guides and suggestions filled with anecdotes from the man credited with bringing professional sports to the level it is today.

McIntosh, Malcolm, Leipziger, Deborah, Jones, Keith L. and Coleman, Gill, *Corporate Citizenship: Successful Strategies for Responsible Companies,* Financial Times Pitman Publishing, London, 1998.

Leading edge companies are increasing their contributions because they are seeing the value of their corporate reputation as a key element of competitive advantage. There is now a movement on to create a new global standard for social accountability called "SA 8000."

Miles, Robert H., *Corporate Comeback: The Story of Renewal and Transformation at National Semiconductor,* Jossey-Bass, San Francisco, 1997:
Miles, Robert H., *Leading Corporate Transformation: A Blueprint for Business Renewal,* Jossey-Bass, San Francisco, 1997.

Corporate transformation requires energy and is led by vision. An architecture or design for the change is required and must take into account the total system of the organization. Strategic planning begins with a clear understanding of reality today and how it is likely to evolve. Every vision must be supported by a well-tailored business model. All business models must link current customer needs with market trends and take into account the real competencies of the organization. Renewal activities should begin with a few very focused activities to promote breakthroughs that can validate the approach, create a positive momentum and springboard the organization. Setting expectations and measurement systems to track performance are important to support the implementation of strategies. All strategic planning should be geared to producing the needed changes in the organization without exposing the organization to unacceptable risk. Feedback from all levels in the planning and early in the implementation stage are critical to revising and improving on implementation as it takes place.

Mintzberg, Harvey, *Crafting Strategy,* in "Strategy: Seeking and Securing Competitive Advantage", edited by Cynthia A. Montgomery and Michael E. Porter, Harvard Business Review Books, 1991.

This article discusses how strategy must be crafted rather than planned. The goal of a strategy planning process is to provide a strategic orientation for an organization from which emerging strategies can evolve as the need arises. Every strategy must reconcile the two themes of change and continuity.

Mintzberg, Harvey, Ahlstrand, Bruce and Lasspel, Joseph, *Strategic Safari: A Guided Tour Through the Wilds of Strategic Planning,* Free Press, 1998.

Showing how different schools of thought look at strategy, the book divides the intellectual basis for strategy and strategic planning into twelve areas including strategy as a process of conception, an analytical process, a negotiation process, a visioning process, a cooperative or collective process, a reactive process, an emergent process and a transformational process.

Mitroff, Ian, *Smart Thinking for Crazy Times: The Art of Solving the Right Problems,* Berrett-Koehler, 1998.

Organizations often have too small a set of stakeholders to assist them in formulating their problem and participating in strategic planning. They also define the problem too narrowly and fail to think systemically and focus on only part of the problem rather than the whole problem.

Moore, James F., *The Death of Competition: Leadership and Strategy in the Age of Business Ecosystems*, HarperBusiness, 1996.
Businesses will work together in new and innovative ways. Businesses must seek leadership positions in their industries and are well served to have advisors at every stage of their evolution. Businesses must look to the "ecosystem" of their industry in order to determine where they fit and where they can lead and remake a market.

Morgan, Gareth, *Imaginization: New Mindsets for Seeing, Organizing and Managing*, Berrett-Koehler, 1997:
Morgan, Gareth, *Images of Organization*, Sage Publications, 1997.
Self-organization will be the new process of organization for work and the spirit of imagination must be encouraged in order to promote productivity and success. Imagination will be the key to developing sufficient possibilities through strategic planning to allow companies to pursue novel and successful new approaches to achieving their objectives.

Morrison, James L. and Wilson, Ian, *The Strategic Armament Response to the Challenge of Global Change*, in "Future Vision: Ideas, Insights and Strategies", edited by Howard F. Didsbury, Jr. pp 115–132, World Future Society, 1996.
Strategic planning is iterative since the world is constantly changing. It is never enough to have a plan. The plan itself must evolve. As Gloria Estephan said: 'Starting over is part of the plan." The process of creating a strategic planning system that captures input from environmental scanning on a regular basis is called "strategic management." The best way to put the role of strategic planning into perspective is that no words on paper by themselves made a high-growth strategy successful. High-growth strategies are a function of "people working and communicating together" toward a goal. There is a clear, non-threatening role in entrepreneurial organizations for strategic management as explained by Morrison and Ian. "Strategic management does not replace traditional management activities such as budgeting, planning, monitoring, marketing, reporting, and controlling. Rather it integrates them into a broader context, taking into account the external environment, internal organizational capabilities and your organization's overall purpose and direction."

Nadler, David and Tuchman, Michael, *Competing By Design: The Power of Organizational Architecture*, Oxford University Press, New York, 1998.
Competitive advantage will be promoted by constantly improving the architecture of organizations. Organizations must seek input from every level of the organization in order to develop a design that promotes creativity and high productivity from everyone in the organization. Execution of business processes will require the redesign of the organization in order to meet the next challenge.

Naisbitt, John, *Megatrends: Ten New Directions Transforming Our Lives,* Warner Books, 1982.

This book includes ideas for future trends affecting American life and business as well as discussing how these trends were identified. A classic "futurist book" the main trends identifed by the author are: 1) movement from an industrial society to an information society; 2) greater focus on the long term than the short term; 3) less reliance on institutions and greater reliance on the self and small groups to solve problems; 4) a move from a national economy to a world economy; 5) restructuring organizations and insitutions from their heirarchical nature to more of a networking or horizontal nature; 6) a shift in economy, artistic and intellectual activity from the northern part of the US to the southern part; 7) a move from a centralized society to a decentralized society; 8) multiple opportunities for lifestyle and work will replace the traditional either/or paradigm; 9) a move from representative democracy to participatory democracy; and 10) a shift from forced technology to a more responsive, balanced high tech/high touch technology that is user friendly and promotes well being in addition to increased productivity.

Napolitano, Carole S., Henderson, Lida J., *The Leadership Odyssey: A Self-Development Guide to New Skills for New Times,* Jossey-Bass, San Francisco, 1998.

There are 37 personal attributes necessary for effective leadership today. Some of these are: vision, integrity, self-confidence, optimism, flexibility, challenger of assumptions, holistic thinking, being visionary, having focus and discipline, tolerance, risk taking, seeking and promoting synergies, embracing change, trusting intuition, establishing and modeling of values. These are all part of the "self" leadership requirements. Other requirements are more "other" oriented including promoting continuous learning, promoting employee development, advocating open communication and honest feedback, creating successful alliances, creating and supporting a powerful work environment and leading others to greater use of and access to information. A third category of leadership traits necessary to lead high-growth strategies is the ability to shape and support a culture where people excel, understanding systems approaches, being current with emerging trends, being able to inspire vision in those one leads, instilling proper core values in an organization, increasing the organization's ability to change quickly and with a strategic direction in mind and being able to both encourage and inspire others to pursue a vision shared by all in the organization.

Navigating Change: How CEO's, Top Teams, and Boards Steer Transformation, edited by Donald C. Hambrick, David A. Nadler, and Michael L. Tuchman, Harvard Business School Press, Boston, 1998.

A key role of CEO's is to release (create, promote, foster) energy within the organization. The keys to top teams are clear goals and governance processes. Boards of directors should be change agents. Transformation often is better supported by intelligent experimentation than rigorous planning. Organizational renewal is critical in turbulent markets.

Oakley, Ed and Krug, Doug, *Enlightened Leadership: Getting To The Heart Of Change*, Simon and Schuster, 1991.

A discussion of the role of leadership as facilitator and as the element in the organization responsible for keeping the organization focused and promoting positive attitudes throughout the organization. In addition, the role of the leader is to encourage and secure significant participation from all employees and members of the organization. A third area discussed in the book is the role of the leader to ask important questions and to promote the sharing of knowledge of all of the members throughout the entire organization.

Oleck, Howard L., *Non-Profit Corporations, Organizations & Associations*, 5th ed., Prentice-Hall, 1988.

A compendium of facts and figures regarding non-profit entities which discusses the mixture of for-profit and non-profit activities within the same organization or related organizations. One chapter focuses on many examples of how non-profits make money and generate revenue to support their cause and their organization. The book also covers every major aspect of operating a non-profit entity from describing the role of officers, boards, committees, employees, accounting, proxies, memberships, bylaws, political activities, affiliations, fundraising, litigation, management techniques, international organizations, bankruptcy and dissolution.

Osborne, David and Plastrik, Peter, *Banishing Bureaucracy: The Five Strategies for Reinventing Government*, Addison-Wesley, 1997.

Strategy, for government or business, must have five components: 1) core strategy based on clarity of vision, purpose and direction; 2) incentive strategy designed to promote the right behavior; 3) customer satisfaction and service strategy; 4) employee and stakeholder involvement strategy 5) culture strategy – a designed effort to instill the best values and behaviors in the organization. The book has 90 tools for developing and implementing strategy that are useful for both government and businesses.

Packard, David, *The H-P Way: How Bill Hewlett and I Built Our Company*, HarperBusiness, 1995.

An autobiographical sketch of Hewlett and Packard and a discussion of the key elements in their strategy, their values and their good fortunes in building the Company. Key lessons learned are HP's reliance on an open door policy, participatory management, demand for innovation and questionning of every aspect of their business by a broad group of people in the company, growing the company from profit rather than outside capital, focus on quality and trust of people.

Peters, Tom, *The Circle of Innovation: You Can't Shrink Your Way to Greatness*, Knopf, New York, 1997.

Constant innovation is required to thrive in the new marketplace where distance means less and where everyone in your organization must begin to act like a business person. Every job should be viewed as a business and branding is the new form of competitive advantage. Organizations must make a careful balance between having well designed systems and having flexibility to adapt and change to new needs in the marketplace. Service needs to be better than excellent. It needs to be incredible in order to be a source of competitive advantage. Talent is also a source of competitive advantage. "Middle men" occupations will be squeezed out by the information technology that makes them obsolete.

Petrick, Joseph A. and Quinn, John F., *Management Ethics: Integrity at Work.* Sage, 1998.
Integrity must be a critical component in the planning, organizing, leading and controlling aspects of business.

Pfeffer, Jeffrey, *Competitive Advantage Through People: Unleashing the Power of the Work Force,* Harvard Business School Press, 1994.
Workforce success is becoming more important as a source of competitive advantage. The key factors in promoting success among workers are: investment in training and education, promoting employee participation and decision making, selective recruiting, incentive pay and employee ownership, creation of teams, long term commitment to workers, information sharing and measurement, feedback and evaluations. Organizations will succeed in bringing about successful changes with some small initial change that produces very visible results.

Pinchot, Gifford and Pinchot, Elizabeth, *The Intelligent Organization,* Berrett Koehler Publishers, 1996.
Workers must have freedom to make decisions within organizations in order to contribute to making the organization intelligent. The seven essentials of organizational intelligence are: employee rights, open and honest communication, use of self-guided teams, equality and diversity, responsibility for the whole by all employees, learning networks, limited governance promoting organizational freedom. The book concludes with a Bill of Rights and Responsibilities.

Pine, Joseph II and Gilmore, James H., *Welcome to the Experience Economy,* in Harvard Business Review, Jul.-Aug. 1998.
Competitive advantage for companies, especially service providers, comes from managing the entire experience of the customer when he or she is shopping for or using your product. Research on how the customer is currently experiencing the service or product you provide is essential to knowing the customer and designing the best product/service mix for your market. Every person in the company should act consistently with the experience that your organization wants to create.

Pisano, Gary, *The Development Factory: Unlocking the Potential of Process Innovation,* Harvard Business School Press, Boston, 1997.
Development process must focus on quality, efficiency and speed. Organizations must support the continuous improvement of their knowledge base and core competencies, the sources of their comparative advantage.

Porter, Michael E., *Clusters and the New Economics of Competition.* Harvard Business Review, Nov.-Dec. 1998, pp 77–90.
Companies create competitive advantage by locating close to other companies, organizations and geographical settings that can serve as suppliers, outsource

agents, buyers and have logistical support facilities necessary for their business to grow significantly. These elements must be of sufficient size in order to contribute significantly to increase the productive capacity of the company. Porter maps out the US into 33 clusters and identifies each. Although cooperation is essential to make the cluster work, competition in each of these clusters is also so strong that companies achieve greater productivity and success than they would if they were located outside of the cluster. Clustering should be supported by public investment.

Porter, Michael E., *On Competition,* Harvard Business School Press, Boston, 1998.

Location will become even more important for companies seeking high-growth strategies since it will be advantageous for them to locate to areas where there are "clusters" or geographic concentrations of firms, knowledge, suppliers, related industries and other supportive institutions. The advantages of inner city locations will increase. Competition should be focused on increasing productivity in the deployment of resources. Competition assures that the need to improve productivity will be never ending.

Better Change: Best Practices for Transforming Your Organization, Price Waterhouse Change Integration Team, Irwin Publishers, 1994.

Key principles to make change successful in operations are: 1) promote honesty and openness; 2) set the right scope for change; 3) know and involve all of your stakeholders; 4) design and employ new performance measures that track your strategies and objectives; 5) seek innovation input from all sources and people available; 6) invest in human capital; 7) promote diversity; 8) have well developed plans and strategies; 9) invest where payback will be the greatest; 10) communicate the case for change to everyone in the organization; and 11) think big and seek great rewards.

Quinn, James Bryant, Baruch, Jordan J. and Zien, Karen Anne, *Innovation Explosion: Using Intellect and Software to Revolutionize Growth Strategies,* Free Press, New York, 1997.

Economic value, high-growth strategies and strategic advantage result from intellect and innovation. Unfortunately, companies do not manage knowledge assets adequately, much less in an exemplary manner. Organizations have several kinds of knowledge: know how-skills; know what-cognitive knowledge; know why-understanding; know why-commitment/motivation; know about-insight/ creativity. Software is critical in collecting, analyzing, storing, leveraging and distributing knowledge. Human beings through using software can capture knowledge and wisdom faster than ever before, control more events, analyze more complex problems, and search faster for new knowledge and information than they could just one year ago. Intellect and knowledge grow exponentially and having the best intellects in your organization is the way to attract other "best" intellects. Knowledge and intellect grow most quickly when shared and leveraged. Innovation is the result of many attributes, including a clear assessment in advance of whether an innovation will lead to the desired market or economic result. 70 percent of all economically successful innovations are driven by a known or appreciated market need rather than some invention that will guide future markets.

222

Rethinking the Future, edited by Rowan Gibson, Nicholas Brealey Publishing, 1997:
This book is based on interviews with thought leaders including Charles Handy, Peter Senge, Stephen Covey, Warren Bennis, Michael Hammer, C.K. Prahalad, Gary Hamel, John Naisbitt, Lester Thurow, Kevin Kelly and others. The interviews cover the accelerating rate of change, networks vs. nations, future of capitalism, attributes of leadership and strategies for growth.

Ringland, Gill, *Scenario Planning: Managing for the Future,* John Wiley & Sons, Inc., 1998.
This book presents eight case studies of scenario planning at work.

Robinson, Alan G. and Stern, Sam, *Corporate Creativity: How Innovation and Improvement Actually Happen,* Berrett-Koehler, 1997.
In theory, an organization's creative capability increases exponentially with its size. This book presents examples and guidelines for making that maxim true in your organization. Six elements play a key role in stimulating corporate creativity: 1) strategic and organizational alignment; 2) self-initiated activity whereby employees are empowered to solve problems as they see fit; 3) unofficial activity where employees take initiatives not directed from above; 4) serendipity and the ability to take advantage of luck; 5) seeking outside stimuli and mixing with companies from other industries; 6) improved communications systems that promote communication between and among people at all levels of the organization (better than a "suggestion" box).

Roos, Johan, Roos, Goran, Edvisson, Leif, *Intellectual Capital: Navigating in the New Business Landscape,* New York University Press, New York, 1998.
The rise in interest in measuring and promoting intellectual capital is the result of the fact that knowledge and information are currently producing increasing returns, where a small knowledge or technical advantage can result in huge returns for the entrepreneurial organization. In addition, the company that gets its successful product first to market is generally the company that recognizes first the future shape of the business environment. Financial assets, including capital assets, alone never got a product to market or provided excellent customer service.

Kanter, Rosabeth Moss, *Rosabeth Moss Kanter on the Frontiers of Management,* Harvard Business School Press, Boston, 1997.
Organizations should focus on creating collaborative systems that promote participation and influence by a broad spectrum of the organization's participants. There are four bases for sustainable competitive advantage: ability to form strategic alliances across organizations and within organizations, speed, continuous improvement, and focus on core competence. Organizations must become more customer-centric, being able to think like customers and placing customer values at the forefront of product design and marketing. Change efforts are well served by experimentation and rapid learning fostered by better communications systems and alignment on outcomes. Management must be able to read trends early and make rapid responses while focusing on the long-term well being of the organization, its employees and management and customers.

223

Rouse, William B. *Don't Jump to Solutions: Thirteen Delusions that Undermine Strategic Thinking*, Jossey-Bass, San Francisco, 1998.

Many assumptions that organizations based their strategic thinking on are false. Seeking big solutions is usually inferior to creating a series of little solutions. Failing to plan for implementation of strategic thinking is usually based on a false belief that because the organization has a plan, it will be implemented correctly. The key to strategic thinking is first choosing the right goal.

Ryan, Kathleen D. and Daniel K. Oestreich, *Driving Fear Out of the Workplace: Creating the High-Trust, High Performance Organization*, Jossey-Bass, 1998.

Promoting open, honest communication and eliminating all "us-them" attitudes within an organization is critical to improving productivity. Establishing trust by including all employees in decision making, by forming teams to combine viewpoints and encouraging all employees to take responsibility for the improvement of the organization will lead to high-growth strategies.

Sadtler, David, Campbell, Andrew and Koch, Richard, *Breakup! How Companies Use Spin-Offs to Gain Focus and Grow Strong*, Free Press, 1997.

The annual market value of spinoffs in the 1990s in the US is $100 billion and there is a trillion dollars of value locked in companies that poorly manage these non-core competency type of divisions within their ranks. This book discusses the difficulties and potential value of spinoffs.

Sanders, T. Irene, *Strategic Thinking and the New Science: Planning in the Midst of Chaos, Complexity, and Change*, The Free Press, 1998.

This book reviews several thousand years of strategic thinkers and concludes that visualization is the key to developing robust strategic plans that address the state of an organization's environment. The book endorses the use of mind mapping, computerized mapping and other visual models to stimulate creative, non-linear thinking.

Schachtman, Tom, *Around the Block: The Business of A Neighborhood*, Harcourt Brace and Company, 1997.

A socio-economic-demographic study of a commercial block in the Chelsea section of New York. The author studies many of the businesses in the area in great detail and provides an indepth sketch of the businesses' strategies, their owners, their successes and failures and the interrelationship between the businesses. The book seeks to capture the "organizational health" of the block viewing the businesses as part of a mini-economic system as well as in their individual right. The book also discusses the interplay between government policies, technological advances, business paradigm shifts and the personal indiosyncracies of the owners in affecting business performance.

Schaffer, Robert H., *High Impact Consulting: How Clients and Consultants Can Leverage Rapid Results into Long-term Gains*, Jossey-Bass, San Francisco, 1997.

Common problems at work include lack of plans, fear and lack of readiness regarding change, a culture that has weak performance expectations, poor work habits, etc. Consultants often go for big changes rather than small initial changes that produce breakthrough results. Strategic breakthroughs are projects that test new ideas and directions with little risk to the organization. Often the key to improvement in productivity is an improvement in communication. Consultants should include specific results in their contracts and base part of their compensation on the successful achievement of these results.

Seeing Differently: Insights on Innovation, edited by John Seely Brown, Harvard Business School Press, 1997.

Innovation is promoted by seeing things differently, such as redefining entire markets, promoting the involvement of everyone in the organization in the strategy development process, developing many options for future strategy, violating the rules of the organization to promote customer service, encouraging and even demanding that everyone in the organization develop innovative ideas, and developing strategies to take full advantage of good ideas once they surface.

Senge, Peter, *The Fifth Discipline* and Senge, Peter, Ross, Richard, Smith, Bryan, Robert, Charlotte and Kleiner, Art, *The Fifth Discipline Fieldbook,* Doubleday, 1994.

These books introduce the concept of the learning organization and suggest a theoretical and practical framework to support organizations building their intellectual and knowledge capabilities through a concerted organizational effort. The Fieldbook gives examples of acutal case studies where organizations decided to improve their learning efforts and translate their learning efforts into greater productivity, profit, customer satisfaction and meeting the needs of their target population. The book states that it is at the systems level, the organizational level , that the plan for improving learning and the implementation of the plan must be focused. A section in the book is called "Seven Steps for Breaking Through Organizational Gridlock" and is adapted from the magazine, *The Systems Thinker,* February, 1993. The seven steps are: 1) identify the original problem/symptom; 2) map all quick fixes; 3) identify undesirable impacts of the quick fixes; 4) identify fundamental solutions; 5) identify shortcomings of quick fixes on organizational development and progress; 6) find interconnections/synergies that can facilitate action; and 7) identify high-leverage actions.

Shapiro, Carl and Vaira, Hal R, *Versioning: The Smart Way to Sell Information,* in "Harvard Business Review". Nov.-Dec. 1998, pp 106–114.

It is very expensive to produce your first information product and costs little to produce more of the same product. Normal pricing models, such as cost models or quantifying savings to the customer or even competitive pricing do not work since the products are one of a kind, have virtually no marginal cost of production and the demand for the innovative product (at a given price) cannot be predicted with any accuracy. How then do you price the product? The answer is to make a menu or pyramid of products, some with this bell and whistle and some with others, and give a broad range of prices for the various products. This menu of products may result from studying all of the possible customer markets and developing products for each segment of the market The customer will then self-select the price range by his or her own value calculation. Research as to why customers chose one product over another will guide future marketing and product development decisions.

Sherden, William A., *The Fortune Sellers: The Big Business of Buying and Selling Predictions,* John Wiley & Sons, Inc., New York, 1998.

The prediction industry, which includes consultants, stockbrokers, investment advisors, meteorologists and others, is broadly defined as having over 500,000 employees and charges fees in excess of $200 billion a year. This book gives the industry rather low marks for accuracy.

Sigel, Lorraine, *Strategic Alliances for the 21st Century,* in "Strategy and Leadership", Sept.-Oct. 1998.

78 percent of alliances do not even cover their costs. Research on needs and alliance prospects is critical to picking the right partner for the right activity. Tiering alliances into groupings is essential for an organization to manage multiple alliances. Alliances require plans, procedures, decision-making structures, open lines of communication, manuals and templates to aid in their operations. Alliances must be monitored carefully and when they are not meeting expectations, revisions in plans and operations must take hold quickly.

Simonsen, Peggy, *Promoting a Development Culture in Your Organization: Using Career Development as a Change Agent,* Davis-Black Publishing, Palo Alto, 1997.

To promote the increase of human capital in organizations, change is required in organizational culture. The culture must support constant learning, flexibility, innovation, adaptability, self-motivation and responsibility. One approach to changing the culture of an organization is to change the employment contract. The keys to a learning environment are trust, openness and promotion of long-term employees through career and personal development. Mentoring is considered as a strong approach since it has been shown to be mutually beneficial to the mentor and mentee. In addition, change must be highly valued by the employees and organizational systems must be developed in alignment with constant learning.

Sindell, Kathleen, *Investing Online for Dummies: Your Complete Guide to Using the Internet to Develop a Portfolio,* International Data Group Books, 1998.

A "how to" primer on how to access key investment sites and how to operate the Internet to invest. The book explains key concepts and terms used in both the Internet and investment worlds. The book is also an investment primer asking the reader to evaluate how much risk the investor should take and guiding the reader through many of the investment vehicles and plays available in the marketplace. The book covers not only stocks and bonds but also such topics as retirement plans and savings bonds, and presents a list of information sources for the reader to become more knowledgable about the world of investing.

Slaughter, Sheila and Leslie, Larry L., *Academic Capitalism: Politics, Policies and the Entreprenuerial University,* Johns Hopkins University, 1997.

Professors are becoming more involved in the marketplace and are becoming more entrepreneurial as state funding decreases as a percentage of total funding.

Slywotzky, Adrian J. and Morrison, David J., *The Profit Zone: How Strategic Business Design Will Lead You to Tomorrow's Profits,* Times Business, 1998.

Strategic planning is again being used in full force with a new twist. Organizations are now using strategic planning to take a broad based look at entire industries in order to determine which parts of the industries are achieving the greatest profit. Organizations are then making strategic decisions to go after this "profit zone" by capturing those business segments that produce the greatest profit within an industry. Examples include General Electric's shift to financial products where there was substantial profits and less reliance on hard products for its profitability. Similarly the book tracks Disney's expansion into the vacation business and the creation of product pyramids where an organization sells its products in both the marginally profitable sectors as well as the very profitable sectors of the market. The book suggests that companies bring together people within their own organizations to search for the profit zones within reach.

Sperling, John and Tucker, Robert W., *For-Profit Higher Education: Developing a World Class Work-Force,* Transaction Publishers, 1997.

Describing Phoenix University, as a for-profit organization, the book explains the advantages of for-profit educational systems as they can be efficient, quickly adapt to market needs, be accountable to their customers for educational effectiveness and pursue an outcome driven education.

Srivastva, Suresh and Cooperrider, David L., *Organizational Wisdom and Executive Courage,* Jossey-Bass, San Francisco, 1998.

Organizations will take a leadership role as change agents. They will need to pursue wisdom with a carefully thought out process and to engage their members to be leaders in achieving change both within their organizations and throughout society as a whole.

Steckel, Richard and Lehman, Jennifer, *In Search of America's Best Non-profits.* Jossey-Bass, San Francisco, 1998.

The best non-profits are developing innovative ways to generate income and are developing partnerships with private sector businesses. Generally, they have a clear mission and focus on one key area and attempt to excel in that area. This book presents an "organizational audit" checklist for non-profits.

Steps to the Future: Fresh Thinking on the Management of IT-Based Organizational Transformation, edited by Christopher Sauer and Philip W. Yetton, Jossey-Bass, San Francisco, 1997.

Many corporations do not manage IT effectively due to cost overruns, failure to plan the projects carefully and perform cost-benefit analyses, and the failure of the employees and management to learn how to use the new IT tools to their maximum potential.

Stewart, Thomas A., *Intellectual Capital: The New Wealth of Organizations,* Doubleday, 1997.

The world has become a knowledge economy and there is wealth in our organizations that we are not protecting, developing, harvesting, nurturing or managing. In addition, our customers have very valuable knowledge about our products and services which is not being tapped into. Citing Dow Chemical's system for managing intellectual capital, a six step process was described. Start with strategy by defining the role of knowledge in each part of the business. Assess competitors' strengths and weaknesses in intellectual capital. Classify your portfolio noting what you have and what you use. Evaluate your intellectual capital and determine what to keep, abandon or sell. Invest in the areas where there are gaps. Reassemble the portfolio and renew the entire process. Human capital is part of intellectual capital. Returns on information products skyrocket as costs of production and distribution are minimal after the first unit is produced. Tools for measuring intellectual capital are provided.

Stowell, Daniel M., *Sales, Marketing, and Continuous Improvement: Six Best Practices to Achieve Revenue Growth and Increase Customer Loyalty*, Jossey-Bass, San Francisco, 1997.

The keys to improving sales and marketing include 1) the ability to listen to and respond to customers; 2) developing processes to improve customer satisfaction; 3) make sales a team approach with team-based rewards; 4) create a culture in the organization where everyone is responsible for marketing in some manner so that sales is integrated into every aspect of the organization; 5) use technology for research, communication and supplying customer needs; and 6) prepare dynamic strategic plans for improving sales and marketing and then improving the improvements.

Strategy: Seeking and Securing Competitive Advantage, edited by Cynthia A. Montgomery and Michael E. Porter, Harvard Business Review Books, 1991.

A compilation of essays discussing the origin of strategy (citing Darwin's work), the relationship between strategy and various functions within an organization such as financial administration, globalization and how to create strategy in your organization. The book also discusses the role of the board of directors in organizations and the complexity of strategic planning in organizations that have numerous forms of business.

Sun, Tzu. *The Art of War*, translated by Thomas Cleary, Shambhala Publications, 1988.

Over two thousand years old, this book discusses strategy and tactics suggested for war. Writing at a time when hand to hand combat was the rule and projectiles could only be transported small distances, this book focuses on the art of deftness, cleverness and the use of strategy to gain competitive advantage. This new translation is taught in many MBA programs and is relevant to the new technological age where many businesses have the same access to basic resources and strategy and planning will make the difference between the winners and losers.

Tearle, Ruth, *The Versatile Organization: New Ways of Thinking About Your Business*, Pfeiffer & Company, 1994.

Organizations must be versatile because success factors change so quickly. The vision and values are the nucleus of an organization and the leaders and empowered workers are the electrons. Organizations must be able to make transitions quickly and exploit opportunities in the short time frame when they are available.

The Center for Creative Leadership Handbook of Leadership Development, edited by Cynthia D. McCauley, Russ S. Moxley and Ellen Van Velsor, Jossey-Bass, San Francisco, 1998.

The distinction between leaders and followers is being erased with people working on teams where they share leadership roles, take turns based on expertise of a team member and work in team led, not individual led environments.

The Challenge of Educating Future Workers, edited by Rima Shaffer, "Futures Research Quarterly" Volume 13, No. 3, 1997.

Organizations must become communities with shared values and vision. Organizations should focus on how each and every employee would like to develop personally, educationally and professionally and strive to provide employment and learning opportunities that foster that development. Change will result in an organization as a result of excellent cooperative learning strategies where all members of the organization learn what is necessary to accomplish the new tasks needed by the organization.

The Corporate Report Card: Rating 250 of America's Corporations for the Socially Responsible Investor, Council on Economic Priorities, Dutton, New York, 1998.

An element of a contribution strategy identified as having a significant impact on a company's rating is community partnerships with non-profit organizations.

The Future of The Electronic Marketplace, edited by Derek Leebaert, MIT Press, Cambridge, MA, 1998.

We now have the capability to have customers actively participate in the conception and development of products. Cyber retailing called "etailing" will create a new economic marketplace where quality (content) will be more important since businesses will not be able to use their geographic advantage as strongly as they used to.

The Infinite Resource: Creating and Leading the Knowledge Enterprise, edited by William E. Halal, Jossey-Bass, San Francisco 1998.

Promotes the view that employees at the bottom of the ladder should have entrepreneurial freedom to make decisions in the knowledge era and that top down approaches will not work. The author believes that globalization will increase economic growth substantially. Essays include the new role for using competition to provide city services, virtual organizations, networked organizations and improvements that will be brought about in organizations through the use of information technology.

The Organization of the Future, edited by Francis Hesselbein and Richard Beckhard, Jossey-Bass, San Francisco, 1997.

38 essays discuss such topics as the increase in temporary employment, worker democracy, organizations with learning missions, human capital, compression of time, diversity, socially responsible organizations, leading across cultures and organizational health.

The Rising Tide: The Leading Minds of Business and Economics Chart a Course Toward Higher Growth and Prosperity, edited by Jerry J. Jasinowski, John Wiley & Sons, Inc., New York, 1998.

High-growth strategies include the deployment of digital technology, the empowerment of workers and the inclusion of employees in all aspects of strategic planning and decision making and linking pay to performance. Based on interviews with 26 CEOs and leading economists.

The World's Greatest Brands, edited by Nicholas Kochan, New York University Press, 1997.

The top 100 brands are listed. An organization's brand image and reputation is in some cases the most important asset it owns. Brands must be based on compelling values such as quality, service, innovation or other area that can be communicated to the market place through every product under that brand name. Balance sheets may begin to use an estimate of brand value on their balance sheets.

Thought Leaders: Insight on the Future of Business, edited by Joel Kurtzman, Jossey-Bass, San Francisco, 1998.

Charles Handy discusses transforming employees of an organization into "members" of the economic organization in an edited interview. C.K. Prahalad suggests including all layers of an organization in constant dialogue about the future direction of an organization. Gary Hamel discusses the need for companies to look outside of their industry to learn how to approach the future. John Kao discusses the need for creativity in the workplace, a "creativity audit" and the value of the "jamming" model from music. Paul Romer discusses the potential development of monopolies in the knowlegde economy. Stan Shih discusses the need for global brands combined with local customer service or "touch." Norbert Walker discusses the economic future of Europe. John Chambers talks about the criteria for success in acquisitions. His company has acquired 29 other companies since 1995. Warren Bennis discusses the key aspects of promoting genius and high-performing work groups. Jean-Rene Fourtou discusses the need for a leader to bring passion and a sense of vitality into organizations through a clear and inspiring articulation of vision for the organization.

Tobin, Daniel R., *The Knowledge-enabled Organization: Moving from "Training" to "Learning" to Meet Business Goals*, American Management Association, New York, 1998.

We do not know the benefits derived from the $52 billion dollars spent on training. The traditional model of training is criticized because it focuses on the wrong goals. The future expenditures in this area should be on creating and financially supporting a learning environment so that employees can learn quickly and thoroughly about the company and its business processes, technical requirements, management approaches and customer needs and behaviors.

Toffler, Alvin, *The Third Wave: The Classic Study of Tomorrow*, Bantam Books, 1981.

The third wave is the information wave that will guide the future of civilization. Electronic information will yield huge changes to our lives, our governmental structures, our families and our social relationship. The book provides an extensive historical account of social drivers and puts the post-1950 period into context in the overall development of civilizations. Building on the production focus of the second wave (build more), the third wave will focus on build to suit the consumer (called the "prosumer").

Tomorrow's Organization: Crafting Winning Capabilities in an Dynamic World, edited by Susan Albers Moohrman, Jay R. Galbraith and Leward E. Lawyer, III, Jossey-Bass, 1998.

Organizations must continuously seek to create new systems that promote internal marketing, networking, effective boards, expanding networks, employee involvement in the strategic planning and decision-making processes, customer focus in every stage of the product design, manufacturing, marketing, distribution and support. Tomorrow's organization will be more flexible, team-oriented and dynamic than in the past.

Tushman, Michael L. and O' Reilly, Charles A, III. *Winning Through Innovation: A Practical Guide to Leading Organizational Change and Renewal,* Harvard University Press, Boston, 1997.

Organizations must strive to improve and innovate in the short term, including implementing innovation that represents a dramatic shift in how the company operates. Managing innovation requires vision, a clear strategy and written objectives. The key to innovation is in the implementation process, not in the idea or strategy development process. Organizations must develop a clear sense of their "performance gap," a statement that compares where they want to be and what they want to accomplish in the future with where they are today. This gap fuels innovation. Innovation results from careful management of the culture of an organization and close attention to organizational politics. Innovation requires the input of the entire management team.

Ven der Heijden, Kees, *Scenarios: The Art of Strategic Conversation,* John Wiley & Sons, Inc., 1996.

Discusses scenario planning from the point of view that the better the business strategic decision-making process identifies the key decisions to be made, the better the scenario planning process works.

Waldrop, Mitchell, *Complexity: The Emerging Science At the Edge of Order and Chaos,* Simon and Schuster, 1992.

Complexity is a review of the research efforts into chaos theory and its applications to the worlds of business and other disciplines. Focusing on life at the Santa Fe Institute in the late 1980s and early 1990s this book charts the intellectual history and practical promise of chaos theory and helps define the scope and boundaries of this emerging scientific inquiry.

Waterman, Robert H. Jr., *The Renewal Factor: How the Best Get and Keep the Competitive Edge,* Bantam, 1997.

Renewal is necessary because change is now the norm. Strategy becomes informed opportunism rather than some static plan prepared years ago to guide an organization indefinitely into the future. Renewal is necessary at the individual and the organizational level on a regular basis. Employee involvement is critical to successful renewal. Organizations and individuals must be aware that old habits trap their creativity, their ability to respond to a new type of challenge or environment and may prevent renewal. Renewal is based on constant learning and appreciation of the newness of the business and organizational environment in which we now work. In order to sustain successful renewal, organizations must base their renewal strategies on their core values and build from the consensus of what the company and organization is about.

Weeden, Curt, *Corporate Social Investing: The Breakthrough Strategy for Giving and Getting Corporate Contributions*, Berrett-Koehler, San Francisco, 1998.

Corporate rates of giving have dropped between 1986 and 1996 from 2.3% to 1.3% of profits. Corporations should donate 2.5% of pretax profits for social investing. Corporate social investment models are being developed to guide older companies and the new entrepreneurs on the block.

Werth, Jacques and Ruben, Nicholas E, *High Probability Selling: Selling Without Pain,* Abba Publishing, 1997.

The old paradigm for selling was to get someone to buy your stuff at a price where you made money. The new paradigm is figure out what the customer really needs, the price that fits in the business model of the customer and sell that to the customer. This demand driven paradigm focuses on the primacy of research in the selling process. Research entails qualifying your prospect in two ways. Does your potential customer need/want your product and is your customer willing to buy it now. If the answer to this research question is "yes", selling is the straightfoward presentation of the economic opportunity to the potential buyer. If the answer is "no", the selling agent should go no further at this time with the potential buyer.

What Works: Assessment, Development and Measurement, edited by Laurie Bassi and Darlene Russ-Edt, American Society for Training and Development, 1997.

Training impacts an organization, its culture, its level of production and its ability to learn. Measurement of the results of training is an important tool in developing the right training tools, in implementing the right training strategies and in creating a learning organization. A learning organization has a culture of inquiry and generativity, extracts and documents knowledge from each of its processes, manages its organizational memory and creates systems level approaches to involve everyone in the learning process.

White, Randall P., *The Future of Leadership: Riding the Corporate Rapids into the 21st Century,* Pitman Publishing, 1996.

Leadership in the future must be able to manage uncertainty. Organizations must leverage learning which will be the driving force behind the growing corporations in the 21st century.

Wileman, Andrew and Jary, Michael, *Retail Power Plays: From Trading to Brand Leadership,* New York University Press, 1997.

Long-term, successful branding is critical to achieving sustainable profits. Brand leadership is created by excellent customer relationships, significant investment in getting your name out in front of the public, appearing to be close to the customer (intimate) and capture of fashion-leading products.

Willens, Harold, *The Trimtab Factor. How Business Executives Can Help Solve the Nuclear Weapons Crisis,* William Morrow and Company, Inc., 1984.
The role of business must be to be a trimtab in society, a small powerful force bringing about desired social changes. This book takes an indepth look at the nuclear weapons crisis and proposes a series of steps to resolve the problem using the analogy of a business "turnaround."

Wind, Jerry Yoram and Main, Jeremy, *Driving Change: How the Best Companies Are Preparing for the 21st Century.*
The 21st Century organization will be customer driven. Since all organizations will be able to achieve, at least in theory, high quality in service and products, the distinguishing features of organizations will be their clearly articulated vision, their speed and learning orientation, their network development and management ability, their information and knowledge base, their agility and open mindedness.

World Boom Ahead: Why Business and Consumers Will Prosper, Kiplinger Books, Washington, 1998.
One of the elements of globalization is the full integration of the world marketplace. Such integration will promote economic performance.

Zell, Deone, *Changing By Design: Organizational Innovation at Hewlett-Packard,* ILR Press/Cornell Press, 1997.
This book uses Hewlett- Packard's California Personal Computer Division as a case study of how to build innovation into an organization.

Zider, Bob, *How Venture Capital Works,* "Harvard Business Review", Nov.-Dec. 1998, pp 131–139.
Venture capitalists invested over $10 billion in 1997, but less than $1 billion went to startups. Government invested $63 billion and corporations invested $133 billion. Venture funds target certain high-growth industries and provide expansion capital at a high price in terms of amount of control and ownership. Venture funds look for good managers. Venture capital may increase substantially as the economy grows.

Zohar, Danah, *Rewiring the Corporate Brain: Using the New Science to Rethink How We Structure and Lead Organizations,* Berrett-Koehler, San Francisco, 1997.
Organizations must take a holistic view and promote dynamic integration. Employees at all levels must be involved in strategic planning and bottom up, self organizing work places will be more productive in the coming era than top down oriented organizations. Organizations must be vision centered. Leadership will not be autocratic, but rather will be servant leadership where leaders articulate the values and the employees carry out the work necessary to achieve the values and goals of the organization.

Index

AAA (American Automobile
Association) 105–6
AARP (American Association of
Retired Persons) 28–9, 84, 126, 144
acceleration 37
acquisitions and mergers 94, 125–9
activity-based accounting 131, 176
adaptive capacity 10
adding value 47, 128
advisory boards 98–9, 154–5
advocates 59
AID (attractiveness/implementation
difficulty) analysis 72–5
alignment 145
alliances 125–9, 166–7
Amazon.com 56, 73, 88
America On Line 14, 73
American Association of Retired
Persons (AARP) 28–9, 84, 126, 144
American Automobile Association
(AAA) 105–6
American Institutes for Research 44
American Medical Association 105
American Society of Association
Executives 105
American Society for Training and
Development see ASTD
analytical tools 39–42
attractiveness/implementation
difficulty (AID) analysis 72–5
competitive analysis 41, 46–52
defining moments analysis 40, 44–6,
146
economic value added 41, 71–2,
131–6, 173
flexibility analysis 41, 52–6
gap analysis 40, 42–3
GE (growth earnings) grid 41, 72–3
growth drivers 41, 61–3, 93–6, 101

implementation forces analysis 41–2,
75–6
industry mindset 41, 65
innovation analysis 41, 52–6
PEST analysis 41, 56–61
Porter's five competitive forces 41,
63
root cause analysis 40, 43–4
scenario planning 41, 65–6
STAIR analysis 41, 69–70
SWOT analysis 41, 67–9
visualization 41, 66–7
see also stakeholders
angels 111
annual plans 150
ASTD (American Society for Training
and Development) xii
competitive advantage 48
competitive analysis 41
conferences 21
economic value added (EVA) 131–2
flexibility and innovation 56
gap analysis 43
goals of 4, 5, 6, 20
implementation forces analysis 75–6
strategic planning 13–14
training programs 148
volunteer programs 29, 126
website 58
ATT 126
attitude capital 89–91
attitudes of employees 170
attractiveness/implementation
difficulty (AID) analysis 72–5
Austin Chamber of Commerce 134
authority in markets 5–6
automation 81
"autopilot trends" 81
AutoZone 123

Avtel Communications 105

Badaracco, Joseph, *Defining Moments*
44
balanced scorecard 17, 173
Barnes and Noble 88
benchmarking 17, 25, 63
benefits systems 124–5, 132, 155–6
Blockbuster video stores 51
blockers 59
board of directors
advisory boards 98–9, 154–5
CEOs (Chief Executive Officers) role
152–3
in non-profit organizations 154–5
role 154–5
selection process 96–8
bond funding 122–4
Boston Chicken (later Boston Market)
51–2
brands 48–9, 125–6
leveraging 105, 106
breadth and focus 148–50
Breakthrough Opportunities Analysis
43
brokerage houses 164
budgetary planning 113
Bush, George 150–1
business plans 150
Businesslike Government (Gore and
Adams) 178–9
buy and hire strategy 102
bylaws 159

calendars 13
cannibalization 52
Canon 183
canvassing employees 147
capacity building 17–18, 81
capital availability 111
capital markets 112
capital raising
angels 111
for companies 116–18
debt capital 117–18
in educational institutions 118–21
and the Internet 111
in non-profit organizations 112,
121–4

receivables financing 118
for small businesses 111
venture capital 111–12, 117
capital requirements 118
catalog businesses 57
categorizing costs 134
Centers for Entrepreneurship 118–19
CEOs (Chief Executive Officers) 152–3
change xii, 10, 27
measurement 53–6
trauma 150
Charles Schwab 56
Chief Executive Officers (CEOs) 152–3
Child Trends, Inc. 84, 173–4
CISCO 126
clarity and emergence 146–8
Clean Air Act 186
Clinton, Bill 152–3
clusters of economic activity 119
co-marketing relationships 118
Coca-Cola 48, 73, 89, 104, 157, 171
commitment 6
communication 12–13, 153
company universities 90–1, 120
company valuation 103
compensation and reward systems
124–5, 132, 155–6
competitive advantage 16, 17
competitive analysis 41, 46–52
competitive disadvantage 49–51
competitive forces 41, 63
conferences 89
Conner, Daryl 11, 52, 133, 150, 161
Conquest Systems Inc. 7
consciously competent organizations
162–3
consolidation 101–4
consumer behaviour 112–13
contract employees 101
contribution strategy 95–6
conversations 153–4
COOs (Chief Operating Officers) 152
copyrights 48–9
core values 10
cost leadership 129
cost management 47, 129–31
activity-based accounting 131, 176
categorizing costs 134
current costs 133

differentiation strategies 130
economic value added (EVA) 131–6
economies of scale 71, 129
and investment returns 133
opportunity costs 71, 131
costs
of education and training 90
of failure 178–84
opportunity costs 71, 131
Councils of Masters 98–9, 154–5
Covey-Franklin Trust 94
creative tension 6
creativity 116
credit card debt 117–18
critical incident technique 44
critical mass 5, 37, 39
culture 10, 55
of governments 179
multicultural competencies 151, 183
current costs 133
customer-centric strategies 55, 165–6
customers 164–5
defining 119–20, 121
repeat customers 119–20

De Beers 52
Death of Competition (Moore) 4, 144
debt capital 117
decision makers 58
defining customers 119–20, 121
defining moments 40, 44–6, 146
Defining Moments (Badaracco) 4
defining organizations 145–50
clarity and emergence 146–8
focus and breadth 148–50
Delia 57
Delphi 99
developing organizational capability 17
development offices 118
differentiation 94, 130
Digital, Inc. 104
Dingman Center 118–19
direct mail 57–8, 161
directors *see* board of directors
Disney 116
distribution systems 100
District of Columbia 58
diversity in the workplace 150–1

domain name values 116
Domino Printing Sciences 87
Drucker, Peter 119

E-bay 88
e-mail 147
The E-Myth Revisited (Gerber) 152
economic environment *see* PEST analysis
Economic Growth Plan (EGA) 149
economic value added (EVA) 41, 71–2, 131–6, 173
economies of scale 71, 129
educational institutions 53–4, 105, 164–5
capital raising 118–21
Centers for Entrepreneurship 118–19
co-marketing relationships 118
company universities 90–1, 120
compensation and reward systems 124
defining customers 119–20, 121
development offices 118
endorsements 105, 118
for-profit education and training 120–1
investment returns 133–4
"leasing" workers 121
repeat customers 119–20
strategic partnering 125–6
Ehrbar, Al, *EVA* 71
emergence and clarity 146–8
EMMAUS 29, 130
employees 27–31
attitudes 170
canvassing by e-mail 147
change trauma 150
compensation packages 124–5, 132, 155–6
contract employees 101
empowerment 168
life-time employment 145
moving between jobs 146
participation 155
recruitment 28–31, 143–6
retention 30, 48, 164
roles 58–9, 155
empowerment 168
endorsements 105, 118

energy 37
enlightened leadership 83
Enlightened Leadership (Oakley and
    Krug) 151
entrepreneurialism 55, 167, 180–4
Equity International, Inc. 106
equity participation 124–5
ERIC 91
EuroDisney 116
evangelism 168
evolving leadership 151–2
export departments 106
external environment 41–2
    see also PEST analysis

fault-tolerant systems 160–1
feedback 147
financial planning 113, 147
First Law of Thermodynamics 38
fishbone analysis 43
flexibility analysis 41, 52–6
focus and breadth 148–50
force 37, 39
force field analysis 61
foresight 66
Future of Capitalism (Thurow) 184

gap analysis 6, 40, 42–3
Gates, Bill 152–3
GE (growth earnings) grid 41, 72–3
General Motors 99
Gerber, Michael 165
    The E-Myth Revisited 152
global information systems 106
globalization 106–7, 151
goals, stretch goals 141–2
government
    culture 179
    essential role of 186
    export departments 106
    policy 186
    scientific research 99
gravity 37
Grove, Andy 27, 68
growth benchmark xii–xiii
growth brakes 61–3
growth drivers 41, 61–3, 101
    Economic Growth Plan (EGA) 149
    values-driven 93–6

growth earnings (GE) grid 41, 72–3
Grundy, Tony
    attractiveness/implementation
        difficulty (AID) analysis 72–5
    industry mindset 41, 63
Guptara, Prabhu 51, 152

Handy, Charles 30, 157
harvesting value 115–16
health benefits 101
Heisenberg's Uncertainty Principle 38
Henson, Jim 116
HERO bonds 123
Hewlett-Packard 74
human capital 89–91
    measurement systems 175

IBM 104
implementation forces analysis 41–2,
    75–6
implementation lag times 68
implementation plans 22–3, 24–5, 82–3
implementation reality 83
incentivizing employees 132
    see also compensation and reward
        systems
inclusion 151
industry mindset 41, 65
Information Experts, L.L.C. 163
information and knowledge 91
innovation analysis 41, 52–6
instant shopping 87–8
integrity 12–13
intellectual capital 89–91
intellectual property 48–9
Internet 11, 36
    and capital raising 111
    conferences 89
    domain name values 116
    and global information systems 106
    growth of 87
    instant shopping 87–8
    and language barriers 89
    management of knowledge 91–2
    sales generation 88
    stable electricity/communications
        availability 89
    and stock control 88
    training delivery 90

virtual teams 92–3
intuitive strategies 9, 11
investment returns 133–4

Jim Henson Productions 116
job descriptions 159
joint ventures 125–9
Joy of Sports Foundation 134
justice system 179

Kaplan, Robert S. 173
knowledge management 91–2, 147
KPMG 157
Kwartler Communications 40

language barriers 89
leadership 83, 151–2, 167–72
learning organization 86, 156–7, 161–3,
    185
"leasing" workers 121
Ledecky, Jonathan 101
Legg Mason Wood Walker 105
leveraging assets 105
life-time employment 145
Lipnack, Jessica, *Virtual Teams* 93
location decision 57
low income people 180–4

Maccoby, Michael, *Why Work:
    Motivating the New Workforce* 55
McKay, Harvey 46
mail order businesses 57
management
    breaking rules/molds 158–9
    rules that cannot be broken 163–5
management by abdication 152
Manpower, Inc. 105
mapping software 118
Margolin, Ben 144
markets
    attractiveness 72
    authority in 5–6
    entry strategies 72–3
    expansion 5
    segmentation 113
    significance 5–6
Marks & Spencer 55, 68–9
Martin, Sally 142
Maryland 58, 180

Maryland Parent Student Teacher's
    Association 22–3
mass 5, 37, 39
materials industry 114
MBA programs 39–40
measurement 173–8
membership concept 157
Memphis Red Birds 123
mentoring 154
Mercer Management Consulting 121
mergers 94, 125–9
Merrill Lynch 56, 87
metrics 177
Microsoft 14, 94, 142
MicroStrategy, Inc. xi–xii
    capital raising 117
    competitive advantage 48
    creativity 21
    defining moments analysis 45
    gap analysis 43
    goals of 4, 5, 6–7, 20
    growth drivers 62
    location decision 28, 57
    pricing policy 113
    retention and recruitment policies
        30, 48, 145–6
    strategic planning 13–14
    supplier relationships 104
    training programs 148
mission statements 6, 7–8, 12, 13
Mississippi 57
Monsanto Company 142
Moore, Jim, *The Death of Competition* 4,
    144
Morrison, David J. 104
Multi-Media Holdings, Inc. 102–3
multicultural competencies 151, 183

National Executive Service Corps 98
natural resources industries 36
net present value 73–4, 133
NetCapitol, Inc. 147
new materials to market 114
Newton's First Law 37–8
Newton's Second Law 38
non-profit organizations 95–6
    board of directors 154–5
    bond funding 122–4
    capital raising 112, 121–4

non-profit organizations – *continued*
  cost calculations 176
  leveraging assets 105
  measurement systems 174–5
  mergers 126–7
  performance-based funding 121
  strategic partnering 125–6
  see also ASTD
Norton, David P. 173
nuclear power industry 60, 163

objects 37
Olalla, Julio 153
Olympic Games 13
open systems 166–7
opportunity costs 71, 131
orchestra leaders 83
Organization of American States (OAS)
    167
organizational radar 84
organizations
  consciously competent 162–3
  customer-centric 55, 165–6
  defining moments 146
  definitions of 153
  historical lessons learned 146–7
  learning organization 86, 156–7,
      161–3, 185
  open systems 166–7
  see also defining organizations
Oser, Andrew 134
outsourcing 16, 100–1

participation 155
partnering 17, 125–9, 166–7
Partners in Education Program 134
patents 48–9, 113
payrolls 100
performance 157–8
performance-based funding 121
personnel *see* employees
PEST analysis 41, 56–61
physics 36–42
  definitions 37
  First Law of Thermodynamics 38
  implications on strategic planning
      39–42
  Newton's First Law 37–8
  Newton's Second Law 38

  Uncertainty Principle 38
planned strategies 9–10, 11
planning *see* strategic planning
    process
political factors 57–9
political power 85
Porter's five competitive forces 41,
    63
portfolio of alliances 128
potential blockers 59
precision 173–8
president's role 152
pricing models 112, 165
privatization 179, 186
product pyramids 112, 165
productivity 155
products
  bringing new materials to market
      114
  differentiation 94, 130
  pricing models 112, 165
  versioning 112–13, 165
profit zone analysis 104–6
profits 166
projects 159

raising capital *see* capital raising
receivables financing 118
recruitment 28–31, 143–6
Reich, Robert 30
reinvention 177
relationship capital 147
repeat customers 119–20
research affiliates 128
retention of employees 30, 48,
    164
return on investment (ROI) 133
reward systems 124–5, 132, 155–6
Richardson Personal Training (RPT)
    26–7
risk tolerance 160
Roberts, Wayne 91
robustness 69
root cause analysis 40, 43–4
Royal Dutch Shell 65

Saylor, Michael 148, 152, 157, 183
scenario planning 41, 65–6
schedules 13

Schultz, Howard 5–6
scientific research 99
SCORE 98
securities industry 164
segmentation 113
selecting boards of directors 96–8
Senge, Peter 157
Sherwood, Dave 142
Slywotzky, Adrian J. 104
small businesses 111
social forces 59
social investing 112
soft failure systems 160–1
software 19–20, 118
spinoffs/spinouts 99
sponsors 58
staff *see* employees
STAIR analysis 41, 69–70
stakeholders 42, 58, 81–2, 83–7
    agenda analysis 86–7
    employees 85
    identifying stakeholders 84
    and learning 86
    and political power 85
    prioritization analysis 87
Starbucks 85–6, 95
Stern Stewart 173
stock control 88
strategic alignment 82, 145
strategic alliances 125–9, 166–7
strategic imagination 39
strategic partnering 17, 125–9,
    166–7
strategic planning process
    aids to 15
    capacity building 81
    and change 10, 27
    comparing strategies 23–4
    constraints on 21–2
    crafting strategies 19–20
    creating new approaches 21–2
    development phase 18–19
    dynamic nature 14–15
    effectiveness of 35
    elements of 14
    employee involvement 27–31
    external environment 25
    flexibility of 10, 11
    guided judgement 23–4

identify current position 20
implementation plans 22–3, 24–5,
    82–3
internal environment 25
key elements 82
key roles 8
monitoring and revising 25–7
objectives 15–18
previous successes 20–1
resource generation 35–6
schedules 13
stakeholder support 24
and strategic thinking 11–12
types of strategy 9
see also analytical tools
strategic risk 121
Strategy Safari 8
stretch goals 141–2
supplier relationships 104
sustainability 5
SWOT analysis 41, 67–9

teams, virtual teams 92–3
technological forces 59–60
telecommuting 88
Templeton, Sir John 171
Thermodynamics, First Law 38
360 degree feedback 147
Three Mile Island 60, 163
Thurow, Lester, *The Future of Capitalism*
    184
timetables 13
tools *see* analytical tools
trademarks 48–9
training 6, 120–1, 156–7
    costs 90
    expectations from 174–5
    Internet delivery of 90
    value of 44

umbrella strategies 9, 11
Uncertainty Principle 38
unit of analysis 94
United Way 121, 125
unity 83, 169
universities *see* company universities
University of Texas 91
US Office Products 101, 102
US Web, Inc. 102

valuation of companies 103
value added 47, 128
value harvesting 115–16
value identification 113–14
values 10, 157–8
values-driven growth 93–6
venture capital 111–12, 117
versioning 112–13, 165
Virginia 58
virtual teams 92–3
Virtual Teams (Lipnack) 93
vision statements 4, 6, 7–8, 12, 13
visualization 41, 66–7
volunteers 28–30, 126

wages
  differentials 184–5
  real wages 180
  see also reward systems
Wal-Mart 157
Washington and Lee University 133–4
Whirlpool 106
Why Work: Motivating the New Workforce (Maccoby) 55
work 37
WorldCom 126

Yahoo 57
Young Business Forum 167